It Could Only Happe

Angie Nawaz has worked s for many years and lives in , Manchester. *It could only happen to you!* is her first novel. Some of this book is based on fact, some on speculation, and the rest on gross exaggeration. You can decide upon which.

I've often said I should write a book. Here it is having finally put pen to paper. I hope you enjoy the read.

I would like to hear your comments about my book, good or bad. Please leave feedback on www.itcouldonlyhappentoyou.com

© 2006 *Anjum Productions*

first published in 2006
second edition published 2007
Anjum Productions

978-0-9554325-0-7
0-9554325-0-2

Dedicated With Love

To Ashley & Steve x x x

Chapter 1 ~	**When it Started**	**3**
Chapter 2 ~	**The Concert**	**9**
Chapter 3 ~	**Office Politics & Gilberts Grape**	**30**
Chapter 4 ~	**The Swede**	**39**
Chapter 5 ~	**The Cat**	**45**
Chapter 6 ~	**More Sick Days**	**53**
Chapter 7 ~	**The Night Out**	**61**
Chapter 8 ~	**Wild Revelations & The Abseil**	**74**
Chapter 9 ~	**Back at the office and Jip's adventure**	**103**
Chapter 10 ~	**The Tooth Brush**	**117**
Chapter 11 ~	**Chocolate - Make The Damn Call**	**124**
Chapter 12 ~	**Another Night Out**	**132**
Chapter 13 ~	**The Bloody Dog**	**140**
Chapter 14 ~	**Phone on a Cheat**	**153**
Chapter 15 ~	**Back in the Office**	**168**
Chapter 16 ~	**Wishful Thinking & Gibraltar**	**182**
Chapter 17 ~	**The Birthday**	**206**
Chapter 18 ~	**The Bonds & Boredom**	**221**
Chapter 19 ~	**Back Home & Dressing Up**	**240**
Chapter 20 ~	**It's almost Christmas**	**256**
Chapter 21 ~	**That New Year!**	**269**
The Last Note		**282**

~ Chapter One ~ **When it Started**

As I turned the page I couldn't believe my eyes. My heart pounded. There it was in black and white in front of me 'The Boss' is coming to town. Well okay town was a minor detail. He is playing in London and, well I'm in Manchester. Just a minor detail though. At least he is this side of the Atlantic. I have been a fan of 'The Boss' for quite a few years now so I just had to get tickets...'I just gotta.' And to think I didn't even know he was touring. Now here I am grabbing my handbag for the oh so lovely credit card. I quickly dial the number. Very quickly in case they had just sold out, God Forbid. Then it would be devastating.

I had reluctantly applied for a credit card thinking I might run up a huge bill. And, I'd probably never use it for those 'essential items' but fritter it way on useless shopping. But, just in case of an emergency I had applied for one anyway. Yes definitely, just for those emergencies mind you. And this is *definitely* an emergency. Okay so I'm justifying it in my mind that I was right to get one all along.

Wow! It gets even better, reading further down the advert The Boss is touring with the E Street Band. My fingers can't dial fast enough. The line is engaged, damn! Quick hit the redial, I just *have* to have those tickets. I couldn't bear the thought of Bruce being on British soil and me missing out. I've never seen him live. In fact I had only been to one other concert before. And a most perfect concert it was too. Oasis at Maine Road.

They were fantastic playing to a huge home crowd. And they were definitely on top form. But could this gig top it I wonder. I'm acting like I'd get front row tickets yet I haven't even got through on the damn phone. I find I'm grinning to myself already thinking what I could wear. Finally! After what felt like an hour of redial I'm through. I quickly ask if tickets are available for Earls Court. I can't get my words out fast enough when I hear those perfect words Yes Tickets are available! Heart racing I ask to buy tickets. The voice at the other end asks how many tickets would you like as they are selling fast...Erm not quite thought that far ahead. Such as who would go with me. I suppose I would need two tickets I could hardly go on my own, but who with. Details, details, we'd cover that one later...

Wait a minute what about three tickets I don't want to leave anybody out? Then again, I don't think I could get three people to come with me. It's in London, and I don't really know anybody else who is a fan. It isn't as if the gig is here in Manchester. At least then I could ask a couple of friends to have a night out and just enjoy the evening with me. I know we would have a laugh but London. It would mean travelling down and an afternoon off work. Plus a late trip back to Manchester plus costs of tickets to travel.

Upon reflection (quick reflection as the tickets are selling fast remember) I answer 2 tickets. Heart beating, I wait for those final words 'your tickets are booked.' At least then you know you have the tickets. Not that I think anybody or thing would stop me but you don't know my luck. But we'll come to more of that later and then you will understand me thinking this way. The nearest seats are a third of the way from the front row. The voice at the other end tells is trying to convince me that they are good seats. Sorry, but by my thinking that puts me a third way back, not third way forward. Oh well, I suppose I should be grateful I've got tickets as I'm sure I'd be gutted if I couldn't get any.

Damn, the gig falls on a Tuesday I was hoping for a weekend. Never mind I'll have to book time off, although we are quite busy... Oh well, that's just tough luck. I've stayed late at work often enough to cover busy periods, so a couple of days off will suffice I think! Obviously trying to justify this to myself again. Excellent! Two tickets to see Bruce Springsteen & the E Street Band. And I'm already getting giddy at the thought. You see I get it about Bruce that other people just don't, well nobody that I know anyway.

The only way I can explain it is he has thee sound, that gravelled sound. And he has a cheeky smile which seems to hide something behind it. Not to mention he can rock like no other. You could call him the Barry White of Rock, one who has a sound of pure heaven which holds a distinct air of mystery and allurement. A sound that puts you in a great mood for or a good night out.

Bruce creates perfect music for blasting in the car or even a quiet night in chilling to his deep yet soft voice. It's a sort of syrup and sawdust sound that cuts right through you. And that's without going into the lyrics. I'd been a fan of his ever since hearing 'Born in the USA' back in the 80's when I was a silly fifteen year old girl. Nothing much changes there then. He was different to the rest 80's influences that I listened to. Such as Spandau Ballet, Culture Club, Annie Lennox, UB40, Soul Music, the great Bob Marley, and of course the god of gods, Elvis. I'd always liked a range of music from U2 to rockabilly. But he had that edge over what was around at that time. His sound was so raw and real, yet so appealingly soft underneath.

So getting back to the concert there is no way I'm going to miss this one. Why does it have to fall on a work day? And we'll have to travel to London in the morning. I suppose we'd need to be there early before tea time. I don't want to be rushing around. I'll just have to book that Tuesday off work, and maybe the next day too? After all I don't know how late the gig would finish. Or how far it is from the train station and what times the trains are. We may have to stay in London overnight. I find myself getting giddy thinking about it again. But who would come with me. None of my girlfriends like him. Well, not enough to travel to London to watch him. And expect them to take time off work, pay for travel expenses. What about Stan? He'd come, I know he likes Bruce, maybe not as much as me, but he does like him. And he'd prefer I go to London with him than troll around London without him. I'll ask him if he's up for it. This could pose a problem though. He has tons of work on and hasn't had a spare minute for weeks.

I don't ask much from him, so that settles it then, the least he can do is spare me a couple of days. Of course when I ask Stan his answer is he can't take the time off work. Being a builder, and in the middle of block paving somebody's drive way I suppose he does have a point. Yet he doesn't seem to mind their drive being dug up when he needs to start another job, or drop off it to go on a quote (even though he doesn't have time to do another job) but hey that's me just being a nag. Living with a builder all you get is 'I can't turn work down.' After pleading with him and making him feel guilty about never having time to going anywhere. And just for good measure adding 'I'll have a good time with the girls without you in London' was somehow enough for him to relent. That's final then, I tell work I need the day off.

The girls at work say the concert might not finish until 11pm so why not make a night of it and book into a hotel. That's a good idea why not. We don't get chance to do much of anything together so lets make a night of it. I can book a room cheap through work as we get a good rate. We can go out for something to eat, we'll have a great time. Oh dear, just had a thought, what about our daughter Bash? She'll have to be picked up from school and looked after overnight. I suppose she could stay at my Stan's or my Mum's. She opted for Stan's Mum then she could call for her friend on the way to school.

We nicknamed Ayeisha Bash whilst she was a baby. When asleep she'd lie on her tummy. When she awoke she'd push herself up by straightening and almost locking her arms, then lift her head as high as she could then drop herself down her tummy on the mattress of her Moses basket. I'd worry she'd hurt her little face dropping herself down like that on the mattress, but she'd just giggle and do it again. And wherever we were in the room she would turn her head as far as she could to have a good nosey and then bash herself down. So we nicknamed her Bash.

All I need to do now is talk Stan into taking the time off work. I'd booked the Hotel just a tube ride away from Earls Court, all plans going well, excellent. Next on the list is the transport, I best check the internet for timetables. The train costs a fortune this could work out an expensive gig. Oh well I *am* going to be there no matter what. We could get the coach to London but that takes forever. Then there's road works, traffic jams or 'incidents' on route to consider. Knowing my luck there's bound to be something going on. The train it is then but I don't mind getting the coach back. We can always take our time returning home to Manchester I just can't take a chance on delays going.

Of course when I told Stan he went ape. Because he's currently in the mentality of every minute of the day has to be spent saving money for our future. But more of that later. Thus meaning take on any work on that you can get even if its twenty four hours a day twenty four days a week. I think its partly for the future and partly because he's a greedy little git. Which alright is good in theory, but you do need to take time out to chill and enjoy life too don't you. So I announce the schedule and what a surprise. Here we go first words are 'how can I spare the time off work when I've got someone's bleedin' drive up, and another job I should have started already.' He's always moaning, sometimes I feel he's never happy unless he has something to stress about. Well he's not getting his way this time, so I can go with or without him. An hour or so later after a blazing row and some tears we both relent. Well mine was under duress, begrudgingly under duress I might add.

So we have decided and when I say we I mean in the singular sense, because Stan decided for us that we can go but we catch the lunchtime train. We'd arrive in London around five and Earls Court is only a couple of tube stops away from the train station. Staying overnight is out of the question (I did say begrudgingly) because Stan has to be back on the job in the morning. Arghh, I could scream because now I have to cancel the hotel. I was really looking forward to staying over. You can imagine this really P'd me off.

But we are still going, and he does feel bad for not sparing time for me (though not quite bad enough for my liking). We decide to get the last coach back and fingers crossed it will be nice and quiet, at least then we can get some kip on the way back. Sorted. And I'm getting giddy again. Just a few weeks till I finally see Bruce play live and with the E Street Band. It should be a great concert because he's known for being excellent live, and with ten thousand people there the atmosphere should be fantastic. If its half as good as the Oasis Concert I went to I'll be a happy person.

As the gig draws nearer I can hardly contain myself, I'm getting giddier by the minute. I've spent the last two days in a dilemma…which outfit. Jeans or skirt, blouse or jumper. Need to be comfy but need to feel good too. I couldn't possibly go feeling like a frump now could I? Jeans and black cardigan (fitted of course) it is then. Plus, I'll be standing up for half the night so no big heels. But me being so small and petite I need some bloody heels or else I won't get to see anything. And its allocated seating, so I can hardly stand on anyone's toes to move them out of my way. Or even fight my way to the front is it? I can guarantee that some big fella will be stood in front of me its sods law. Suddenly, I can still hear Stan whittering on with himself about time off work again. He is beginning to get on my nerves.

I wanted to enjoy this gig, not have him dampen my mood. And if I hear one more reference to 'him missing work' I swear I will put poison in his tea. Well okay then maybe just a laxative or two, just enough to keep his mouth shut ha ha. Okay, I'm joking but even a jury would sympathise with me. I remind Stan he can work till he's sixty five years old, and work will still be here when we get back. God, is it not enough that he works six and seven days a week all year round. Always putting off holidays and taking time out (more of that later).

I have just enough time to I send a quick email to Antonio:

Hey Antonio my friend. Guess who's going to see Springsteen tomorrow? Not you… it must be ME then!   :-)

Reply: Thanks For Nothing Ring me later tell me how it went
 :-(

Antonio is a fan of Bruce's he was gutted that he had meetings that clashed. He might get to see him in Europe in the next week or two, I'm sure he will wangle it somehow.

~ Chapter Two ~ **The Concert**

Concert day arrives and I definitely can't contain myself now. To get in the right mood I blast a Bruce CD at top note. Whilst getting ready I must go through my routine. It's yet another thing that gets on his nerves, waiting for me to be ready. Does he not know that it takes at least twenty minutes before you can start on the hair/make-up ... after having a bath and condition hair, that you need to cream self down with moisturiser, and only then can you start on drying hair. Oh, and then there's the make-up to apply. Will put on slightly more than usual as we are going out.

Well I am going out and he is only tagging along purely out of guilt. Not that he really wants to be there, he's going for me really. Before it was yes he quite liked Bruce, now its suddenly descended to he's ok. Purely for my benefit you see, just to wind me up. Because, yet again, I'm interfering with his 'work.'

He's shouting upstairs 'for gods sake are you not ready yet' I think four times so already. I shout back you cannot rush perfection... of which is wasted on him because he didn't find this funny at all. It's just another reason for him to get irritable. I'm finally ready only to be told 'you don't look any different.' Yes, its wasted on me this time because now I don't find it funny. I have to bite my tongue not to reply... its not for your benefit. But he is not in the joking mood today, where as I am.

Then the moaning starts again. Even though he asked three times this week 'Could he not have played Manchester. We could have had a good night, and gone for dinner or something' I want to reply 'why so that we don't hinder bloody work' but instead grit my teeth and smile sweetly. Of which he takes the hint that now is a good time to shut up. Now he knows I'm not amused. I tell him again 'For the last time, he was not playing Manchester on this tour, don't mention it again or we will end up having a row, I want to enjoy this day.' The other one he keeps saying is 'I should be at work now' have I heard that four times this morning or is it fourteen times? I can't remember it has been that many, and we have only been up three hours. The day can but only get better. At this rate I'll be ready for topping myself by lunchtime.

We arrive at Piccadilly train station only to find a heaving queue for tickets. Every man and his dog seem to be in front of us. If we don't hurry we will miss the damn train. I can feel Stan's temper rising from three feet away. How he's managed to keep his mouth shut without sarcastic comments I don't know. I try not to have eye contact, I can feel myself ready to start laughing. You know that nervous laugh that starts at the most in appropriate time.

Is it my fault I didn't have time to pick the tickets up before. Or was it, I didn't think so. Although I do pass Guide Bridge train station every night, on my way home from work. Five minutes away from home. Best keep quiet that I could have got them from Guide Bridge or he will skitz. Luckily, I manage to buy the tickets with five minutes to spare before the train leaves.

As we are running for the train I'm still grinning to myself thinking about the concert. I feel like the cat that's got the cream. Now all I need is to find a comfy seat with a table and grab something to eat. You see being so busy getting ready we've not had lunch yet. As the train pulls out of the station a couple of guys come walking down our carriage. You know the type…loud scally types making sure they phone everyone they know on their mobile phones. The I'm Mr big because I don't work and can chat with my mates all day on mobiles.

As they walk nearer I pray they don't sit near us. A few hours with them shouting about will surely end up with an argument. They'll get on our nerves that much that sooner or later we'll end up asking them to shut. They sit a couple of tables away. I feel that nervous laugh starting again. I can feel a trauma coming on. Luckily things get a little quieter. I can hear a few blokes at the end of the carriage having a laugh and a few beers but not being loud. Thank God.

I'm getting even giddier thinking seven hours to go. But what a pity we didn't get front row tickets (I'm still gutted about that). Never mind it could have been worse I might not have got any tickets after all. I'm just enjoying my coffee when one of the scallies gets his phone out for the tenth time in as many minutes. Then he shouts 'Yeh I'm on me way to Earls Court.' My ears prick up at this point, could they be going to the gig too. They don't look like Springsteen fans. Just as I start to see them in a different light he spouts 'Yeh, trying to sell tickets for the Springsteen Concert, I've got a quite a few tickets and they're good seats too'!

My ears are still alert only to hear him shout 'Yeh, I had some tickets for his Manchester Gig but didn't manage to sell them all. At this point I choke on my coffee almost spurting it all over Stan. Who at this moment in time is sat opposite me and glaring. And from what I can feel his eyes are like a pair of lasers burning holes into my head. I can feel my cheeks start to flush, very quickly and that nervous laugh starts again. Yes, I'm definitely feeling the trauma. Now if I was with the girls they would have found this hysterical. Stan on the other hand did not. I mean, its not as if I could have predicted a gig in Manchester. Is it my fault I didn't see it advertised anywhere.

Yes he's definitely annoyed. The fierce eyes and burning forehead are a slight give away. Oops, I think I may be in trouble now. I sort of blink and peep up through my fringe, hoping he would finally see the funny side of it. But no, he doesn't feel sorry for me. Even though I'm looking very sheepish, or is it squeamish, due to the heat my body is generating at this moment making me feel a little sick.

He usually feels sorry for me when I flash big eyes at him, but not today. Ayeisha always says I have Jasmine eyes, Jasmine from the Aladdin film. And with one flash from them and I could get away with murder, well not today. I'm sure that if he could get away with strangling me now he would do. I can already feel the words of a rant ready to tip of his tongue. How's able to contain himself I'll never know. Although the look he shot me had enough energy for me to self combust. It's like sitting with a pressure cooker ready to blow. Oh well only 3 hours of train journey to go, silence and no eye contact seemed the best option.

After an hour into the journey he finally found the will to speak… 'So he isn't playing in Manchester then, only London? I could have been in work, finished a little early…and on he goes. At this point I can feel tears start to well up in my eyes. Not because I feel sorry for myself, well okay just a little, but because he's on about bloody work again. What is his problem? I don't often ask for his time, effort or attention and he knows it. I'm beginning to get angry now of which he can see by my face which is probably purple through temper.

He decides softly is the best option, as I am a premenstrual female who is ready to blow. And he probably doesn't want a scene on the train. After all we've not been left home more that an hour. He must have felt sorry for me, as he backs down saying 'never mind we might as well enjoy the evening now.' At last it takes a bloody miracle, but he finally comes round to my way of thinking. Although he did do his damndest to spoil it, he realises keeping me happy is the right option today. That, and he feels guilty for going on so much.

Take a deep breath, relax and let's enjoy the day. Now we have the tension out of the way I know we will have a great time. He just grins at me like he knows I'm the cat that's got the cream. We both start laughing, feeling ridiculous arguing over something so silly. We finally made it to London, and manage to find our way around the underground and managed to lose the ticket touts. When we arrive at Earls Court there's already a large crowd assembled.

I'm trying to convince myself that if we edge ourselves forward we could get nearer to the front even though we are booked in seats. But I suppose I'm that type of person who always wants more, or so Stan reminds me. 'Well what self respecting female wouldn't ha ha.' He chooses to ignore my comment. Once inside we find our seats... ok a third from the front, which some people would think this great, however not me. Difficult to believe I know but I don't sulk, just feel very jealous of those on the front row. Which to me is only human nature.

I ask Stan to get something to eat, one thing I do not want is Stan getting irritable because he's hungry. He's a complete nightmare if he's hungry. Thankfully he returns with a bag full of goodies. There must be enough in there to feed six of us! So far so good and then row in front of us arrive. I knew it, I just bloody knew it! I take one look ahead and stare blankly at Stan. Of which he bursts out laughing not quite believing his eyes either. The guy who decides the best seat in the house for him is the one in front of me, although he has half a dozen seats to choose from.

He must be at least six foot tall! I could have bet £10,000 that the biggest guy in town would be blocking my view. Its almost as if someone upstairs says come on we haven't had a good enough laugh yet so lets get her going some more. Of all the seats here, why on earth could he not be behind me or even at the side of me. I ask you, is it me or what. But you will come to understand things like this are the norm around me.

The concert gets underway and everybody is as loud as can be, the atmosphere is electric. There is a screen for those at the back, but I don't want to watch a screen. I'm devastated, I have to keep standing on my tip toes to see a little of the stage. Security are keeping people in their seats and not even letting them stand in the isle. They almost tried to keep us sitting down! That's enough to cause a riot. At a rock concert, sitting only? I don't think so. I could stand on my chair to get a better look. And, doing this I am *still* only the same height as the guy in front. So I figure that this should be ok. But then the Gestapo arrive telling me get down off the chair.

But I can't see a damn thing so when the security walk away I'm back on my chair. I have to or I won't see a thing. The guy in front stands a little to the left, so I'm getting a much better view. Just as I am getting back into the concert 'Gestapo Guy' is back again. I can't risk it again.

Stan feels really sorry for me knowing I can't see a bloody thing. He suggests I stand in front of him with my heels against his chair legs and he'll hold me up. Technically I'm not standing on the seat, because my feet are straddled against the top of the legs around the chair. Well yes next to the plastic seat, but, not quite on it. Security tell me to get down. To which Stan shouts 'she's not standing on the chair seat, she's leaning against me.' So he goes off in a huff. Ah, my lovely, lovely Stan. He's now forgiven for being a 'git.'

Now I'm happy I can see. With a great view of the stage, and more importantly I can *see* Bruce. This is fantastic, he is amazing live. The entire band is on top form. And Clarence the saxophone player gets the biggest cheer of all as usual, and rightly so! The crowd are getting louder and louder as Bruce does an encore. Nobody wants this to end, so we get even louder.

Just as the concert is reaching fever pitch Stan shouts 'We should be going soon to get the coach' What! I almost have heart attack. I didn't intend to leave early, and right before the finale! I reply 'Its going to finish soon anyway it's almost ten thirty. This keeps him quiet for a few moments. I can't believe what I heard, and I'm still gutted we weren't at the front, now he wants to leave early! I mean what on earth was he thinking about.

Suddenly, I notice a some people are slowly edging forward through the isle. Quick Stan! I shout lets go to the front but he says 'No Security are sending people back to their seats.' As the second encore starts, everyone surges forward again, too many for the Gestapo to hold back. Sod this I thought, I'm off to the front. Security couldn't tell everyone to get back, so I might be lucky enough to sneak through.

I throw my handbag to Stan, as he's shouting something back about going in a minute. But I'm already rushing off down the isle before it registers what he is saying. Within seconds I'm in front of the stage. The sound from the speakers are so loud they almost burst my ear drums. I manage to squeeze myself to the barrier the same as everyone else, there is no way I'm going further back now.

I can't believe it, right in front of me Bruce walks to the edge of the stage. Everybody starts shouting and screaming, stretching their arms out shouting for Bruce to come to our side. By now Security have given up and leave us at there. At least I think they have because quite a few people are still behind me. Slowly Bruce walks towards us again but this time reaching out to our hands. The noise from the crowd is almost unbearable. Most people are bigger than me, in fact everybody stood there is bigger than me and manage to lean out further than me. I'm already on my tiptoes reaching out as far as I can. Then some kind person shoves a bloody flag in my face so now I can't see anything. But within a moment Bruce appears right in front of me. I can't believe it I feel like I'm going to burst.

The crowd roars in a frenzy everyone screaming and pushing. I'm getting squashed against the barrier and feel like I'm going to faint. I desperately try to stop myself fainting and hope he stops in front of me. But instead he goes past further down the row. Everyone shoves to the side thank God which allows me to breathe again.

Before I can catch my breath back Bruce appears right in front of me again. My God this is fantastic, though I doubt he could see anything with lights shining in our faces. He carries on singing whilst walking along the front row and holding out his hands again. I can't believe it this is perfection. Did I really get to the front from all that way back.

As the Band does the final encore, security pull everyone back demanding we go back to our seats. Well I'm sorry but after the time I've had getting here I have no intentions of going further back. Especially now I'm only a few feet away. The concerts almost finished anyway a few more minutes aren't going to make much difference are they. And besides how much space do I take up anyway, I'm only six and a half stone wet through.

There's no way am I going back now. The view from front row is fantastic and I've just seen Bruce's face. Little Stevie the guitarist has just pointed to the crowd, almost as if to thank us for our support. I'm so giddy I could burst. The Gestapo are back looking at us all, trying to figure out who was actually there. By this point I don't know how, but I've managed to squeeze onto the end of the seats of the front row.

A girl besides me glares at me like 'you cheeky cow, your not supposed to be here.' I of course look very sheepish and smile, then just stare ahead. She very kindly let me stay there and enjoy the remainder of the concert. How nice was that, I think she felt sorry for me. The security guard stares at me, of which I cheekily smile back and stay where I am. He sort of questions himself to say was she or wasn't she there already. I just ignore him like I don't know what he is on about. Jeez, that was close. The finale was brilliant, nobody wanted it to end. There was no supporting band, just Bruce and the E Street Band for three tremendous hours. God, front row I can't believe it, I saw him close up almost touched hands like those at the side of me.

This has definitely made up for being stuck way back. The Band have left the stage, it's definitely over. What a fantastic night, then it dawns on me where is Stan. He was behind me at some point. I best get back and try to find him, he won't believe I got to the front. Now everybody is pushing to get out. They've rushed out of their seats like ants. Stan is in the isle waiting for me and I'm grinning away like a Cheshire Cat grinning from ear to ear. But Stan is definitely not smiling. In fact his face is like thunder. This wipes the smile straight off my face in a blink. I'm definitely not smiling now.

I feel my face start to flush, probably from the blaze I can feel coming from his face. Stan slams my bag towards me and starts ranting about missing the coach. Oh my God, the bloody coach! I had been so excited I'd completely forgotten about time. Stan's temper looks ready to burst. I try to pacify him saying lets push forward a little to squeeze through everyone. But Stan is not in the mood for niceties, and trying to push his way through hundreds of people is not a good idea.

Funnily enough everyone else has the same idea pushing towards the exit. I try telling him its okay, when we get out we can rush for the tube. That was until we finally get out the main doors and see the Police outside. They are holding everyone back in the queue, stopping them from pushing forward towards into the tube station. They're only letting a few people through at a time. Oh no, at this rate we will be walking home. Yes, I can feel Stan's blaze coming through.

If you put a radar machine on his anger, you'd have picked it up from Papa New Guinea. I can feel a trauma coming on. I don't dare laugh through nerves he'd probably strangle me. I think we've got less than fifteen minutes to get to the coach station, but with this crowd it could take at least an hour. We try to push forward but to no avail. The Police are only letting a few people at a time go.

Finally, what seems like forever, we make it into to the tube station, only to be lost in maze. And, when we do find the right platform it's heaving. When the carriage pulls up, people are trying to squeeze aboard. But there is definitely no room. Reluctantly, and really worried, we wait for the next one to arrive. Which feels like an hour of course. It's like all of a sudden everything starts to happen in slow motion. I'm sure I'm having palpitations.

I can feel myself holding my breath, literally begging for our tube. When it does arrive we all surge on like bees in squeezing back into a hive. I'm feeling like a beetle being swamped by Ants. I have an urge to scream to everyone 'Get Back' somehow, but I manage to restrain myself. I pray its only seconds to our stop. Arriving at our stop we run out to the main road like mad men. It's quite a walk to the coach station, and we are unsure of which way to go. Especially a quick way. Not even having enough time to walk we run down the street as if chasing a handbag thief. To top it off its been raining, the ground is wet and slippy. Of course there isn't a taxi in sight.

We run as fast as we can down the road. Yes, I am actually legging it. Well trying to bear in mind the last time I can remember running I was at school some fifteen years ago. Right now, I feel like I am the most unfit person I know, and I feel angry for it. I get a stitch in my side that hurts like hell. Stan is about as sympathetic as a robot, shouting 'we have to run faster now move it.' I feel like I've got a personal trainer like Harvey bellowing at me to work harder. All I can think is faster, I'm bloody dying here. Stan grabs hold of my arm to practically dragging me down the street, shouting 'I cannot believe you can't even run down the god damn street.' Again, he's not amused, it's not my fault I can't bloody run. I couldn't run for a bus if my life depended on it, but here I am expected to be Linford bloody Christie.

I cannot help but think to myself what if we are going in the wrong direction? But, just I am starting to have my fifth panic attack of the day, we finally get sight of the station. Thank God for that, I couldn't have ran a step more. Feeling rather anxious, I'm look for our coach to come around the corner. That would just be typical wouldn't it as we arrive at the station it would be pulling out.

I ask Stan 'I doubt it would leave dead on time, it might hang on a minute or two if all the seats are booked but not filled yet.' Surely it wouldn't just go? He doesn't reply, either he cannot face the thought of it going, or he's too angry to speak (or both). We're both looking for our coach. I'm pleading with God for it to be there. It's amazing how in certain times of need you suddenly become religious. Okay, so it happens a couple of times a year. But at those times you suddenly become so insignificant yet very desperate.

I still can't see the coach, maybe its running late. It does happen after all. Yes I know now I'm clutching at straws. My mouth feels so, dry but I cannot summon any words. Only a few coaches are in the station and there doesn't seem to be much activity ie, a huge queue waiting for the Manchester coach. We ask an attendant where our coach is… of which he replies 'it's already gone.' GONE! He did say GONE! Didn't he. Or am I dreaming this and it's my nerves making me hear what I don't want to hear. Then Stan sort of gasps. Yes he did say GONE! I don't think he's going to take this very well. Feeling very nervous, I gulp for air. You could see his face start to boil at the bloke. Not directly at him but a reaction to what he'd said. He turns to me and shouts you've got to be joking. We've missed the God Damn coach! The attendant sort of takes a few steps back looking worried at the inferno about to rage.

People start looking at us although Stan doesn't notice this. All he can see is us two, without a coach, stuck in the centre of London. But *I* can feel them looking at us. Almost as if they're only an inch away from my face. I'm feeling very embarrassed that we've missed the coach, but feel even more embarrassed that he is holding centre court giving a performance of a lifetime. If only I knew then that this was just the beginning.

At this point his voice goes up about ten notches. He starts ranting and raving 'Its all your fault. You just had to have that extra ten minutes didn't you, You just couldn't leave on time to make sure we got the coach could you. What the hell are we supposed to do now' then he stops for breath.

I can feel my face burning, tears are pricking my eyes, but I'll be damned if I cry in front of these strangers. They may be strangers but at this moment it feels like the whole world knows me personally, and that they're all tuning in. Of course he doesn't hold back. As if the ranting wasn't quite enough of a sideshow, he now starts to pace up and down, boiling with temper. When I say pace I should say stomp, heavily.

Everyone is still looking. I can't bear to look at their faces, I just see a blur of heads around all facing me. At this point he is screaming how selfish I am, then slams his bag down onto the bench (yes the bag of goodies that I insisted he go bloody buy, the ones I now bitterly regret asking him to buy). Defeated and deflated, I sit on the bench. I am still trying to breathe because I think I stopped five minutes ago at the 'It's Gone' point. But Stan doesn't just slam the bag down in temper. Oh no, he goes for the big dramatic launch as if he's trying to break the bench with the bag. I'm worried about looking at the bench because it went with such a force. I wonder if it's caused any damage, he then continues to stomp again. Now I feel like I want to die because I know everybody's eyes are still all fixed on us.

Then, in a mixture of defeat and temper he plonks himself down on the bench asking 'what the hell are we supposed to do now.' All I can think is we'll have to wait here and get the early coach back to Manchester, which would probably be about three or four o'clock in the morning and I just want to cry. At the most inopportune moment my mobile phone bleeps a text message through. I best answer it could be Ayeisha. But it's not Ayeisha. It's a message from Antonio: Hey my little friend how did it go?
Was the Boss great or what you lucky thing?

Sulking I think to myself yes I'm feeling really lucky now Antonio. Stan shoots a glaring look to me. As if to say is that all you can do arse around on your mobile. Best not to make this any worse than it already is I put the mobile away. Just when I think things couldn't get any worse the attendant walks warily towards us, almost looking like a frightened rabbit.

I pray to God (thus being quite a few times in one evening so far) *Pleeease* don't say calm down. Stan would just love to get into an argument with somebody because he needs to burn all that charged up energy that the temper has fuelled. The attendant stands awkwardly in front of us blurting out 'I'm sorry but the coach station is about to close.' Poor thing he looks really nervous and blinks fast a few times adding 'You'll have to leave now.' My mouth drops open because I haven't got over the shock of the missing coach yet, I can't cope with this one.

If I didn't die ten minutes ago I am surely about to now. Neither of us can think. Me because I'm still trying to fight the tears back from the last few moments. And Stan because he's still trying to calm himself down.

Pleadingly, I ask can we wait for the early morning coach to Manchester. But he says they are locking up the station until the morning, everybody has to leave. Yes, I want to cry, but I'm still stunned into silence. Stan decides this is the right time to jump up saying 'We'd better go then hadn't we', then storms towards the doors whilst shouting 'I don't believe this.' Still in shock I tag along behind him worried about whats going to happen now. After all, it's a long walk home. Our audience are still staring at us but I try desperately not to give any eye contact.

Once we are outside he seems to think a lecture of how selfish I am is warranted. I, on the other hand do not. He rambles on but funnily enough I am so not in the mood. Although I should be grateful, the ranting has mellowed into a mere shout. I feel guilty enough, but I'm damned if I am going to feel guilty because he's too selfish to stay in London for one night. Then make me be out to be the bad one.

Christ, if everyone heard him in the Station, they would have thought I'd dragged him to a nightclub got us both drunk and then made us miss the bloody coach. It was hardly a bad thing what I did, stupid thing maybe but it hardly puts me in the category of sinner does it? Then he asks if it was worth it. I suppose now is not the time to answer. Feeling sorry for myself like I have the whole world on my shoulders, Dump more guilt on me why don't you? I reply.

This is where I loose it. I shout back saying he is the bloody selfish one. It could have been great. We could have been at the hotel having fun, enjoying the evening together, and having a drink or two. But Oh no, he just can't spare one bloody night. There would have been no stress about being late for the coach. No upset about having to miss the ending of the concert, as if I would have anyway. But I'm supposed to feel guilty about a bloody night out. I've just recovered my breath from the stitch, I'm upset and humiliated by the ranting and all those strangers, as if I've known them all my life. I've had enough so I storm off down the street in the opposite direction. I can feel the burning sensation of tears start rolling down my face.

It's late, its dark, and now its starting to rain again. I don't have a clue where I am, or, where I'm going. I can hear Stan shouting 'Angie' down the street but I'm fuming. Like I want to go back their for more grief. He can sod off, if he can't spare me one night, then f**k him. He shouts he's sorry and he's angry because we have missed the coach, and for me to come back.

But I'm still stomping down the street in a rage upset and not giving a damn. Catching me up he tells me 'Don't be stupid wandering off on your own like that' but I'm too upset to listen. 'Stop it' he shouts grabbing hold of my arm, 'come here.' I refuse to move. He doesn't say sorry, or let's find somewhere to stay, no just 'come back here.' I'm probably too angry to accept his apology anyway.

I just stand there, trying to think through my temper and tears. I don't want to go with him, but I don't want to walk around London on my own either. I don't know where I am or what we are going to do. I mean, there isn't anybody about to ask directions or find out where we are. For all I know it could be some dodgy area. I just stand there upset. Stan said 'Come on let's find the train station and see what time the last train is, you're not walking around on your own.'

Begrudgingly, we walk in the same direction sort of together. Neither of us speaking, both still fuming, we try looking for a sign for directions to the train station. God knows what people would be thinking if there is CCTV near the station. They'd be sat behind the camera's going 'look here's another pair; lets see who wins this argument.'

We eventually find the train station. There are lots of people still about but it's cold and noisy. We ask what time the next train is. I figure the next one would be around one or two o'clock in the morning. Then people could arrive back in Manchester around five or six in the morning. This sounds pretty reasonable to me. But of course life isn't that simple is it, especially as it is me. Because the next train isn't until five thirty in the morning. Brilliant. Just bloody brilliant. I ask Stan what more could possibly go wrong. Which is something you definitely shouldn't say, not if I don't want to tempt fate. Stan is too exhausted to shout any more. I think the ten minute stomp here has helped calm him down.

Okay, so we have to hang around the train station for the next five or six hours but at least we are inside and safe. Everybody around us seems drunk, drunk but happy, trying to find their last train home. Well okay, they did look a right sight. But at least they look like they'd had a good time. We on the other hand look distinctly unhappy. Stan asks should we try to find a hotel, or go into the café for an hour and get something to eat.

I think its pointless trying to find somewhere to stay at midnight, and then have to be up at four in the morning to come back here. It's not worth it. I think it's best to just sit around here whilst people are still about. Then go into the café when it's quiet here when everyone else has gone. At least we'd feel safe in there when the station is empty. He agrees, so we just sit in silence a little more. I feel cold and damp, the seats are freezing, and the atmosphere between us is like ice, just to add to the ambiance.

My mind wanders off wondering what Bruce and the gang are doing now. Probably enjoying a great after show party and swigging champagne. At this point a rail guard, our good old friendly rail guard comes towards us again 'I'm sorry the last train is about to leave soon, if this isn't your train then you'll have to leave now were closing the station.' I gasp again! I don't believe this, twice in one night, surely we can't be that unlucky. Here's me thinking at least we'll be indoors, safe and dry inside the station.

Where the hell are we going to go, it's midnight and outside is pitch black, the streets are quiet and the rain is pouring down. We ask if it's alright to wait for the early train as we have missed our coach. I'm sorry he replied but we have to empty the place then lock up. I breathe another big sigh of desperation. We don't speak, just walk out of the train station together. Isn't it funny how things look in daylight. I mean you feel you can deal with anything in daylight, but night time puts a different prospective on things.

Walking out of the station that night felt even worse than walking out of the coach station. I know anger had something to do with it but I did feel there were options open. Now I'm feeling rather scared it's a little late in the day to think what options are available. The station looked quite different when we arrived earlier today. It was vibrant, hundreds of people were milling about doing their thing. Traffic was passing by and the atmosphere was great, with smells around such as baguettes and coffee in the air. Now, it was quite frightening. The road looked dismal and dirty.

Suddenly, I'm rather thankful I'm with Stan. I suppose it was stupid walking off alone like that, but at the time you don't think that, your temper runs your emotions. Thinking about it now, it was silly to be alone in the centre of London at midnight with no knowledge of where is a safe or where is a bit dodgy. I'd be a sitting duck target for weirdo's, and believe me where ever I am there is surely to be a weirdo around.

There's no point in arguing, deflated we agree to let it be and try and deal with the situation. We look for a hotel or Bed & Breakfast. After all we are in the centre of London, there must be hundreds of them around. Or so we thought. The first few we ask are fully booked. There were large hotels with lots of rooms, but 'no rooms at the Inn.' So on we plodded, passing a few more. Again no vacancies. It's gone midnight, the rain is pouring down, I am tired and want a bed. At this moment in time, I'd sleep anywhere. I'd doss on somebody's floor if they offered, because trudging around like this sheds some light on how it could possibly be for homeless people. At least we have money for a room, should we ever find one. What on earth do homeless people do. I'm overcome with 'self being' thankful I have a job, a job I moan about daily, a job that helps pay for a mortgage, my car, clothes and holidays.

Times like this remind you how insignificant you are, how something can change within a moment. The moment for me is depressive, and full of self pity. If I sulk any more I'd be tripping over my chin. We seem to be going round in circles. I'm sure we have just passed that building twice already. It is then I have a 'Eureka' moment. Suddenly remembering when I booked the hotel, I put the phone number into my mobile phone. Just in case we couldn't find the hotel after coming out of the gig.

But I am cringing. Cringing at the thought they'd have my cancellation in the diary, then here having the cheek to ring for a room. And at this time of the bloody night. Well, desperate times call for desperate measures. I'll have to embarrass myself by ringing for a room. This is one night I am not going to forget in a hurry! Then I have my second Eureka moment, I don't have to give my name, I can put it in Stan's name, Bingo!

I ring quickly. This is going to be really embarrassing because I can't even remember where the Hotel was. And more importantly I don't know where we are! When I finally do get through the line is terrible and I can't hear a damn thing. I shout loudly down the phone 'Do you have any rooms available' hoping they'll say yes. They keep repeating something, but I can't quite make out what they are saying.

How apt! Phoning up and embarrassing myself to see if they have any vacancies. And, to top it off, I hear a train go past over the bridge. The racket rattling through the empty street is ridiculous. That must have been the last train. Was it just as a reminder? Either that or a slap in the face. I take it as a slap in the face. I'm shouting down the phone if they have any rooms and can hardly hear them. After a minute of shouting back and forth I get the jist of things, no bloody rooms!

We hadn't brought much money except for travel and food. We thought we wouldn't need any travelling to London and straight back again. The oh so lovely credit card is looking decidedly glum now. I was so looking forward to our trip, booking a room, staying over and have some fun. Now, now I feel like I begrudge paying for a room. Before it was for an enjoyable evening, now it's a necessity upon desperate measures. What a night...What a bloody night. Funny, I'm not feeling too excited now.

We're getting quite desperate, where do you go in the middle of the night? The Police Station and ask for a room? I suppose they would say yes if you don't mind spending it with forty drunks. I feel very vulnerable even with Stan. Gods knows what I'd feel like should I be on my own. Stan doesn't like the area we've wandered into saying it looks a bit dodgy.

We best get somewhere that feels a little safer. Yet its pitch black and we don't have a clue to which is the best way to go. Suddenly all the houses and buildings look the same, again. Surely we haven't walked in another circle, we can't tell. The B&B's signs are still showing no vacancies. The hotels are full It doesn't seem a thriving major European city, if feels like the back of beyond.

I felt like crying again but don't. Mainly because I don't want to hear 'I was right when I said we should leave early...I told you so.' I'm already going to be reminded of this one at every opportune moment for the next 10 years anyway, of how I stranded us in the middle of the night, how selfish I am. Maybe I should get the inscription 'I told you so Selfish Cow' on my coffin. There isn't even a soul around to ask for directions, or help.

Turning yet another corner we find a B&B. The owner with a strong Scottish accent says he is full and asks if we are from Manchester. He then starts rambling about how he loves Manchester United Football Club and Manchester even though he's a Scot! He's really sorry about having no rooms and tells us to ask at another B&B down the road and around the next corner. A friend of his runs it, we might be lucky.

I mumble he couldn't have liked Manchester that much or he would have let us stay in their lounge and just sit on the settee until 5am, and we would have still paid for a room. Stan just stares at me as if to say 'there is nowt like cheek.' Off we go again, around the corner to the B&B he mentioned, and ask if there are any rooms. Yes we have one left. Thank God!!!

It doesn't have its own bathroom, it's a shared bathroom, but does have a sink & toilet with a double bed. (Under the circumstances, I was hoping for single beds or even single rooms). However, now is not the time to complain, we are very grateful for the room all the same.

We can't sign in quick enough and whilst we are paying another couple arrive without any luggage and asking for a room. But they are told we have taken the last one. Now I really feel bad. I look at Stan and whisper 'Couldn't he let them stay in the foyer.' Again he just glares at me then says 'They'll just have to do what we did and carry on looking it's not our fault.' But they could be searching for ages and it didn't look like a great area to be stranded in. Again I feel really bad. I even say to him they could sleep on our floor if they want, but he glares at me saying don't be stupid.

We go to our room without speaking. We don't undress we just lie on top of the blankets, no apologies no making up. I'm cold and get under the blankets still refusing to apologise. Exhausted I drift off to sleep trying to forget the whole episode. Well most of it, maybe not the part of reaching the front row, this manages to bring a little smile to face.

We wake around eight am. There is nothing to do but freshen up as we don't have any spare clothes. The atmosphere is still frosty. Venturing outside it's a lovely spring morning fresh and sunny. Again in the daylight it looks different. People are milling about, shops open with lots of activity. It doesn't look so bad after all. We pass a bistro and decide to stop and get breakfast. I'm desperate for a cup of tea. You know that feeling when you are dying for that first cup of tea of the morning. Its absolute heaven and feels like the best cup of tea I've ever tasted. What a day to be arguing on, well maybe not arguing just not speaking.

I sit watching people going around their business. It should have been a fun morning. Getting ready in the hotel and maybe have an hour or two in London before we come back. I can't help but feel such self-pity. If I think about what has happened I'll surely burst into tears. One bloody day to spare for an evening out, is it too much to ask for. Is it me being selfish? I can't believe we are sitting here like this. What should have been a lovely morning being giddy about wagging work. Well, I know I'm not wagging work but there is something great about you chilling in London, having breakfast in a Bistro whilst everyone else is in work. This makes you feel like your wagging it.

I absolutely refuse to apologise. I feel as I usually do, that I have done nothing wrong. I look at him thinking why are we like this again. He looks back at me knowing what I am thinking. But all he can summon is 'Don't look at me like that' as if *he* hasn't done anything wrong. Which usually means don't look at me with those big brown eyes, I am not feeling sorry for you or give you your own way. I look away feeling sorry for myself even more, if that's at all possible.

After breakfast we walk towards the coach station. He says its pointless rushing for the train now. We only have to pay extra to buy new tickets. We might as well go to the coach station and amend our tickets from last night. By the time we get back it would be pointless him going into work now anyway. But by my thinking he works for himself anyway, so why put yourself under this pressure. Always taking on more work than he can physically do. Then expecting to fit the work of five days in two.

Why should I feel guilty for asking him to come. If he wants to work and have no life then why do I get the guilt trip. No, I won't have it. He says I'm the most stubborn person he has ever met. I presume he means besides himself. After all this was my thing. I had asked him to come, he didn't have to take me up on it. He could have stayed at home with Bash, and then been up in time for his precious bloody work. Oh no, he tells me I'm the most aggravating person he has ever met. Again, I presume he means besides himself. I absolutely refuse to grovel. I am not going to say sorry.

I'm not even sure if I would accept his apology yet, well should he offer one that is. Would he have done the same, I ask myself. Would he have missed the end of an England football match to make sure he got the train home? I don't think so somehow. He'd rather have walked than missed the ending. Could you imagine if I made him leave ten minutes before the end and England score in those last few minutes, it would have been 'the' part of the match. Would he then have listened to me bleat on and on about having to leave. That he would have to miss the end and then listen to me moaning about getting home.

The finale is the crescendo of the evening how could I possibly have missed that, and that's without me getting to the front row. He wouldn't stand there listening to me moaning, there is no way he would budge, and he knows it. I can't help but feel really sad and he knows it. So eventually we talk, Stan apologises for not sparing more time. And that he wants to make more time for us but explains he needs to get through more work so we can have more money behind us so we can enjoy our future. I finally say I'm sorry that we missed our coach. Not an admission of guilt you understand for me making us late for the coach, just the fact that we missed it. Once again, he reminds me I am the most aggravating person he knows. I, on the other hand don't quite see it the same way. He puts his arms around me gently kissing me, saying he can't believe what we are like, and that he's sorry. I have my lovely, lovely Stan back now. The rational kind and gentle Stan. Well for a short time anyway. I might as well make the most of it.

I remind him how annoying and aggressive he is to my aggravations and stubbornness. I also remind him how he completely showed me up when deciding to throw himself around the coach station, and topped it further by slamming his goodie bag around. But he tells me how he kept his hands from my throat is a miracle. And he has the cheek to add that I'd drive the Pope mad, even the Pope wouldn't be able to keep his hands off me. This of course makes me laugh, I can but only ask why does he look like Antonio Banderas. No Stan does not find this funny, of which makes me giggle even more.

He is really sorry for all the ranting and raving. The security have probably kept the display on tape so they could have a good laugh at it the next day saying to the next shift 'you'll never guess what idiots we had in last night. Just watch him ranting and launching himself about.' We spend the afternoon making up, aw my lovely Stan. There isn't any point spending all that time sulking and not make up now is there.

We laugh about the last twenty four hours, not quite believing how ridiculous things got. I mean of all the carriages the ticket tout just had to sit in our carriage. And how it spoilt what was a good day and a great concert. At least I'll have something to remember my first Bruce concert by. I wonder what would happen the next time I see Bruce in concert. Would I get to the front row again, maybe next time I'd wangle some back stage passes! You never know.

~ Chapter Three ~ Office Politics & Gilberts Grape

Back in work I give the guys in the office a recount my of my saga. It gives them a good laugh if nothing else. They are of course in hysterics at the re-run. One asks 'Isn't that just a typical day out for you then Ang.' Which come to think of it I think they may be right. I always seem to be on the tail end of something. It feels like riding a wave, you know the wave is coming you can feel the current building up. All you can do is ride it out because you don't know how to stop it. But one way or another you know its coming. Later on you will find out lots of 'odd things' somehow happen around me. Be it to me, around me, or around friends of mine, but it sure as hell is in some close proximity to me.

Working in a busy Customer Services Department we of course think of ourselves as the hub of the company. If there isn't anything happening in our office, then it's not worth knowing about. I suppose we also happen to be the loudest office on site. We process the orders and export the goods ie. We get to take all the crap. The phone calls orders faxes, allocate stock raise invoices print paperwork and if we are really lucky we get to prepare the rest of the hundred and one documents needed to export the goods around the world. You can imagine we are busy all day, every day. We each have our own countries to look after and just for good measure share a chunk of the UK market too.

Some of our customers are more demanding than others so we try to keep the customers we get along with. Because we work with them daily we get to know our customers which makes our life easier. Some of our team and I use the word 'team' loosely, are more team players than others. Being such a busy office we all have to muck in together. If we are busier that usual or having a bad day we help each other out. Or that is how it's supposed to happen. Except and I'm sure you know how it is some of us do all the helping but get nothing in return. Yet it always seems to be the same few that never help out. This eventually causes a few 'ripples' in the office.

Our flexi-time is supposed to help us cover office hours, staggering our hours between ourselves to make life easier for us. Again the flexibility suits some of us more than others and a few take advantage of it whenever they can. Well one in particular, Claire who had just turned forty and approaching her mid-life crisis. She struggled to get childcare cover or so she claimed. Her childminder could only do two afternoons a week, mid week. At first we put it down to circumstances and helped accommodate this for the short-term. Then when her childminder decided to get a full time job Claire looked for another minder. And guess what the new minder could only part time too.

What a miracle two minders who only work mornings and the same two afternoons. What a bloody coincidence! Maybe they belong to a cult or something and have meetings in the afternoons. It's a bit of a phenomena. It's funny because I've never heard of this before. If it didn't affect the office we probably wouldn't mind so much but we had to cover her work. It stinks of taking the mickey and the office was feeling it too. Wouldn't we all like to finish early three days a week to trawl the shops or go to the park.

Claire didn't help matters either by refusing to look elsewhere for a minder. You can imagine how this went down in the office. She took a full time job but doesn't want to do the work. Which is fine but then go find a part time job. But she wants her full time wage with part time hours. Our boss did his best to hide in his sanctuary but the singletons marched into his office demanding she be made to pull her weight. After all why should they cover her work just because they don't have children.

This caused a few rows but she complained her family lived in London and Scotland and has nobody around to help her. We tried helping and asked friends living near her of who their childminders are. We gave her the phone numbers but she refused to contact them, saying she doesn't know who they are. We were furious that management let her get away with it. But she turned the taps on crying at every opportune moment making them feel guilty. This went down like a lead balloon because the others could see right through her. At first Antonio sympathised with her then saw she was very manipulative and declared he did not like her.

We dealt with her phone calls when she went home early and sorted problems out that came with the call. We could hardly say to a customer call back tomorrow. It affected our service levels and our morale. This meant she couldn't have her equal share of work because she wasn't there to answer the damn phone. To top it off she claimed she was doing most of the work because more orders were entered by her. Yes single line orders, our orders could have thirty product lines on them. Does that mean she does more work? I think not. One thing you don't do is start with office politics because you won't win. Even Margaret Thatcher would have problems taking on this office. Should anyone upset the balance of the office then it became like a pack of wolves baying for blood. Everyone was used to pitching in but this ruffled everyone's feathers for sure. When we complained we got nowhere fast leaving us even more deflated.

Claire was separated from her husband Duncan. He ran his own business and couldn't be relied upon to do his share for the children. Yet he would phone her constantly throughout the day. She claimed it was to speak to her because he was so concerned. Claire couldn't see that he rang her to see what she was cooking for tea. Could he come round, could he bring his shirts to be ironed. He still had washing to do but couldn't do it if he was coming to see their girls. And each time like an idiot she'd tell Duncan to bring the washing along too.

Yet he could never phone to say he'd pick the children up or cook their tea and take them to the park. He wanted to be single and have his family too. And she was the doormat letting him. Of course she couldn't see it like that. She claimed what a Good Samaritan he was always keeping in touch and calling round and didn't the sun shine out of his backside. We however wanted to slap his backside. Although we did feel sorry for her we also wanted to shake her, tell her to wake up and smell the roses. He isn't interested and he'll soon stop calling once he finds himself another woman to do his shirts.

Each of us wanted to phone him up and tell him 'Look Pratt,

sort your life out and do your share looking after the children like parents are supposed to.' But she'd probably get us sacked if we did. Then she'd end up taking him back and we'd be the bad guys. We all knew he was only interested in himself. And the outburst about childcare comments from us did not go down very well at all, then she turned into the colleague from hell. If it wasn't Claire feeling ill then it was one of the children. Of course they were never off colour like normal kids. Oh no, they were always seriously ill. If one of ours picked up a bug from school we would have looked after them, give them some medicine and they'd be running around in no time at all. Not Claire's she would phone for the doctor to come out on a home visit. If it was that bad you would have got the husband home and taken the child to the emergency room. It came to a head when she was in the doctors almost every week for herself or her children. When the doctor refused to give any medication she ranted that he was useless.

The doctor was probably ready to strike her off his list, of course we thought this was hysterical. Antonio revelled in this one and came round to our desks pretending he was a doctor on call carrying Smarties asking if we'd like a sweetie it will make us feel better. Trudy decided to be as silly as the rest of us and made Antonio a little red cross to pin on his shirt. Lawrence asked if he needed an apron making, then stuck A4 pieces of paper together in the shape of an apron. Antonio grabbed a black laptop case pretending it was a doctor's bag and paraded up and down the office shouting 'Doctor on call, Doctor on call.'

We fell about laughing until our boss came into our office to see what all the racket was about. He took one look, saw that we were in hyper mode and turned his back to us walked through the door and shut it behind him. I suppose he knew we were just letting off steam. Otherwise we would be letting off steam in his office and do our weekly moan. He was right because we were on a high from laughter that all the work was completed far faster than usual.

As parents most of us knew what its like to juggle work and home life. But the way Claire was behaving was ridiculous. The least she could do was attempt to look for childcare. If only to show willing to the rest of us otherwise look for another job. She played on worrying leaving her children with someone she didn't know. But that's the same for all of us, you carry on looking until you find someone you do feel comfortable with. We thought her children's sudden sickness was always exaggerated. Even more so when her doctor told her she was being dramatic, that should calm down for the children's sake and again refused to prescribe more medicine. He told her children need to build up some resistance to minor bugs, otherwise there body will never be able to fight infections. We all thought this was perfect her own Doctor calling her a drama queen. We interpreted this to mean she was liar. Either that or she was suffering from Muncheison Syndrome.

We all sympathise when children are poorly but even our sympathies had worn thin after months of this. Her absences were a weekly event. She would play our boss like a fiddle turn the taps on with floods of tears then rush home. I mean how many Doctors appointments could a person need. This was without going into the mental state we all thought she was suffering. It didn't help matters when I sowed the seeds for a lifetime feud by saying I wouldn't have the husband coming and going like its a bloody hotel then never being around to help with the children. She didn't take kindly to this and didn't speak to me for weeks after. Like this was some kind of punishment for me.

Other colleagues thought we were heartless until they saw for themselves the minute she left work she was grinning away, and ran straight to the shops buying chocolate and cakes. Not really what you'd expect when your child is ill. And you certainly wouldn't be smiling, I thought you would rush home.

To add to the trauma she had what could be considered a split personality. When we arrive in work normal people say the usual pleasantries of 'morning.' Depending on what mood Claire was in you got either a miserable forced hello in return, and if you're really lucky you got the 'grunt.' Now the 'grunt' had different meanings for different moods 1) Morning, but I can't be arsed
2) A forced Morning but I don't want to speak 3) No it's not a

pleasant morning now p*** **f. Now how difficult is it to be pleasant. Courtesy comes free and helps maintain a happy office environment. We didn't think it was much to ask. After all we are at work for eight hours a day it would be nicer to have a pleasant day that a miserable one. We don't expect you to like us or even be social, it could be helpful even for your own sanity by being pleasant.

It's not as if we love being at work, we only come in for the entertainment value. Because there's always some saga or other going on. And we being the friendly colleagues that we are take great delight in each others dilemmas. It's the only thing worth coming into work for lately. Although I'd rather not be in work, I yearn the moment I can say I'm leaving. I feel like I'm trapped on a hamster wheel only to be let out when I'm sixty five if I'm a good girl. If not we'll keep you here until your seventy!

Argh, I feel I am living in Dullsville, dull dull Dullsville. I wake up with that feeling someone is about to say 'Guess what your real life is here and that was just a bad dream.' Then you're woken into reality with a *grunt* that feels like a slap in the face. It has the effect on making you feel like you have road rage and it's only the beginning of the day. The frightening thing is companies actually tolerate this behaviour and expect you to work in it.

I've worked for other companies and it's always the same. These types are used to manipulating situations to suit themselves. You see if it was a sore you'd put cream on it. If it was a broken limb you'd put a plaster cast on it. But how do you treat a grunt. If I was the manager I'd make all people like her stand in a corner facing a blackboard with the words *I must learn to smile* staring back at them. Do you think the penny would drop eventually? Yet, on other days it's like Claire had had a frontal lobotomy overnight. She'd come into the office pleasant, even giddy. It was like her behaviour befitted auditions at a Butlins holiday camp falling over herself to be nice to you. At first we thought she'd finally come round to her senses. But it was never consistent and change daily. This began to scare us because she wasn't rational, what was she after.

Now have I missed something from yesterday. Had she taken happy pills or something. Had she finally made up with everyone realising her miserable behaviour was causing an atmosphere and now wants to be nice. I suppose pigs can fly. But these occasions never lasted long and woe betide anyone if we were laughing at something and she was in one of her moods. She made us feel like we had a vendetta against her and then she'd be even more miserable, if that's at all possible. It couldn't be helped because ours was a vibrant office people calling in all the time. There was always some story being told and often about me. The saga of Bruce, the train, Stan and the hotel kept the office entertained for a while. But the saga with Claire ran on and on.

We couldn't figure it out did she feel her life was crap or she wasn't being centre of attention. Was it because she just didn't like working, or more to the point that she didn't like you. Now the latter could be accepted if it was just me, but this wasn't the case as she was like this with everybody, on any given day and for any given reason. Her personality changed with the wind. The grunting followed with slamming phones, stomping and stropping, and general huffing and puffing.

We nick-named her Grunting Gertrude, which eventually became Gertie for short. Often referring to her as What's eating Gertie's Grape from the film Gilberts Grape. When her mood started we'd email each other around the office: What's up with Gertie no early finish has to put a full day in Aww poor gal

E-mail reply: No she can't think up an illness so no rushing home

E-mail sent: maybe she can get cowshed-itus

E-mail reply: What's that

E-mail sent: You know, miserable cow... needs to be put in shed for a few hours, otherwise 'itus' might be spread

E-mail reply: What you mean like foot and mouth disease... come into contact with it and it spreads to anyone you speak to

E-mail sent: Ha ha ha, now go away I have work to do or I'll have to report you.

Email reply: Don't worry we're sending her to grumble weeds camp, she might get a few ideas for more sick days.

This had us all laughing and helped to vent some pent up

frustration for a while. Infuriatingly it's like treading on eggshells around her. Becoming wise to her we sympathised with her less and less over the coming months. Things came to a head when even some customers complained about her gruff attitude. This time management had to speak to her thinking or rather hoping that this would resolve the issue.

Instead she became worse, even claiming we got the customers to complain. Here I learn a valuable lesson that with some people you just never win. Nothing will ever be enough for them and you will always come off being the 'offender rather than the offended.' It will all be your fault, they will always manage to manipulate somebody into thinking they are the victim. I mustn't understand the situation, because stupidly I thought if you caused a problem with others at work you get spoken to about it, get it sorted, end of.

But this was me being rational. Her attitude meant we get rewarded by her attitude by gaining her offended customers, hence more work. Can you imagine how well this went down? Not only does she swan home on a whim, she gets to do less work, and when she pulls her face we get to do even more. She has a problem that needs sorting, but can doctors treat grunting and arrogance. I must remember that one, if ever I am in management don't solve the problem put the work onto others.

I'm sure other companies have this problem all the time. Speaking of which we had seen a booklet which says 'if there is a problem, all route causes lead back to management.' We thought of framing it to put on the wall. I suppose its true management get paid to take responsibility and all route causes do lead back to them. Somehow we don't think this will go down well. We take it on as our office mission statement, referring to it often.

Gertie's moods became more frequent and the consequences became worse. With her temper flaring up so much that she threw a pile of files and a paper weight across the room at a colleague and narrowly missed Jenifer's shoulder. All because Trudy stood up to her giving her a piece of her mind which brought it to boiling point. Our boss was forced to start proceedings against Gertie. But she was only given a warning due to her mental instability rather than the incessant sulking. We wanted to throw a party put a few balloons up and maybe do a cartwheel or two down the office. Okay a little over the top, but a year of grunting and stomping, enough is enough. You'd think she would realise what she had become.

Instead it was like a time-bomb waiting to go off. Gertie's face had become contorted like Mrs Trunchbull's spitting and snarling like it was all our fault. But our fault for what, for not accepting rudeness of speaking one day and not the next, or being grunted at. We had tried talking to her, joking with her and sympathising. In the end we ignored her out of shear weariness. We just got on with the job and if it was work related we'd speak to her but more concerns or pleasantries unless she changed her ways.

We decided her problem was hormonal, and as Doctor Antonio concurred, hormonal it was. Even the other departments didn't like to confront her about work never knowing how she would react. We all have bad days and need to be by ourselves but this was like daily torture. Things got even more interesting when a Swedish woman joined our office.

~ Chapter Four ~ **The Swede**

When the guys from the warehouse heard a new girl was starting, and not only a new girl but a Swedish girl called Olivette, they couldn't get their arses into our offices fast enough. They eagerly hoped or rather expected a blonde bombshell, legs up to her armpits and a double for Claudia Schiffer. It was hilarious watching them drool over the vision they were expecting. However, when she arrived they were rather disappointed. The Swede turned out not to be a natural blond with her hair dyed a grubby brownish blond.

Olivette certainly had the big legs but not the sort they were hoping for because her legs were big. She had huge arms and shoulders that an American football team would drool for. By the looks on the guys faces she frightened them. She wore her hair in pigtails finished off with round glasses, saying this made her look 'girlie.' The jury was still out on that one. The guys asked which butch girl she wanted to look like, chunky spice. One said her hands were so big they were like shovels. But they were all far too chicken to put her strength to the test. It's funny because they never rushed to our offices with the same enthusiasm after Olivette's entrance.

Later when the guys got to know Olivette they'd do impressions of her when she'd gone home. Pretending she was a sumo wrestler in a blond wig they'd bounce around the room having us in stitches. They were of course as polite as ever to her face. I think they were more scared of a back hander from her that would probably put them in hospital. When Olivette first joined she was interesting and bubbly, just the sort of character we needed to blend into the office. She had lived her first early years abroad then spent most of her schooling in England with her English father. It was her mother who was part Swedish part Russian. Olivette kept us entertained for a while. She always had a funny story to tell about somebody that she knew. When Gertie realised Olivette received more attention from us than her it seemed to put her nose out of joint. At first it was a little difficult for Olivette having to put up with Gertie's outbursts too. Then Gertie suddenly cheered up deciding to befriend Olivette. We felt a slight relief because a happy Gertie made life easier for the rest of us.

This temporary sanity didn't last long soon enough both seemed to be vying for attention. If it wasn't Gertie taking centre stage then it was Olivette. The comedy show became a competition between them with each of their stories getting wilder and wilder. As the weeks went by it became a ritual of 'I did that' or 'I know who that happened to as well', or my mother's brothers' girlfriend did that twice as good and my granny is bigger than your granny.

One classic was Olivette's cousin's nephew was a 7ft 6in giant whose children have to be taken to hospital every year for check-ups. Apparently they grew too fast for their age. Of course the others wasted no time in taking the mickey doing impersonations of Pinocchio whilst hiding behind the door. I tried desperately not to laugh hiding behind my computer, but had to leave the room for fear of choking to death from laughter. And Olivette wasn't a person easily amused at herself.

Then the mood swings started with Olivette. At first we thought it was due to spending too much time with Gertie. But then they stopped speaking to each other, and so it carried on but this time twice as bad as before, we had two of them to contend with. Twice the moaning and twice the misery. How the hell or we supposed to cope now. Olivette moaned about the coffee machine, moaned about the filing system, wanted us to move the fax machine closer to her, wanted us to move the tables around so she could be central to everybody, her chair didn't fit the table, could she have a new table to fit the wires. She wanted to keep a check on us all more bloody likely.

Luckily our supervisor stepped in saying the wires won't reach. Antonio hinted at happy pills for the office instead of free coffee, which neither seemed amused by. If that wasn't bad enough we had to stand by and suffer the two of them competing for having the worst headache, worst illness and worst life. Please God if you're out there release me from this misery, is it my lot in life to have this each and every day.

Surely there are better work environments than this. We each go home at night spending the evening moaning about work and how crap it is. Stan of course laughs it off saying it's probably me winding them up. I point out they are doing this to the office and not me. He tells me not to worry it won't be long before we can go travelling and give the rat race up. This alone keeps me going.

I have now come to realise that most offices have this distinguished mix of personalities. Their traits are more prominent in some than others. I could bet a thousand pounds you will always find one of each personality within any group of offices. One will be a martyr one quiet who plods on with work, another will be flamboyant always wanting to be centre of attention. One will be loud or aggressive, and another will be the pacifier. If your lucky will have the office clown, always happy and keeping everyone in a cheerful mood.

And one will be stroppy git who thinks the world owes them something. You will probably have a control freak everything having to be in order. And maybe you will have a 'Sebastian', but more of that later. And if you're really lucky you will have the opinionated one, only their opinion counts because the world revolves around them.

We however, got the double pleasure of moody ones. One of those who'd stoke the fire and start a row then walk away as if they had nothing to do with it but merely an innocent bystander. Maybe it was competition between them, or that they were too alike and soon realised they didn't get on. Each tried to say the other wasn't good at her job, trying to get others on their side, we kept well out of it.

Gertrude was moody and arrogant and Olivette became dangerous. The guys named her Olive from on the buses. Olive didn't need glasses but bought them saying they made her look intelligent. If ever there was a fire to be stoked Olive seemed to be at the bottom of it. Olive started stories at work saying 'I can tell you but you can't tell anyone else.' Which was odd because the day before she would have been a misery and today she wanted to confide in you. We became wise taking what she said with a pinch of salt making sure we didn't divulge private information to her. You could guarantee it would be twisted then repeat it to others.

Another character we worked with was Larry King. He was okay sometimes quiet and sometimes a little strange. He too had a liking to Friday's off. What with Gertie and Olive pushing for Fridays off it left us little time for taking long weekends. It soon became a battleground and we were in the middle. Some days Gertie ignored us and Olive would be best friends to us all with a manor befitting Mrs Santa. The next day it would be visa versa. Larry often put himself in the firing line with the girls for taking 'Friday illnesses.' And to think we worried if our Italian colleague Antonio would fit into the office, little did we know he would become one of us. We never thought Antonio would get used to us, being Northerners we can be pretty straight talking. When we do have something to say it's usually with a wicked sense of humour. We often joked people wouldn't understand us because they've never drank our water. We can offend by our directness, often mistaking it for ruthlessness.

Yet Antonio fitted into our wave length quickly soon becoming one of us. He appreciated that most of us worked as a team. He had always been left to struggle on his own before. Antonio didn't take to Olive or Gertie. At first speaking to them pleasantly but soon came to realise you don't judge a book by its cover, the cover can be pleasant and the horrors lie beneath the page. They said how stylish he was coming from Milan and both wanted to pet him. He thought they both had a few bolts loose, as did we all. Even Larry tried to keep a wide berth.

Antonio entered cycling competitions and one day came into the office in his cycling gear. Gertie was quite taken with this telling him how well he looked in shorts. We of course thought it hysterical, I did my usual hiding behind my desk. Poor Antonio his face flushed bright red, he couldn't disguise the look of terror written all over it. A few days later when we thought things had quietened down Gertie announced she was taking her skirt off to show Antonio her legs. I could feel a trauma coming on for poor Antonio is this yet more ridiculous attention seeking.

Brazenly she walked around to the middle of the room

whipping her skirt above her waist. Without the slightest embarrassment she shouts 'ha got you going.' Thank God she had shorts on. I say thank God but they were lycra, you know the ones that go tight to the knees and make everywhere that shouldn't bulge. Just because she was tall didn't give her the entitlement to think she had Claudia Schiffer's legs.

If she was looking for male company then she picked the wrong guy because Antonio had been dating for a while and was pretty serious about her. Poor Antonio ran through the office hiding behind the door, in view of half the office did vomiting motions to his mouth. I'm in hysterics whilst the others sit in disbelief wondering what is coming next. Parading in bathing suits for attention. Antonio went home feeling sick, saying he'll have nightmares about chubby knees, bulging legs and large fat bellies.

Antonio's girlfriend is a very pretty girl, a natural beauty looks like Helena Christiansen. You know the type, flawless skin, not an ounce of fat on her and a lovely personality to match. So the sight of dear Gertie's bulges came as a shock to his system. For months after he said he suffered flashbacks. The rest of us decide its worth while coming into work just for the entertainment value alone. Our boss couldn't believe his ears when he heard this one.

When Gertie went on holiday a picture of her mysteriously arrived on Antonio's desk with a note on it saying missing you already. Winding him up about Gertie kept us entertained the whole time she was away. We'd email reminding him to phone Gertie. Shouldn't he be checking if she needs her suntan lotion topping up, or she might need a drink taking over to her sun bed.

Somehow he found this quite distressing and threatened to leave if we carried on any more. He ranted that we were stupid and childish in Italian. Of course the others carried it on for a few more days just enough to make him squirm. He knew our sense of humour and that we couldn't let this one go by. He was just a little paranoid that Gertie had a thing for him saying she frightened him.

Most people in our department were okay well quite funny in fact. Trudy forever organised often dragging herself into work no matter how ill she was. Jenifer liked her own way. Olive pushed a few buttons with her stories which were always a little too convenient. I'm fascinated with people who have unusual hobbies finding them really interesting. With Olive, her hobbies weren't strange they were too far fetched to be believable. She was always in competition with everybody. She skydived but was very overweight, she was a marathon runner but no medals or certificates to show for it. A synchronised swimmer but never had photos of her group. Jenifer asked if she could watch her skydive then Olive conveniently hurt her knee.

You could have a laugh with Geraldine, or Jerry for short, although she did have a habit of getting loud sometimes to the point of embarrassing. She was a vivacious Afro Caribbean woman who was often loud and wild when outside work. And quite funny inside work so long as she was kept on a tight leash. Our boss thought she was barking mad. What worried me was we were often on the same wave length finding the same things amusing. Then their was Jenifer who could be a little opinionated which in itself was great entertainment value. Gertie was of course self centred with world revolving around her. At any cost and blamed everyone for her shortcomings, even if they weren't in the room. Sebastian could be either delightful or very matter of fact, camp and outrageous all in one and loved to shock. Antonio was calm loved to be in charge but never bossy just precise.

And Larry was Larry, forever laid back and went with the flow. Sadly some thought he needed to find his backbone. Tony worked in another department but was in ours so much he became part of ours. He was always willing to help a mate out and loved the antics going on in ours. His department was so quiet it always made his day when it all kicked off in ours. In all, our mix of people made for a fiery pot at times. Although most of us wanted the offices run smoothly, there was always something ready to boil over.

~ Chapter Five ~ **The Cat**

One morning driving Ayeisha to school I catch a glimpse of a cat. It was stood on a wall set a few feet back from the roadside. As I approach the bend the cat decides to jump forward onto the pavement. When I say jumped it actually sprung as if from a jack-in-a-box. Instead of staying on the pavement the cat jumped straight in front of me. Not having time to stop I swerve quickly trying to miss it. Thank God I didn't go into the other lane of traffic. Managing to swerve just enough to get me out of the way I'm thankful nobody got close behind when I feel a thud. My teeth start to tingle I think I've hit the cat.

Holding my breath I hoped it was something in the road and the cat is still on the pavement. Ayeisha shouts 'Mum, you've hit the cat.' Trying to calm her down I tell her it could be something in the road. But knowing damn well it will be a miracle if we haven't. I can feel the nerves kicking in. My stomach is churning up, indicating I pull over to the side of the road. I tell her to stay in the car, I don't want her seeing the poor thing injured she'll be really upset. A few people carry on driving circling to go around us. This is awful I can't believe nobody stops to help.

Approaching the cat I can see it doesn't look good at all it's lying still in the road, looking lifeless in fact. Walking nearer to the cat my mouth starts drying up making me feel like I'm walking the plank all alone. When a guy stops to offer help. Thank God someone else who can take control. I'm not very good in a crisis. I ask him if it's still alive, peering over the cat he's not too sure. 'This is awful what do I do, where's the nearest vet? 'It looks pretty lifeless to me' he tells me 'I don't think it's alive.'

The poor little thing it looks dead there's no movement at all. He tells me we should put it at the side of the road. Are you sure we should just leave it. He sees I'm upset then tells me 'Don't worry, they sometimes perk up later and jump up.' 'Oh God' I shout you mean it's still alive I best take it to the vets.' Staring at me blankly he says 'No, I think its dead.' I look at him stunned because a moment ago he said it could still be alive. Then the penny drops, I realise he just said this to save my feelings. I feel a lump come to my throat. He says its best to leave it at the side of the road. There is nothing we can do and the owner may live nearby, at least if they see it they can bury it.

I thank him for stopping to help. Walking back to the car I can feel tears prick my eyes. Ayeisha gets upset I tell her I'm sorry that there was nothing I could do. We look at each other depressed, I still have to take her to school and get to work myself. I feel awful having to leave her at school but there is nothing we can do. I felt really shakey in need of some caffeine. I tell the others in the office what happened. They are really nice fussing round me trying to make me feel better. Lawrence is back in the office this morning from meetings in Europe. He rushes over to get me a drink. They are really sweet and sympathise but I don't feel any better. I should have known it wouldn't last long and was a big mistake telling the office.

A short time later when my phone rings it's the warehouse. 'You've not seen my cat have you, only it didn't come home this morning.' 'Thanks a lot' I shout to the others. They hid behind their computers saying they're really sorry but it is funny. I don't find it funny at all, trying to compose myself I carry on working preferring to forget the phone call. Then I receive an email addressed to myself and around twenty others at work: *Have you seen my cat?* I don't believe it the gits, they know how upset I am.

Shortly after another email arrives *Have you seen my cat? Last seen running down Audenshaw Road.* Everybody bursts out laughing again.

Then another arrives… *Have you seen my cat? Last seen running down Audenshaw Road, being chased by a mad woman*

Then another… *Have you seen my cat? Last seen running down Audenshaw Road, being chased by a mad woman with long black hair*

And another *Have you seen my cat? Last seen running down Audenshaw Road, being chased by a mad woman with long black hair, driving a Fiesta*

'Funny, very funny' I shout out. They can see I'm not amused which makes them laugh even more. Then another arrives…'

Have you seen my cat? Last seen running down Audenshaw Road, being chased by a mad woman with long black hair, driving a Fiesta, with a picture underneath of a Cat upside down.

And then another... *Have you seen my cat? Last seen running down Audenshaw Road, being chased by a mad woman with long black hair, driving a Fiesta' with a picture underneath of a Cat upside down and the caption 'I last looked like this.'*

Bloody B******ds, this carries on all day, they find it amusing the guy told me it would jump up later on. What after drinking lucozade they laugh. Even people who work for the company but not on site carry it on. I can't believe how heartless they are. Well I can, if was happening to someone else then I'd probably be laughing with them. But it's happening to me so I don't find it funny at all. Later in the day, they bring me a coffee and biscuits as a peace offering. I suppose I should know them by now if something happens I should expect a ribbing. Jerry keeps popping into in the office making meowing noises as if looking for a lost cat. You'd think that a female colleague would be a bit sympathetic, obviously not. They don't mean anything by it they're just making entertainment of it for the day. If it wasn't my turn we'd only be laughing at someone else.

When I get home I tell my sorry tale to Stan stupidly expecting lots of sympathy. But he decides the best option is to laugh at me. I stare back at him not amused. He realises running over the cat has upset me he puts his arms round me saying stop being silly it was an accident after all. Adding 'At least it won't happen again all the cats in town will avoid your car now' I choose to sulk. Trying to cheer me up he offers to make tea when he suddenly realises a video tape we had borrowed from the shop is late back. It was a wildlife film Gorillas in the Mist. We had tried buying it but couldn't get hold of a copy anywhere and decided to make a copy of the film before returning it to the shop. Like you do, and lots of people do it. We only want a copy for ourselves. It's not like we want to start up our own video club or anything.

Later that evening I noticed a tape on the side. Just as I'm about to moan about things being left out I glanced over at the tape and noticed it wasn't one of ours. Staring at the tape I feel myself gasp. Oh my God no it can't be! It is, it's the tape from the shop. We've only taken the wrong bloody tape back giving them our copy and we have the shop's. Oh God I feel another trauma coming on. I try desperately not to but laugh with nerves no matter how I try holding them back. The nerves are rushing through my body like quicksilver. I shout to Stan 'You've sent the wrong tape back, you'll have to take it back and get ours.'

He looks at me blankly 'No I'm not taking it back you wanted the damn tape you can take it back.' Sarcastically I shout 'But you copied it.' But the membership is in your name he replies quite matter of fact and too smug for my liking. I can't I plead almost in tears and he knows what a mard-arse I am. He knows I'd rather leave the country than have to go and face them. And knowing they know what you've done. Oh the thought makes me cringe with dread and I think I've stopped breathing. Jolting me back to reality he shouts 'You wanted it now you're taking it.' I cry 'But you know you taped it.' Only because you asked me to he replied as if he was completely innocent.

I've never even got a parking ticket, a speeding fine, nothing, and now I could get in trouble because of this. I went to bed feeling really anxious. Not being able to sleep I spent the whole night tossing and turning. Still feeling traumered in the middle of the night I wake him up pleading with him again but to no avail. The next morning he lets me go to work worried sick. All day the thought of facing the shop made me feel sick. It's not as if we could pretend it's a blank tape of ours because we clearly labelled it Gorilla's In the Mist. I groan with pain at the thought. How could we have been so stupid. I wouldn't mind but we've never made a copy before. Trust us to get caught out first time.

I spend all day expecting a phone call from the shop. Each time the phone rings my stomach turns over. Home time came and still no call. Stan hasn't rang either. Maybe they hadn't noticed I try convincing myself. Knowing full well they take the tapes straight out of the cover to put them onto the shelves so they *must* have noticed. Driving home my stomach churned all the way. Not one to be a drama queen I'd convinced myself they'll have phoned the police. When I get home I beg Stan again but he's adamant.

There's no way I can face the shop, I can feel the tears start to well up. I'm not that hard faced whereas Stan can be. He knows it would be such a trauma for me.

After more pleading and watching me squirm for an hour or two he finally gives in. In return I agree not to moan if he goes fishing every weekend for the next 10 years. A smile of relief comes over my face. I start laughing with nerves as he leaves. And yes I wait at home in the safe zone. When he finally returns I can't believe the police aren't with him. Stunned I ask what happened. Not phased at all he told them we gave them our tape by mistake and gave them theirs back, bold as brass. I'm sorry but I don't remember any 'we' going on. I distinctly remember Stan put picking the wrong tape up, but what the hell I'm not going to argue. He laughed that they gave him a really sarcastic look when they handed our tape back. Phew although I'm saved I can't relax for a while after and don't go into the shop again. Well not for a year or so. I wouldn't mind but I'd been a customer of theirs for years. Oh dear, best give it a wide berth for a while, a very wide berth.

Cringing seems to be an art of ours. A while back Stan's Aunty came to visit. He hadn't seen her for a few years and I had never met her before. She arrived exhausted from the journey and went straight to his Mum's house. We stopped by to say hello, as Stan took his coat off something flung out towards his Aunty. 'Ouch' she shouted as the object hit her leg. I couldn't make out what it was at first. I just saw her face wince in pain. Stan stepped towards her trying to apologise but stood in the way so I couldn't see what had hit her. As he stepped down to pick the object up I could see dots of blood coming through her tights. I couldn't believe my eyes. What on earth had he hit her with?

He turned around to me holding one hand over his mouth and his darts in the other cringing with embarrassment. He'd forgotten the darts were still inside his coat pocket and flung them into the air as he took his coat off. Thank God only one of them struck her leg. He kept apologising but she insisting on no fuss saying she was alright. The poor thing had to sit there holding a damp tissue on her bleeding leg, what an entrance. And if that wasn't enough there was more cringing to come.

Stan had always kept a menagerie at home. He kept anything that moved really. I've always liked rabbits, chinchillas and cats, when I'm not killing them that is. With Stan its Birds. Big birds little birds owls, hawks, anything that flies except budgies. Bash had her own two rabbits and named them Rosie & Jim after the TV programme. Rosie was a lovely looking fawn colour that didn't like to be picked up. Jim on the other hand was a gorgeous white fluffy thing with a big daft face that loved to be cuddled. He thought he was a teddy bear.

Bits kept sticking to Jim's fur. Stan cleaned him up and checked him over. He had a worried look on his face and thought something was wrong with Jim. He thought there might be a tumour on its tummy because it looked like there was a squashed walnut whip. Then he bursts out laughing saying 'it's only his bleedin' nuts.' Right on cue Ayeisha wanders into the garden. I have to turn my face away because I can't stop laughing.

Whilst we were having tea with his Mum and Aunty, Ayeisha shouts 'My Jim's got nuts in his belly.' I almost choke on my tea and stare at Stan who's going bright red then starts laughing nervously. Aunty Louisa looks at us both curiously. I squirm and wish for the ground to open up and swallow me. Stan saves the day saying 'That's right your rabbit's been eating nuts hasn't he'. Stan then jumps up saying he needs the bathroom and makes a rush for the door. He stands in the hallway grinning at me knowing I can't look Aunty Louisa in the face or she'll know we are laughing at her. I have to sit there cringing desperately trying to hold my face as straight I can. She knows something is going on but unsure why we are acting stupid. Either that or she thinks we are just strange. The git I'll swing for him when we get home.

For a few weeks now I've been going to keep-fit with friends. Well I say keep-fit but it's actually self defence classes I just tell Stan it's keep-fit. Can you imagine the comments from Stan *You.. in self defence, what are you going to frighten them with your mouth.* No I don't need him winding me up or laughing at me for that matter. I want to surprise him when I can do it properly. That however might not be some time. The guy teaching, Sensei, taught another friend of mine and she was ready to take her black belt. Whenever we watched he'd tell us to join in but we always chickened out. After a while we thought what the hell what's the worst that could happen. A few bruises and some embarrassment.

Sensei reassured us not to worry it won't be Karate just self-defence. We decided after a few months of bottling out to give it a go. The only problem is we have to practice on each other. I don't mind practicing moves on a guy, but on a female who is a friend is awful. We all feel really embarrassed about it and fall about laughing. Sensei shouts at us to try harder. We can't help but do the moves really girlie. Sensei gets furious with us shouting what would happen if a guy tried to grab you in the street dragging you down an alley. Do we think he'd pull our hair and gently ask us to go with him, or do we think he try hurting us any way he can. This gives us a wake up call and all put more effort into it.

Back in work I've been telling the girls what we have to do at self-defence. They sit intrigued laughing at the re-enactment at the sight of me trying to be assertive and angry. One move is where a guy grabs hold of your wrists and pulls you. You have to twist your hands in circular motions trying to push his hands away, and hurt them if possible. As I'm showing my moves Antonio walks into the office. He asks calmly why don't I try it on him. Now I'm four feet ten tall weighing six and a half stone. He on the other hand is twice the height and twice the weight. The girls laugh and tell him it's hardly a fair match. But I'm feeling a little confident. Besides I've been doing well in training. Go on then I tell him try grabbing my wrists. But before I've managed to get ready he's already grabbed hold of them and tells me to get out of that. I try to moving my hands as we had practiced.

Why is it that you don't seem to have the same effect when doing it outside of the training room. I remember what to do going over it in my mind when he says 'when your ready.' This gets me mad and I try to move but his hands don't bloody budge. I try again, but he's like he's got a vice to grip me. I try again but to no avail. I stand there looking defeated. Well it worked last night I sulk. Antonio then grabs hold of my elbows, lifting me up and proceeds to walk me back to my desk. The others are in stitches at the sight of him picking me up. He sympathises with me saying its good that I do self-defence, but keep going for lessons for a while little girl. They all burst out laughing.

Sarcastically I tell them it's not always a six foot gorrila that grabs hold of you. It's usually some weak pathetic man who needs to feel control over women. It's a good job I get on with Antonio. He has such a great personality that you couldn't get offended by him, even if he was showing me up. Antonio finds me amusing saying he had never seen anyone so small as me which makes everyone laugh.

At our 'keep-fit' evenings we hear Sensei saying if ever he got into a fight or somebody wanted to fight him he has to warn them he is a black belt, otherwise he would never be able to teach again. We find this hysterical. Could you imagine being out and someone gets cocky. You have to shout at them get back I'm a black belt whilst holding your hands up in fighting stance. I chuckle to myself I must try this one out on Stan. He'll think I'm loosing my marbles. What's even more ridiculous is we'd never be able to get our paper belt, let alone black belt. We'd be there with the infant group every time.

~ Chapter Six ~ **More Sick Days**

Fridays became popular in the office because we all wanted Friday off. At first we tried working around each other or rather around Gertie and Olive if they weren't pulling a sickie. But soon Larry became a problem too mysteriously catching the Friday sickness. We wondered what the symptoms were because they always started on a Thursday night yet nobody else caught the symptoms. They probably midnight meetings with each other bringing voodoo dolls of the rest of us in the office, instead of giving us an illness, they pile our hands with more work.

Larry made excuse after excuse to get Fridays off when suddenly out of the blue it came out he had a girlfriend. I use the term *girlfriend* loosely, the woman he dated only turned up Fridays. We were more than intrigued because he'd never mentioned her before, yet now it seems she was his long term girlfriend. He spoke of her all the time yet never phoned her from work claiming she was busy in the day. When anyone tried pinning him down about her job he evaded the question or changed the subject to work. Larry claimed they only spend weekends together to keep the relationship alive otherwise they would bore each other. But all he does outside work is watch television and go shopping, he doesn't go to the gym, swim, walk, cycle nothing. The only consistency in his life is work and he's bored with that.

It later transpired that the weekends were actually a couple of hours on Friday night. The girlfriend never mixed with work or his neighbours they never socialised out at all. I know some people don't feel comfortable mixing easily, Stan certainly isn't. But we do spend time together watching a film or going for a meal, we take Bash out for a day trip or go to the park. Occasionally we'd catch Larry on the phone to the girlfriend. It never sounded like he was making a date with her, more like he asked when she could fit him in. When he realised he was overheard he'd brush it off saying he was just making plans for the weekend. Worst was to come when he slipped up that he left money on the table for her. He got all flustered and claimed it was to treat her to something nice.

We all became alarmed, even Gertie said it was nothing short of prostitution turning up for an hour or two a week and accepting money. Which it did sound odd but Gertie was the last one to speak on relationships. Antonio asked does she bring her washing of which Gertie got embarrassed and walked away to the fax machine. Larry claimed they had dated for years yet none of her children were his. Apparently the children came along when they had broken up for a while and didn't want the children involved with anyone else. Jenifer asked if they were by the same guy but Larry didn't take kindly to the Spanish inquisition. How boring she cried, just when we were getting to the nitty gritty. Larry insisted the girlfriend Kimberly was the love of his life and would live together when the children are older.

We felt sorry for Larry. Sorry that he believed in a relationship that wasn't a real but a fleeting of the night. There wasn't there for emotional support, caring or sharing for each other. If it was just for sex then fine you don't claim it's the romance of the century. Larry said they get on each others nerves. Can you really get on somebody's nerves if you only spend two hours together. Of course Olive said she had lots of friends in relationships like this. 'She would' I said 'that's a Friday night drunken eleven o'clocker not a relationship.' Jerry overheard me and giggled. Antonio hinted to Larry if he was single he would join a dating agency to meet people but Larry looked offended. The others agreed it was some sort of infatuation on Larry's part. Trudy managed to lower the tone telling us Kimberly would arrive in a uniform. I said if he socialised more he would meet the right person one day, but Trudy replied 'of course he would she would be a traffic warden or a nurse' we couldn't help but laugh.

Olive and Gerties sickness ranged from the dentist, the doctors, a sick child or relative and I think Olive's Granddad had died at least three times in six months. This must be quite record. You name it they came up with it. Both wanted their way even if it crossed with one of our holidays we still had to cover their work. Larry wanted Fridays off to get ready for Kimberly which became known as Larry King Night. We took bets on if she would turn up, little did he know Trudy's friend lived around the corner.

Trudy asked her to spy on Kimberly, which turned out Kimberly looked very street wise and stayed less than two hours. Monday came and Larry spoke of their lovely weekend together. What between Larry, Gertie and Olive it became a free for all. Whoever came up with the best excuse got the day off, if they hadn't phoned in sick already. They performed if they couldn't wangle the day off, surely other offices didn't run like this.

This particular morning I'd had the morning from hell. Forgetting Ayeisha's lunch which is sat on the kitchen table, forgetting a letter for her school trip which is sat at home in her gym bag and she doesn't have gym today. And guess what, yes it has to be handed in today. I turned the car around to return home only to find traffic twice as busy. All I can picture is work piling up on my desk. You can imagine I'm really late and not in the best of moods. When I finally get to the office I shout morning to all. Trudy says morning in a very weary tone not at me but to let me know there is a problem. I glance over at Olive to find a dozen bottles of pills lined up along her the desk. Now is this for a) attention b) letting us know she had a sickie coming up c) sympathy d) all of the above. I really can't be doing with these antics today my phone is ringing off the hook and a pile of orders need processing.

First things first I turn the computer on and get a coffee. When I walk back to my desk I find Olive holding her hands to her stomach and whining with a face like she is going to cry. I drop on my chair exhausted with it all and the day hasn't even begun yet. Looking over my computer I roll my eyes to Trudy. She smiles back sarcastically admitting yes another day of hypochondria is in store. We ignore this display as she wants attention and I've got work to catch up on. When Olive first joined us we gave her attention and constantly checked she was alright. We'd get her a drink and Lawrence ever the drama queen would fuss round her propping her cushion up. When it became a weekly occurrence we ignored it, only for her ailments to get more bizarre. No skydiving this weekend I mutter out loud.

Now we could play this two ways completely ignore her then be accused of being unsympathetic. Or play her at her own game and ask what the tablets were for trying to catch her out. She was usually on something else the week before. Why a dozen bottles though, you don't get this amount of pills when you've had a liver transplant. But hey, I'm no doctor just the poor sod who has to put up with the female hormones.

Normally I would disagree with guys saying we play on 'women's problems' but on occasions I hate to admit it but they are absolutely right. This time I think women's problems stretch to mental instability too. The whole office already thought a spell in a psychiatric ward might do. Jerry came in shortly after and couldn't believe her eyes. She just shot me an angry look to let me know she'd cottoned on too. She switched her computer on in a fit temper knowing she had to bite her tongue or all hell would break loose. We tried desperately to ignore her but the constant groaning from behind her computer is driving us mad. If we had a radio we would turn it up but we don't. Unfortunately for us the groaning gets louder. Now you may find us a little harsh, but this was a Friday and Friday is 'Larry King Day' one of them was going home early and he who groans the loudest will win.

By ten thirty after being ignored for long enough Olive feels more of a display is needed. She stood up holding her feet wide apart and leans her arms right across the table holding her hands on the table to give her support. Then she proceeds to gyrate her rather large hips around in a circular motion whilst groaning out loud. It looks like she's trying to give birth to the table whilst high on drugs. Is this what happens when you take drugs and start to hallucinate. I'm that shocked I start feeling the nervous laugh come on, if I look at the others I'll burst out laughing.

Antonio and Gertie had been at the photocopier not realising what was happening. When they walked past Olive they see her stood up as if bearing down on the table and panting, having no idea what is going on. I grab hold of my phone ringing Jenifer. She asks 'what the hell is all this for, shouldn't she be sectioned' then shouts 'I'm sure there are laws about this kind of behaviour.'

Trudy walks out of the room disgusted at the latest outburst. I mean what the hell do say to someone gyrating over there desk? She's almost six foot and twenty stone giving birthing impressions across the table, it's embarrassing for God's sake.

Embarrassed for her I try not to giggle but it's so ridiculous. I turn away pretending to looking at the computer for my information for my fictitious customer. I can't give her eye contact or I won't be able to contain myself, I can already feel laughter building up, my throat's going dry and tight desperate trying to hold down the laughter. On the phone to my fictitious customer I announce I'll get back to them as soon as I can.

I stand up and without looking at anyone announce I'm going for a drink and leg it out of the room as fast as I can, only to find Trudy hiding in the ladies. We both burst out laughing, and I'm laughing so much that my stomach hurts. We were quickly followed by Jenifer who is raging 'What the hell was that performance for? 'I think she's trying out for a part in Coronation Street, I mean with acting skills like that she is wasted in this job.'

Jenifer can't believe she's hankering to go home again. Does she not realise when your employed you are supposed to work a full week, and we have to do her work when she is not here. And what about Gertie, has she not started playing up yet she seems to be in good spirits so far. That would be all we'll need the three of them playing up. We are all worried because Jenifer needs to get her desk sorted out before going on holiday. With Jerry on another project for the boss she can't help out, we don't want a mess left for us whilst Jen's away. What a dilemma.

We're not back in the office five minutes and Gertie's making phone calls. Oh what a surprise another sickie coming up. Gertie says her daughter isn't too good she needs to go home, again! At this rate we are falling like a pack of cards. Now is this the daughter she thought had scarlet fever last month, or the daughter who she thought was asthmatic or maybe it was the flu again. Gertie made some reference that it's probably because her doctor didn't prescribe medicine for her last time and that he was so unprofessional. He ran out of pills because of Gertie and Olive more bloody likely. It's a wonder there wasn't a prescription shortage in Manchester because of hypochondria circulating.

Maybe its Gertie and Olive's need to be in competition with each other. Whatever it is they both leave by lunchtime leaving Larry sulking because they got in there first. The timing was perfect really, the company was looking at incentives to lower sick days. They asked for suggestions, my god where could we start without getting sacked. We could get rid of certain staff and bring in new healthy people for starters. We came up with extra day's holidays allowing one or two days to be used for sick or emergency days. We could do a raffle and those who don't throw sickies can have their name entered into a draw to win a car. Of course we latch onto this idea making something of it. Mainly how to exclude certain people from it otherwise it would be sods law the sick day crew would bloody win. Otherwise we'd have to break the car down into who gets what.

Larry would be entitled to win the wheels and Gertie would get the steering wheel. Antonio adds Olive could win the wheel nuts, but isn't entitled to the wheels due to lack of days in the office. Trudy gets the chassis and I get the bumper to protect the local wildlife the bloody gits, Jenifer and Jerry can share the boot and Antonio gets the pedals and seats. Lawrence isn't here so gets nothing and the boss probably gets a Porsche. When Olive and Gertie hear of the car incentive they think it's a great idea and are looking forward to entering the draw. The cheeky gits, this has got to be a joke. Do they actually believe they're entitled to enter, the mind boggles. Maybe they thought the rules are that you can enter if you have less than five days sickies in a month? Even then they'd be pushing it a little.

Any urgent bookings get written on the board in the office. We gave it up when we were too busy to keep up to date. Decided to put it to a far better use it became our top customer's board. To get on the board you have to be the most annoying or just plain stupid ones. Our highlight is who gets to the top for being the most aggravating. We rate them by giving them stars. We ask if we get to nominate Olive, Gertie and Larry to the board, but they'd actually out do each other by the hour. Tempting I know, but best not to upset them any more than possible. The board is reserved for special customers who don't know what they want or when they want it, expecting you to manage stock for them. Since you don't work in their firm its obvious you know their business better than they do.

My special customer of the day was Collins & Co who phone up placing an order. Normally they take large quantities to get the extra discount, but it won't be ready until tomorrow afternoon. We have a small pack available but will be the higher price due to extra packaging. And I'll have to make an extra carriage charge, it's late in the day and have to get an agency driver, of which they agree to. I tried offering an order to despatch late tomorrow that way they can take larger quantities they want. But no they insist on the small order arriving in the morning. They thank me for helping them out of a fix. Okay the customer is always right or so we're told.

The next morning I receive an irate phone call from Collins & Co saying I've sent them the wrong products. Initially I presumed the warehouse have sent the wrong items, until they mention small packs. I ask them to wait on the line whilst I check with the warehouse and press the silent button. The warehouse insists they've sent the correct order in small packs. I go back to Collins & Co telling them the order is correct, that's what the lady ordered late last night. The woman starts ranting again we've sent the wrong items. Patiently I ask her to hold the line I'll check again. I shout *for Gods sake they are telling me lies again*.

Trudy glanced up amused. Keeping composed I go back to the phone explaining it we didn't have the items they requested so the lady agreed yesterday to the smaller packs. Insisting it was our misunderstanding she wants the order returned and the correct one sending out, today. And she refused to pay the carriage charge. I had to bite my tongue knowing I chased around for half an hour getting a special driver in. I'd asked our boss for his approval. He says return the goods and send out what they want. They are too big a customer to upset. We both know they're lying. Smarting through gritted teeth I get to tell them they are getting there own way. What makes it worse is I know damn well it's the same lady who phoned yesterday. Instead of admitting she

59

made a mistake she implied I'm the liar. What would I know I'm merely the customer services girl.

Slamming the phone down and frothing at the mouth I charge to the board shouting 'COLLINS BLOODY COLLINS' and put them straight at the top of the board. Still not satisfied and to everyone's amusement I charge back to the board underlining Collins with big red lines. Oh well another good start to the day. Having a messaging system on the computer we are able to print notes on paperwork for the warehouse. Although I'm tempted to put a note on for the customer to see I'm not willing to be sacked over it. Instead I enter a note on the system that only we can view. To ensure nobody misunderstands them in future 'If Collins & Co asks for small quantities.. Do Not Send Them.... Even If They Insist Do Not Send Them because THEY DO NOT KNOW THEIR OWN MIND!!!!!!

I think whoever processes an order for them should get the message now. Then I shout down the office 'When a customer says yes they obviously mean no.' The others find my strop quite funny because they know I'm furious after jumping through hoops for them. Whilst I'm not yet telepathic I can only listen to what they want. There is one consolation Gertie & Olive are in work both happy and well for today anyway. I thought Olive would have told us she phoned for an ambulance after the other day and all that pain she was in. Maybe she's a healer in her spare time hey.

~ Chapter Seven ~ **The Night Out**

Deciding we need to chill out we arrange a night out with the office and can invite friends too. The more the merrier at least then we won't all talk work. We haven't had a good night out for ages and decide on Manchester. Meet up for a few drinks then go over to the gay village on Canal Street. It's always a good night there and if it's a warm evening everybody stands outside the bars alongside the canal, it's usually a great atmosphere. We don't get trouble there and the girls feel safe. The only possible upset would be the odd girl crying over a guy in the toilets and maybe a transvestite consoling them telling each other the woes of men.

On Saturday about ten of us will be going out. Being away for the weekend Jenifer will miss out on any antics going on. Larry says he will come but we know he won't turn up. Everyone was up for it except Olive that is. She's probably suffering from an invented disease undiscovered by medical science, and hoping to prove us all wrong in not believing her. Like that's going to happen. Trisha works in the purchasing department and will be in Manchester Saturday and wants to join us. She can be very loud and quite a handful. She's been everywhere done everything and had most men in town, or so she claims. She doesn't work in our office but often pops in out of boredom.

Working in our office for the last few days working on spreadsheets for us we can hardly say no. Besides she's usually up for a good for a laugh. Come Saturday night as predicted neither Olive nor Larry turned up, but surprisingly Gertie did. It's really busy in town, music is blaring full blast and the dance floor is heaving. Trisha is on top note being loud as ever. She's getting drunk quickly I hope she doesn't start being bitchy. We can all be bitchy but when you've had a drink people can go too far.

Trudy asks her to behave herself tonight but she's spoken too soon. 'Of course' she says then turns to Gertie telling her she's glad she's over the depression then swanks over to the dance floor with her friend. I turn away choking on my drink. I can't believe what she just came out with. We'll get the wrath of that for the next two months now.

Gertie is definitely not amused. We don't see her smile again, instead preferring to spend the evening glaring at my friend Sadie. Of course Sadie is freaked out saying what had she done to upset her. Poor Sadie felt like she had a stalker in the background. It turned out Gertie was jealous of my friend for not being a frump for her age and having a slim figure. What a ridiculous thing to say about someone you don't know. My god what is wrong with people, Trisha had upset her not Sadie.

Antonio slopes off to get the drinks in. Sadie and I decide to give Gertie a wide berth and head off to the dance floor. The first thing we see is Trisha dancing in the middle of a bunch of guys making a play for one in particular. Bearing in mind most of the guys in here are gay guys there is little chance for her, so why the big floor routine. It's positively cringe worthy, almost as bad as watching David Brent do his dance routine. So far the guy seems to be enjoying the exhibition.

As the night wears on Trisha gets louder and more outrageous. We can't help but laugh. She gets the guy in bear hug and lifts her feet off the floor with the poor guy trying in vain to hold her up. Still not satisfied she twirls him around the floor, swinging him so hard he crashes to the floor. Not content with this she rolls herself over on top of him. Then says 'Oh dear, look at us.' Clamping her legs around his she flings her arms around his neck pretending she's stuck shouting help me up. Trudy came over joining us on the dance floor not quite believing the sight in front of us.

Pretending not to be with her we get our drinks from Antonio and watch from the side. All we can do is laugh at Trisha, as she tries to walk off the dance floor she's swaying all over the place. In a drunken stupor she manages to pull two guys over with her. Their drinks spill over everyone much to the delight of Gertie. After the bitchy comments she received earlier she revels in this one. All we can see is two pair of pants a white top and a skirt waist high. Her backside is on full view to the whole world and far too much cellulite on show for my liking.

I think that a woman of her age with that many dimples should well and truly cover it up with a sensible skirt, or even trousers to be on the safe side. With her clothes ruffled and dirty she looks like she's been dragged through a hedge backwards. Hurting her arm in the second fall didn't help either, she's now blaming the guys for the spilt drinks in the kafuffle. Nearly wetting myself with laughter, all I can think of is how the hell will she explain this one to her boyfriend. Knowing he's due to collect her shortly.

We take her to the ladies trying to tidy her up a little. She looks a right state, her hair is all over the show her pale skirt is filthy with all dirt and drinks rubbed in and her make up is a mess. Looking like she's been rolling around in a field Trudy takes a photo of her 'Something to show her on Monday morning' she said. If this didn't stop her from drinking again nothing will. Antonio says he's never seen such a disgraceful display by a woman in his life. Apparently women from Milan are more refined. We could hardly argue with him looking at Trisha. We walk her to meet the boyfriend trying to explain she fell over a little drunk. Which technically is the truth, we just don't mention her legs wrapped around a gay guy and the free entertainment on show!

Come Monday morning we hope Trisha comes into our office she still has the spreadsheets to finish. When Trisha finally arrives we spend much of the morning laughing at how drunk everybody was just to gage her reaction. She looks a little embarassed but says nothing. We mention *that girl who was the star of the show* again she says nothing. She looks decidedly sheepish about the whole evening trying to play it down says she remembers nothing.

We of course delight in telling her what she got up to and make up a few stories for entertainment value of seeing her squirm. We haven't had this much fun since the dead cat incident. I'm enjoying somebody else being on the end of a ribbing for a change. We carry it on for a while before telling her the truth. Then just for good measure Trudy sends her photo of Trisha to us all, which somehow she did not find funny. Somebody must have forwarded it to the shop floor because they printed a copy putting it on their calendar. I thought this was going a little too far. Luckily it was taken down before she found out or there would have been fireworks.

Olive came in work not impressed that all had a good time without her. More strangely though Gertie was in high spirits. Being in such a good mood she's brought in biscuits for us to share. She's joined in the laughter commenting how great the night out was. Hello, was this the same person I asked to dance with us because I felt sorry for her, only for her to growl at me she wasn't in the mood for dancing. Hadn't she spent the whole evening being miserable. Why are people so bloody awkward, if you're nice to them they want to clash, if you ignore them they want to clash. Now we are life and sole of the party.

Maybe she thought about what Trisha said and it's finally sunk in. Or maybe I misunderstand scowling for smiling even though I drank very little. She's so unpredictable, usually miserable and moody then on occasions pleasant with everybody. Could Gertie be a twin and we have the wrong twin today, hence the niceness. The jury is out on that one, but which ever one it is we make the most of it because it sure won't last.

We have a lottery syndicate at work with quite a few of us in it. When ever there's a rollover we spend our time dreaming how each will spend our millions. We're obviously not planning on it being hundreds, only the big three week rollover counts. We talk of how we'll miss work *surely not* and how we'd enjoy not coming into work Monday morning. We'd be busy cashing the cheque. Trudy says she'll still come into work to do a hand over. Jenifer and I stare at each other in shock saying in unison 'you'd come in work.'

Trudy says it's because nobody would be left in the department. Jenifer and I grin at each other again knowing Olive and Gertie will be left because they didn't want to join saying 'I never win anything.' Oh dear what a shame they'd have to turn up for work because there won't be anybody to cover for them.

Jerry says she'll have the amount we win, as we're all convinced we will win, tattooed on Trisha's arse, after all we are convinced she will show her arse. This has us in hysterics, we laugh at how we'll photocopy Trisha's backside and send a copy around the company.

Antonio comments 'and it won't be the first time.' Trisha's face flushes with embarrassment, her expression suggests she is thinking has this already happened. We all go sheepish hiding our faces behind the computers. If she sees us laughing she will know for sure, then we will be in trouble. We suggest a leaving present for those who aren't in the syndicate. Jerry suggest putting a photo up of the syndicate. I suggest putting a note underneath saying 'missing you already...guess who.'

Trudy says with cheque amount underneath in big bold numbers. Its days like this that keeps us going. Getting giddy we say how we will spend the money, but it'll have to be a big win because I'm already on my sixth million! I watched a programme about Entrepreneurs and how they made their millions. One guy made his through magazines, another sold mobile phones, another through property. One said when he was young he didn't know how but he knew that one day he would be rich. I laugh with the office saying I feel like that too. I don't know what I am going to do in life, or how I'll get there.

Of course the others rib me but how great would that be. Rich enough to enjoy life with freedom to do what I want. Nothing flash or spectacular, but it must be special. A little retreat or hideaway something like Richard Branson's Nectar Island. That isn't much to ask is it? Having a single parent mother who had to flog for a pittance all her life never having opportunities that are open to people today makes me want that even more. And we'll have to win soon because I want to do and see everything whilst I'm young enough to enjoy it with my family and friends. Yes that feels right, we can dream can't we.

Typing away at the computer I'm off into my own little world. Asking do I see myself still sat here when I'm sixty five. I bloody hope not, Stan said if he has to work until he's sixty five then he'll top himself right now. The thought of it fills both of us with dread, the clock ticking away by the second watching until five o'clock...praying for it to chime when you're sixty five. I enjoy working and meeting people and working on projects and problem solving it's the camaraderie of it all. But the monotony of nine till five for the next thirty years sends shivers down my spine.

I'd love to work at something I enjoy doing, trouble is I don't know what work I'd enjoy doing. I've never come across anything to hold my attention for long enough. Nothing appeals to me that I could envisage me still doing it for the next thirty years. I'm looking for three days a week, lots of travel involved and excellent pay. I've still not come by it yet.

I ask the others if they saw the programme and my vision of 'I'm gonna be rich it was meant to be.' Of which they fall about laughing telling me being rich won't make me happier. Of course they're right but it helps to have a better lifestyle. And there would be more satisfaction to being self made than just winning it, oh I'm so misunderstood.

We all agree winning is still a lovely option. I laugh telling them I keep saying to Stan he's just not aware of my many talents. They tell me they haven't discovered them either and fall about laughing. I tell them Stan says 'Yes I could have been an astronaut, if only I could get my arse out of bed.' Oh I'm so misunderstood (again). Laughingly they ask if I'm on planet Ang again. I grin and bear it because it is funny.

Stan works too hard renovating properties often working seven days a week. He just won't turn work down no matter what project he's on. When I speak to him about it he doesn't listen, insisting it won't be for long. He wants to earn enough money to retire on or semi-retire but sooner rather than later. I warn him he won't be here to enjoy it if he doesn't spare time for his family.

Ayeisha is growing up fast if we're not careful we'll miss out on sharing things with her. At this rate she'll have to put herself through University and won't want to be with us. She'll be travelling with her own friends. Stan tells us he wants to enjoy holidays but never has time to spare. He realises time is passing us by and agrees to book a holiday, we decide on Sri Lanka. He says he can buckle down when we get back.

Wanting to enjoy the moment whilst we can we think three weeks will be good, enough time to chill out and enough time to travel around experiencing some of the country. Otherwise we go for a shorter time, and it will be time to come home before we've even relaxed. I'm getting giddy again, it doesn't take much to please me. Before we book I best check with work and make sure nobody else has booked the same weeks, office politics and all that. I ask for the time off but my boss refuses, the others look relieved too. I know they're thinking if Olive and Gertie throw sickies its puts a strain on them.

But that's not my problem I'm entitled to my holidays. It's ridiculous, I have to plead and beg, the boss says if I get three weeks off then everybody will want three weeks off. Well actually they won't, some don't want to go for more than a week and others can't with one commitment or another. It didn't help that we want to go in the next few weeks either. I phone Stan and tell him the news, of course he goes ballistic, a huge company can't cope if I have a few weeks off. He's ready to storm in work and give them a peace of his mind.. Diplomatic as ever. For once I agree with him but I ask him to be calm and see what happens. I do what I'm best at and go into sulk mode.

A while later I'm summoned by the boss. He asks if I've thought about going for two weeks, sulkily I inform him two weeks isn't enough. Besides we'll be paying a fortune for two and three doesn't cost much more. It will cost far more to go back for another week and see all that we wanted to. He can see I'm upset and tries to compromise. He can offer three weeks my face lights up with a beaming smile. But he tells me it has to be over the Christmas period. The beaming smile freezes into a false smile, one of those like you've seen someone you want to avoid but catches you out, and it's written all over your face. I'll have to discuss it with Stan first I tell him. Leaving his office I feel like scowling like Gertie, he knows I'm not impressed.

Bloody hell we wanted to go now not in a few months. It was bad enough when we was going whale watching last year and it fell through because we faffed around for so long before booking it that the places were sold out. I'd swapped and changed our dates that much it was embarrassing. Work thought I was playing chess on the holiday board, by the end of it I gave up in defeat.

This time I'm sticking to my guns or we'll never go away. I can't plan ahead with Stan for more than a week let alone months away. Of course Stan took it well, threatening to tell that cheeky b******d what he thinks of him. I try to calm the situation explaining my boss isn't being awkward. But Stan shouts 'That's because its convenient that offices are shut down for ten days at Christmas we're supposed to be grateful they allow you to go on holiday, besides we don't know what our situation will be like at Christmas I've worked through the last two Christmases.'

Yes this was going down very well. He has a point though. I go back to my boss and tell him if we can't go now we can't go at all because we don't know what work commitments Stan will have, if he has another house to renovate he can't just leave the job for weeks. I choose this moment to remind him that we have spent the last few months covering all the sickies in the office, hoping for some leeway. Instead it backfires saying 'that's why I can't give you three weeks off now, should they be sick whilst your away then the office will be in trouble.' Stunned into silence I don't quite believe what I'm hearing. Because of those bone idle gits my holiday has to suffer.

I haven't done myself any favours though because it makes me feel like I'm a waffler. One minute saying I'll book at Christmas then know damn well I'll end up changing the holidays again. What is it about the British culture being indoctrinated into working for forty eight weeks of the year and being grateful for the few they allow you off. In Spain they take a few hours a day off for lunch, they know how to enjoy themselves. We however feel agitated if we don't work when its daylight. It's like we are all ants on the production line, give a hundred percent and definitely no playtime. We are sucked into this mind frame, stay here long enough and you morph into the rest of them.

Maybe I should throw sickies like the others then they'd be grateful when I do turn up. Work don't seem to mind when we're busy working through our lunch hour time and time again when we are busy or covering others when they're sick. I don't mean genuine illness but the one day sickness with a miraculous next day recovery rate. I drive home in a depression. Is it me am I the mad one. Everyone rushing home like ants. Nobody talks or acknowledges each other. Everyone races down the streets drawn like magnets. We're all in a rat race and nobody gets off the wheel until they drop. Sometimes we are side tracked through road rage or through accidents, but the daily monotonous routine never fails. I wonder how long we can last like that.

I refuse to bend to the rules, be desensitised into accepting the regime. Only going along with it whilst I have to. If I say I'd like to retire by forty five people gasp *and your complaining.* But I don't see it like that. I've worked from being fourteen years old and feel there are enough people in the country to keep it going without everybody working until 'normal retirement age.' Isn't it enough to spend 1,920 hours a year working, then times that for every year until retirement. It doesn't bear thinking about. Maybe it's me, I'm mad and everyone else is sane. I don't see anything wrong with leaving work early or taking three week holidays. In fact the holidays should be minimum two weeks three times a year. Why should we feel grateful for the peanuts we get.

Stan and I could have bought the flash car or bigger house we both work hard enough. I know people who have done and are still trying to keep up with the Jones's. When this isn't enough they re-mortgage to the hilt and do home improvements then they have to work until they're sixty five. I worry for them. Don't they want security or peace of mind that a little money in the bank will give. They don't think like that only thinking about today. We talk to Ayeisha even at her young age warning her of getting into debt and the only debt you should have is your mortgage if necessary. People who live on credit cards accruing debts all over the place have to work twice as long to pay the interest back. She laughs at how ridiculous it is to spend all your money on material things that you probably already have. I shall remind her of this when she's eighteen, I wonder if she'll think the same then. I've always wanted to be involved with charities but know I'm too soft a person that brings the job home with them getting too emotionally involved. I'd also love to run my own business but two people self employed in the same house isn't practical. In case of emergencies one of us needs a regular wage to cover for the other. Plus with Stan investing here there and everywhere it would be hell trying to manage money and it's not worth the stress.

Stan is forever finding me businesses to run. Cafes, chip shops, paper shops, sandwich bars, you name it he's found one for sale for me. He doesn't understand the pressure we'd both be under and the time away from the family necessary to build the business up. What if we want to go on holiday, we could hardly close for three weeks and still expect a business to still be there when you get back. This idea alone makes me know it's not practical.

By the time I'd got home my boss had phoned. He's only changed his mind about our holiday. He asks can I take them in about six weeks time that way it doesn't clash with anyone else. Yippeee! Time to get the brochures out again before Stan changes his mind again.

We've often thought of getting away abroad somewhere maybe Australia. Ideally Stan would like to up sticks and emigrate. My ideal would be six months here and six months abroad. But it's hardly practical and rather costly too. It's a nice idea but leaving family and friends behind permanently, I'm not sure it's something we could do. For a year or two it would be a great experience. The thought of being alone and isolated somewhere doesn't appeal. Besides Stan is hardly the sociable type, if anything he is anti social. He doesn't mean to be. He just can't cope with people and says they talk a load of waffle. It's hilarious watching him having to be nice. If he knows people well he'll tolerate it but even then it has to be in small doses. Take last week for instance the three of us were walking through Ashton Market. Stan bumped into a guy he used to work with and stopped to say hi. After two minutes of polite chatting I could see Stan's eyes wandering off track. The poor guy was in mid speech when Stan abruptly replies, 'I've got to go, its nice seeing you again' then starts edging away.

Ayeisha looks at me in horror not believing what she witnessed. Walking away I'm embarrassment for the poor bloke. Yet Stan bold as brass talks about what shopping we need to pick up not even realising how ignorant he was. 'Stan that was really rude to ignore him.' He claimed he didn't ignore him trying to say I was exaggerating. Ayeisha shouts 'Dad, that was terrible, you really embarrassed me then.' He bursts out laughing thinking it was funny saying 'you know what I'm like I don't do the nicey nicey chit chat.'

He genuinely feels there is nothing wrong with this behaviour. How on earth would he get on if we were abroad. You have to make an effort be friendly and mix otherwise you'd never meet people or you'd be totally isolated from society. I couldn't cope with complete isolation. We laugh at him 'if you were on a deserted Island like Castaway you have to work as a team to survive, they'd banish you to the other side of the island.' He replies 'you wouldn't need to banish me I'd banish myself to the other side.' The guys at work can't believe some of the stories about Stan. I'm sure they think I make it up, but then you couldn't possibly make it up, could you?

Work encourage us all to take the initiative to work out solutions, not just sit back and wait for problems to escalate. If it helps get the job done efficiently then it helps you and the company. I wonder if any of my *solutions* will work on Stan, it would be a start wouldn't it. Work are big on training and this months 'way forward' is evaluating and measuring. Anything and everything, even taking to putting charts up all over the show for how we can achieve better. Yes we really need to look at these whilst walking round the office trying to get the job done. Our boss asks what training courses we are interested in.

Sending Gertie on a communications course would be good, although she informs him she's already a good communicator. Lots of jokes went around about that one. Olive wants to do the management course. To manage what I ask myself, how to manage your desk in four days instead of five. I've got the 'how to manage time & people' and 'how to get the best from a team.' We all know the answer to that one. The skill is knowing how to delegate, how to get other people to do your tasks whilst you look busy.

The course turned out to be interesting, showing us how to get rid of someone you don't have time to speak to. When they walk into your office gently take their elbow or arm with your hand and start talking to them whilst walking them through the door at the same time. This is great we try it out on everyone back in the office.

Instead of walking with you like is said they should, they look at you like you've lost the plot, wondering why the hell your holding onto their arm. We all fall about in hysterics. We could keep this going for weeks. Jerry is doubled over with pain from laughing. Antonio says he'll try it on the next person to come through the door. So far he's tried it on Trudy and our boss, well they did ask how it went. I can't breathe for laughing so I can't do it. When Trisha pops in Jenifer has a go. Now knowing their personalities, and the fact we can't keep straight faces, Trisha thinks she is being accosted. This is priceless. It was worth going on the course just to see how ineffective this can be. Even if it doesn't work how it was intended, it does bring the office together. We haven't laughed so much since Trudy's photos and the dead cat incident.

You can see people walk towards our office hear the noise level and walk on by. I think they must be frightened to enter, or what might happen to them. It does lift the mood for a while. Trudy's communications course explains how different people are. I think we are all aware of that one. However, it says how you can approach a person but respond differently because of their personalities, or that some don't respond at all. She shows us a grid reference of personalities. We all fall into categories such as a people person, a tank, a logical person etc. It shows how to read people by knowing if they are able to think things through logically. It they are good with figures and can predict specific outcomes they are probably a logical person, not a people person who tend to be accountants or in a similar role and not social workers.

Logical people aren't often interactive people often preferring to work alone. We think of Gertie, she on the other hand thinks she's a people person crossed with logic, because of her good social skills, although she doesn't have too many takers on this one. A tank is someone who acts now ignores the consequences deals with them later. They don't ask opinions as their opinion is the only one that counts, to them anyway, saying they tend to be natural leaders. These are often people in authority who are able to take the responsibility of their actions. Though their actions are not necessarily the right ones. Priority to them is get the job done, and their way. My god it's like looking at an epilogue of Stan, the words leapt from the page. I take a copy home to ask Stan questions from the grid. I ask him how he perceives himself he thinks he's logical! Ayeisha and I laugh, we look at the Tank grid 'act now think later' she is in total agreement 'his opinion is the only opinion that counts/act now and think later.' Thinking about it I hardly needed the grid to tell me that did I.

~ Chapter Eight ~ **Wild Revelations & The Abseil**

At the local fair Trudy won her sons two goldfish. Having never had fish before she commented how hard can it be. This was to be her first mistake but hey we all make mistakes, some are more costly than others. The main thing was she tried for her sons and it's her good intentions that counted. By the end of the week she was a little concerned the new fish didn't look too healthy. Sadly by Monday morning one goldfish died, and not wanting to upset her sons she told them it was just sleeping and rushed to a pet shop to replace it. Explaining her problem in the shop the assistant told her some fish won at the fair die soon after, and she was just the unlucky one. The fact that he'd said she was 'unlucky' put her mind at rest.

Less than a week later Trudy again said her fish didn't look too healthy. Now hang on a minute haven't we been here before? If it was me I think alarm bells may have started to ring at this stage. But not Trudy she was convinced she was *meant* to care for pets. We ask her which was it the original one or the sleeping but now alert one. She said the original one. She says this might be her fault. Laughing at her we ask what on earth is she feeding them. Or maybe she didn't realise they need feeding. She might think they feed on plankton like in their natural habitat.

We politely suggest she reads up on how to look after fish whilst she still has fish to practice on. Sadly we were too late. The original one had gone to sleep too. We plead with her not to buy another. Well, not until she sought medical help for the existing one. Trudy being Trudy is now on a mission to have herself some fish. Telling us she has to get it right she won't accept not being able to conquer this. Even if she has to go through a hundred fish practicing she is going damn well get it right.

We start running a book on how long the survivor will last. So again on the way home she stops at the pet shop. She asks the shop what went wrong and was advised to buy a bigger tank rather than the small bowl she has. Off home she goes, again, this time armed with a new tank and a new fish. Oh dear I sense another funeral coming on. Do the boys not realise the fish are changing by the day, and that one has now been so desperate it's jumped right out the fish bowl when it saw her coming.

Another week later the third fish is looking like it is on its last legs, well fins. Trudy had to tell her boys something because even they noticed it was too asleep. This time one fish has gone back to the fair to look after the other fish because it's missing them. How sweet and economical with the truth, trust her to come up with that one. Worried again, she went back to the shop asking what is going wrong and how she looks after them.

Apparently every time the fish came to the top of the water she thought they were hungry and fed them. Again, and again, and again. She was overfeeding the poor things, and whilst they're desperately gasping for oxygen she's throwing in more food killing them again, and again. We ask her whether the pet shop allows her back in the shop yet or do they run shouting murderess. I think even the fish jump out of their tanks at the sight of her coming down the isle ready to choose another gasping not me.

We threaten to put her picture outside all pet shops with 'Warning, woman often seen entering pet shops, murderess at large, do not let this lady into the shop or near any fish.' Surely the pet shop would refuse to serve her this time. Shouldn't they have a moral obligation to the fish, isn't there a rule about cruelty to animals. I'm sure it covers marine life as well. When she pays a visit to the pet shop this time, the assistant gives her careful instructions of fish etiquette. He's only gone and given her more to practice on.

Somewhat shaking when handing her the new alive and kicking fish he's given her a pump to keep the water fresh too. We put her on probation yet surprisingly these survive for a considerable time. I think the children have taken over the upkeep of the fish?

Lots of changes are happening at work now a European Group have taken over the company. Deciding its necessary they bring in their own 'International Management Team' obviously since our management ran it quite successfully over the last ten years.

Lucky for us we have their valuable knowledge knowing that we could not manage before. They believe in the 'tweedle dum tweedle dee' approach, two managers checking on each department. We've nicknamed them Noah, always coming in two's. I don't think they understand us if anything they find us strange. They certainly don't get our northern humour.

Whilst at the coffee machine I saw one of the new managers stood before me in the queue. In a big dramatic way he says 'Hi Angie', I didn't realise I was that popular. It's probably Customer Services Week coming and he wants to make friends. 'How goes things in customer services then' he asks me with enthusiasm. I tell him we're really busy trying to keep it short and sweet that way he won't keep me long. 'So what do you do about the phones ringing all the time ' he asks. Mmmmm, now is this a trick question I ask myself. Is the answer; we answer what phone calls I can, or you can only answer one phone at a time. Pondering which answer I think its best to break the ice with a joke. 'Oh we don't worry about them at all, we just take the phones off the hook' I reply with a smile.

Sarcastic I know, but a little humorous I think. Let him know we do have a sense of humour. Apparently not, his face he goes a very pale grey then he seems to gasps. Bloody hell surely he didn't think we've taken the phones off the hook. We are a little professional for god's sake, well we do try to be. It was a joke I reassure him, this is the first chance I have had to get a coffee, with the phones all morning. Our northern managers would have got the sarcasm straight away, knowing our wicked sense of humour. Sadly it was wasted on tweedle dum. Oh well, I did try. It did work though, they steered clear of our department for a short while.

Because it's been so busy in the office the new management are sending Sebastian a Spanish guy over from their offices. Sebastian speaks Spanish obviously and also fluent in Italian and German. He'd lived in the UK before when studying and for his first two years with an international company. God help him here, he'll need all the help he can get with this barmy lot. We were concerned he may not fit in because of our northerness but he fitted in perfectly, well after a few hiccups. He didn't look at all like we imagined, half expecting a replica of Antonio Banderas with luscious locks of jet black hair.

The girls were a little disappointed because he was quite the opposite with short cropped spiky hair coloured blond at the front. He was very sweet with a delightful accent, it became clear that he was very flamboyant and particular. We sensed another drama queen entering. His vocabulary was excellent, in fact speaking English better than us. His full name was Sebastian Salvatore Senon Mauronta, meaning a revered saviour and lively one, and Mauronta is a medieval Spanish name. From the sounds of it he has a grand lineage back to medieval times, Gertie and Olive best watch out or he'll be putting a bad omen on them. This spooks Olive for sure who becomes cringingly pleasant to him. Jenifer has the pleasure of training Sebastian. He thinks for English people we are a little forward or even harsh. But then we are northerners saying it as it is. I don't think it helped when Jenifer was training him he didn't understand how we worked. So she went over it again, and again. In the end with sheer frustration she flicked the back of his neck with the tips of her fingers and cried 'you just don't listen.' I couldn't help but laugh at Jenifer's frustration but Sebastian wasn't amused by it at all.

There was no need for that he shouts back in his Spanish accent and nearly crying. He was used to dealing with people and working on projects. Now he had to get on with the nitty gritty every day work necessary to get the orders out. Sebastian you need to concentrate more, we work differently than the Spanish office. 'But you should not hit me' he whined. 'This time I'm only joking' she said 'but next time it would be harder' this time slapping him lightly on the back of his head. 'And don't be soft only babies whine' she laughed.

Of course this made us laugh even more. It was so ridiculous that it was almost funny watching Jenifer fussing that every thing had to be just so. Telling him procedures must be followed properly and 'you must listen when I'm talking.' Not meaning any offence she was just larking around. She was sick to death of training people then they go off and do their own thing. Worse still with nobody else knowing where the hell they were up to. Hurrying him up she tells him we have a lot to get through so let's get a move on. I try to lighten the mood and break the atmosphere suggesting it is getting a little late. Maybe you should try again first thing in the morning it might sink in a little bit more with a fresh mind. Because they'll have to go over it all again tomorrow anyway.

Positively sulking Sebastian didn't look like the revered one today. He went a little introvert. Well I thought it was funny Jenifer flicking the back of his head. She wasn't meaning it aggressive it was just her way of joking. She thought she was laughing with him. Somehow he wasn't feeling the joke. Lawrence thought he was sweet and had taken him under his wing. Lawrence would wouldn't he. He seemed to be going more camp each time he came back to the office. Spending most days working on assignments for the company Lawrence hadn't spent much time with us.

Lawrence was assigned back to our department working on a 'measuring project.' Counting what orders where put on the system, by who, how long does it take to process, how long before the orders were despatched. Being in his element with his new role he flounced around becoming more outrageous. He was sweet taking Sebastian under his wing but he seemed to be getting camper by the week.

Wearing bright or garish things to work it wasn't as if he wasn't outrageous enough already. He once came to work in three quarter length pants not quite the attire for the office. I think the new management would choke on their coffee. As usual Lawrence entered the office like a peacock strutting to get as much attention as he can. This morning he had remnants of glitter on his clothes it turned out he hadn't been home all night.

We didn't mind giving Lawrence our attention because he was such a softie and didn't have a bad bone in his body. Although he did love a good cat fight over guys, he didn't like oppressive behaviour or listening to Olive and Gertie's moods. Before Lawrence had felt a little threatened by Olive and Gertie but now felt he could be more relaxed. In fact it was quite entertaining watching him try getting the best ailments out of them both. Egging them on seeing which could out do the other, having us in stitches with his antics.

We wondered how long it would take for them to click. Now he had a best friend to impress he was on top form more than usual. Lawrence would sit in the hot seat begging us to ask him about his night before. Wanting us to talk about his all night parties and the new friends he met. The hot seat was a spare chair in the office and if we needed to get information from anyone, we would invite them to sit down on our chair for a while. Once comfy we would gently interrogate them. This time he confided he had 'news' for us.

Apparently he was coming out of the closet. We all look stunned and not because he has come out of the closet. But because he actually believed we thought he was still in the closet. I think the glitter and hot pants skipping down the office was just a little give away. We humour him saying 'Wow.' He flutters himself around even more. He gushes 'I can't believe I've confided in you guys, I think I need some caffeine' and then out he flounced. We wondered what drugs he may have been on.

Sebastian had missed the 'coming out' announcement whilst being on a tour of the company. When he returned he seemed very quiet yet he had been quite bubbly before. Come to think of it he was a little quiet before the tour. We thought he might be homesick. Concerned we ask if he is alright. 'No' he replied rather sulkily. We try to cheer him up telling him about Lawrence. But he chose not to listen to the gossip or comment. Ignoring us all he sat down. What was a funny few moments had now turned into deflation. We didn't want this to carry on, after all we've had enough of Gertie and Olive's moods in the past. Now with Gertie or Olive we wouldn't have asked or we'd have suffered their woes all day. But with Sebastian we were concerned. It almost felt like dealing with a child.

I ask if Sebastian enjoyed the tour. He didn't reply in his excited manner but sulked that it was alright. Then said he doesn't want to talk because he is upset. I don't believe this whats wrong now. I haven't done anything wrong, I only wanted to help. I feel my face drop and the rest of the office start grinning. A little shocked I ask Sebastian what I have done wrong. Almost in tears he said I laughed at him when he couldn't grasp the training. I try telling him I didn't laugh at him not grasping it, but laughed at Jenifer trying to teach him.

I prompt Jen to ask him what is wrong after all she is supposed to be looking after him. She sheepishly asks Sebastian if anything else was wrong. This time he leapt from his chair shouting 'Actually there is something wrong but don't want to talk about it.' Bemused at the outburst we wonder what else can be wrong. We know Gertie and Olive haven't been near him yet. For once it cannot be their doing. Jenifer tells him if he doesn't speak about it we can't help. Sebastian walks to towards her taking centre stage saying 'If you must know you really upset me, so much so I could not eat my dinner.'

Stunned she looks at the rest of us pleading for help. Gertie then stomps through the office concerned somebody else is getting attention and being made a fuss of. She strops past ignoring the domestic, probably because she is not centre of attention. What on earth can he be talking about, then it clicked, the flicking his head and the little slap. We know he wasn't amused but surely he didn't take her serious. I know we had all laughed with them both when it happened, but he was deadly serious. Jenifer looked so embarrassed thinking this was a wind up but could tell from our faces it was not. I tried hiding behind my computer desperately trying not to giggle, thinking this serves her right for being bossy. We could see it written all over her face as she squirmed with embarrassment. Especially with the rest of the office watching. Which of course made me giggle more with the nerves kicking in.

Sebastian shouted 'I felt ill all night, I even worried about coming into work today.' Jenifer was shocked and tried to get herself out of the hole saying that Trudy had laughed too. This annoyed Trudy 'Don't try dragging me into it.' Sebastian moaned 'Angie laughed as well.' Why does everything always come back to me. He then says looking directly to Jenifer 'But you were the one who offended me most of all.' The office had all been giggling but this wiped the smile off their faces. And poor Jenifer looks as shocked as ever. Olive, Antonio and even Larry come fussing round like clucking hens. Trudy hovers at the back slightly suspecting it could have a little to do with her.

I did feel sorry Sebastian being so serious. He is a nice person but this was a little ridiculous. I hide behind my computer giggling some more. My god, if he is being like this over something silly, then how the hell is he going to cope when it really kicks off in the office. But he then goes for the kill 'You tried to embarrass me in front of the office.' Jenifer cringes with embarrassment as she tries to tell him it was only a little fun. He looks directly at her eyes piercing hers waiting for her explanation.

She looks to me for support because he had a go at me first. I shrug my shoulders because I've already said my piece. Plus I don't want to make it any worse than it already is. I do feel sorry for Jenifer in a way. She looks so embarrassed, she doesn't know what to do in front of us all. She tells him 'I didn't mean to upset you, we were only training and we laughed because you weren't taking any of it in, it was only a bit of fun, honestly Sebastian.' She was hoping for a little warming of the atmosphere. But he replied 'I've been upset I could not sleep. I'm really shocked because I never thought a guy could be so sensitive. But then again Sebastian is a little different than most guys I suppose. Poor Jen. Where in the training manual does it say about dealing with this one. Normally we'd tell him to stop behaving like a big tart. But he really was upset, which made us feel awful because we did all laugh at him. As a peace offering we go and get him a drink and a bar of chocolate trying to fuss him a little and calm him down.

We tell him not to take us so seriously and that we were only joking. If Jenifer didn't like him she would have ignored him and not joked with him. He thought we didn't like him that's why we laughed. We try telling him not to be silly we all like him. We are just not used to guys being so sensitive. Coming from Manchester this is not usual behaviour from a guy. Christ, he's not going to last a week with us at this rate. Jen apologises profusely, telling him not to bottle things up but let us know if something bothers him, we won't be offended. We didn't like seeing him like this. Jenifer treads gently with him for a while realising he was such a sensitive soul. She says she is genuinely sorry.

I just hope Sebastian doesn't get in the middle of Olive and Gertie or they'd eat him alive. At some point Olive and Gertie will start a war as usual. We just hope he doesn't start crying. We had wanted another guy in the office able to stand in between them both when the going gets tough. And not jump for the extra soft tissues. Thankfully Sebastian settles down and accepts the peace offering. He does eventually accept our humour. Although he did say it was an acquired taste. Seeing the office fuss round Sebastian seems to annoy Gertie even more. You can almost see the steam coming from her ears. This is worth it just to get her back up. We decide to be gentle with Sebastian as he's not the typical bloke you'd meet.

Although we do wonder how is he going to react with the guys here. If he thinks that we are bad, or rather Jenifer's bad, he wants to see how direct the guys can be. Some of the guys from the shop floor can speak rather harsh and mean it. Not to cause trouble but saying it as it is. We give it back just as good, you have to stand up for yourself otherwise you'll get walked all over. Unless it gets serious we play the game. Which is great because you get the best of both worlds. Holding our own when we need to and be delicate females when in need of a favour. Then they feel sorry for you and help out. Well everyone except Olive and Gertie, they tend to run from them like scared rabbits. But then again wouldn't most of us.

Sebastian was a quite a character we hadn't met anyone quite like him before. He was fascinated by people, when he lived in London he had met friends from Manchester. He loved to meet people, it didn't matter who or where. He had a passion for food shopping in his lunch hour, often coming back with phone numbers of complete strangers. He would spend lunchtimes in the supermarket discussing with shoppers what they had in their baskets. He said he could read people just by what they had in their baskets. Telling us if they are the plain boring type, creatures of habit with a can of baked beans and a loaf.

Sebastian would make beeline for people he thought interesting because they'd have great ingredients to make wonderful dishes. Sebastian told us single people are on the look out in the Supermarket. We asked how he knew they were single. Single people shop with a basket not a trolley. They buy single items not large packets. He'd strike up a conversation with the boring ones trying to tempt them into buying something more exciting or exotic. I have been shopping for my family for years. And I have yet to be accosted over the frozen peas section. It must be the Spanish accent that does it or people might think he's a weirdo harassing them in the ice-cream section.

More worryingly I often pop into the supermarket buying things just for me that Stan or Ayeisha won't eat. It never crossed my mind people would think I'm out on the lookout for a date. I had never noticed what people had in their baskets. Since Sebastian arrived I made a special effort to people watch. It's funny to watch people buying, falling into the boring pies frozen pizza's and a few lagers to the Jamie Oliver I can cook categories. I suppose Sebastian has a point. Sebastian is so charming you couldn't be offended by him. He has amazing conversations with men and women in the supermarket. Although we are convinced he hides behind a counter waiting for somebody to pick foods he likes he pounces on them. He says talking about food helps strike up a conversation claiming it a great ice breaker.

If a stranger accosts you and asked what you're cooking for tea you'd think you've found a weirdo wanting to come home with you. But Sebastian got away with it every time. I'm surprised security had never challenged him before. But then again he probably chatted them up too. It was even funnier when a television programme asked where the in place to get a date was, the supermarket only came out as the top place. I don't believe it he's even got his own dating agency going. Its probably one of those 'pass it on' things, you leave a card with your number on the delicatessen then somebody else picks it up or forwards it on to another stranger.

When he goes to the supermarket we take bets on if it's possible for him not to come back without chatting somebody up. Lawrence bounces into our office knowing he's missed out on something but not quite sure what's going on. Plonking himself down in the hot seat dramatic as ever asks what's going on. We tell him nothing more than usual we need to get back to work otherwise the boss will start moaning. If we encourage him to stay we'll never get any work done. He takes the hint realising we have been messing around for long enough for now. We try getting back to the grindstone when he says 'I'll spare you the drama for another time then, and by the way you need to throw me a coming out party. He still hasn't realised we've already accepted his coming out before he came out.

Sebastian went to a 'party' shortly after arriving in Manchester. To think he only has a few friends in Manchester he was certainly getting around. As ever we were all intrigued as this party was only attended by professionals, or rather male professionals. He was pretty coy about the evening saying very little at first. Normally after a party you usually say who was there or who embarrassed themselves, or which friends you met up with. I naively thought he had just met up with friends until he said the 'all male professional' theme. It then sounded like a specialist club, and only being allowed into the club should the glove fit. We obviously did not fit the glove. He commented he hadn't met most of them before and neither did he say which friends invited him.

Alarms bells started ringing, was it friends or a friend of a friend who invited him. It was an unusual mix of people too to say there were only a handful of people, a barrister, curator, policeman, solicitor, dentist and company director. I asked if it was a dinner party but he said no although he did have a few nibbles. He gave me a big cheesy grin saying it was a really good party and everyone had a great time. I'd have thought half a dozen people getting together for an evening isn't really a party. Trudy smiles saying he's being far too coy about the evening, we must introduce him to our hot seat.

Our hot seat came in handy should we want to grill anyone. If they are fool enough to sit in the hot seat then they had to tell the truth. Shortly after Sebastian sat in the hot seat, so of course we had to interrogate. At first he claimed they were just friends of his. When asked did he know any of them he said no but he did know one guy through an acquaintance. Did he drink a lot at the party? 'Yes quite a bit.' Did any women go the party.. 'No.' Then his phone began to ring, he jumped out of the chair ready to answer it when Olive beat him to it. Jerry leaned as far as she could over the office without falling off her chair to listen. Jen asks him are you sitting comfortably, we can't help but laugh. He confessed the party did get a bit wild. Asked if he behaved himself he tried answering yes, but the grin gave it away. The last thing he can remember is being barely dressed in the swimming pool with a guy on either arm. Laughing it was great fun. I was in hysterics I couldn't believe what he comes out with at times. I shout at him 'for god's sake you did take precautions didn't you? The mother in me coming out again. He insisted he did, but if you are so drunk would you remember.

Sebastian finally came out with it telling us he is fully fledged gay. Of course we got very little work done this afternoon, laughing with Sebastian. People keep passing by probably wondering what the hell we are laughing at this time. He says it is tinged with sadness because although his family love him they never accepted his sexuality, hence moving to London to study and become himself. Lawrence told me he found me amusing that I'd be shocked at Sebastian. I knew it wasn't that I was shocked, but because I wouldn't do the 'kiss and tell' to the whole office. You know the sort the tacky tell the office who you've been with, when and where. I thought this was only something teenagers do, or what lonely people feel the need to do, finding out what others are up to because they don't have a life of their own. Yet our office on the other hand thought quite differently. They were all quite happy to inform us of old acquaintances.

No wonder Jerry was taking a keen interest because she was quite happy to tell all about the guys she'd dated. In fact she was in her element giving all the sordid details. When I say it was dated it sounded more like a list of brief encounters. I wondered how she could remember all their names as the list was quite impressive. It was quite embarrassing really listening to all their conquests. But it was hilarious to hear about when they almost got caught. This became the great entertainment of the office for a while, keeping us amused for hours. Why is it when laughing at others we find this a greatest source of entertainment. Yet I know if I heard that Stan sits discussing me with his work colleagues I'd be mortified. In fact I'd wring his bloody neck. As much as he's a pain in the arse I know Stan is a real softie underneath. Being very much a man's man, of which I like, he's also really caring. There isn't a day goes by when he doesn't tell me he loves me, except of course those days when we are going off on a raging row. Because Stan has a bossy controlling side to him, always having to get his own way, people just see him as a steamroller in tarmac. What they don't realise what a great sensitive side he has. And that he can be so witty he'll have Ayeisha and I laughing till our sides hurt.

Unfortunately for me Stan is one of those painfully truthful people. If you don't want the answer to a question then you don't ask Stan. He has this awful habit of saying things as it is and quite mercilessly. No matter how much you don't want to hear the truth. He never thinks to say things diplomatically then you still have the truth but without the upset, oh no he goes guns for glory. He'll as easily tell me I look great in an outfit, as partners should do, as he would saying it does nothing at all for me. Especially when you don't want to hear it.

If I ask do I look fat in a particular dress he has no qualms telling me my backside looks big, in fact he goes as far as saying your fat makes you look fat. When I sulk at his comments, of which I often do, he tells me 'if it looks good I'd tell the truth just the same, would you prefer I lie to you. Well of course I would. Then he'd follow on with 'The trouble with you is you only want the answer if it's the right answer for you.' Well obviously, who wants to hear they look a mess. Don't we all want to hear you look lovely? You'd think he'd learnt to lie just a little if only to please me. Back in the hot seat Lawrence said he has only ever fancied men and that women do nothing for him, even though he gets on great with women. He divulges of having lots of one night stands, and now looking for a more meaningful relationship rather than a one night stand. He feels he just hasn't met the right person yet. I suppose it is difficult, with millions of heterosexual people out there many still find it difficult to meet that right person. For somebody homosexual surely their chances of meeting Mr Right their chances lowered because there are less people to choose from.

Or would this work in his favour, having less people to go through finding Mr Right could you find your soul mate a whole lot sooner? Lawrence feels now is the right time to meet that someone special, to share things with, evenings, holidays, laugh at silly things that other people just don't get. Lawrence never wanted a family. He was keen to be an uncle but never the thought of children to restrict his life, or want the responsibility for a child. He just wanted a partner. But felt such angst at not having somebody in his life. He also revelled in the outrageousness of his past too. Not trying to be outdone Sebastian got back into the hot seat recalling a chance meeting with a woman called Roxanne whom he met on a flight to Los Angeles.

Roxanne was a complete stranger who emptied her life story out to him on the flight. I mean this is the most obvious thing you do on a flight home isn't it meet a stranger pouring your life story personal details and all. Although to be fair he was in the habit of meeting the strangest of people. They saw this motherly instinct in him making people feel they could confide in him, or they thought him like a substitute girlfriend. Roxanne poured her heart out to him telling about a guy she had previously met on the plane bound for England, yes another stranger I might add. She'd talked to this stranger for an hour or so then when in London went back to an hotel with him, apparently feeling a connection with each other on the plane. That and the need to sleep with a stranger as you do?

Now at this point I'm sure alarm bells would be starting to jingle just a little at this point. I think I'd pretend to be ill and move seats letting her pour her life to somebody else. But not Sebastian oh no he encouraged her to tell all. What's more he wouldn't find this story odd in the slightest, like this happens to him every day. Because Sebastian had this way with people, you could imagine him sat there giving her his full attention. Roxanne then goes into graphic details of how this guy had told her on the plane he fantasized about sleeping with a stranger, and he fantasized about being with another man as well (well he got his first fantasy anyway). I bet Sebastian couldn't believe his luck being sat next to Roxanne, he'd have been in his element.

Apparently Roxanne's stranger fantasized about being with a man only because another man would understand how he felt about his needs. Now hello earth calling! How the hell does this happen? Had she been desperate, easy or on drugs I wonder. I'd be more concerned if this guy was a mass murderer or just let out of a lunatic asylum. If that is what he discloses to a stranger within an hour or two on a flight then what would he want to divulge in private. We couldn't help but fall about laughing.

But did Roxanne worry of the stranger's character? Oh no she wasn't put off in the slightest, in fact she wanted to marry this stranger. She was arranging a visa to be with him in Los Angeles, permanently! Sebastian insisted it was true. I'm sorry but you meet a stranger on a plane, you don't even know his last name or where he lives. Nobody knows where you are or who you're with and you go off to a hotel to have sex with him. Now is it me, have I led a sheltered life, or is this just a tinsy bit odd. Yet Sebastian didn't think it odd at all. He couldn't see why we would be concerned at all. He looked bemused saying 'what if you met somebody and hit it off in an instant.' Maybe if I felt a connection with someone and that's a big if. But this guy was talking fantasies before the aperitifs had finished. They both sounded unstable to me. We all burst out laughing at him again. But he couldn't understand our humour, he thought we were laughing at him not the situation.

We tried explaining this wasn't the normal experience you have on a flight when going on your holidays. We'd be more concerned of getting the window seat, if your meal is good, where is your luggage. Not Sebastian, his norm is to have a Jerry Springer moment on the plane. I have visions of who'd be sat behind them listening to their conquests and choking on their coffee. Maybe she wanted Sebastian to be the 'other fantasy man' and she was sounding him out. We laugh telling him half expected to see a photo-fit of her on crime watch in the future. He trots off sulking that our amusement is not to his liking. This obviously makes us worse, I mean what can top this. We ask the rest of the office if anybody else has a holiday experience to share with us not that we are running the Jerry Springer show.

Somehow our holiday stories don't quite match up to his. I'm so glad I work here. Can you imagine the fun I'd miss out on working for another company. I wonder if all companies are this. Would they get away with it. Right on queue Jerry keeps with the moment and forces herself into the hot seat. To say the hot seat that has become very hot this week is an understatement. Jerry claims she's a little embarrassed about this one and it mustn't go out of the office. Which of course we lie through our teeth reassuring her it won't go any further. But what we didn't clarify was further from where so technically we're in the clear.

Jerry thinks a bloke she knows seems *familiar* to her. She rambles on about not remembering it clearly because she was drunk and thinks she may have had 'thing' with him. We ask her to clarify what she means by 'thing.' She thinks she couldn't be sure if she had met him at a club in town. If it is him she remembers taking a shortcut down the back streets towards the taxi rank. But now thinks they might have stopped on route a little to get to know each other. She says they only kissed but can't be sure as she was really drunk. Oh really what a surprise. If its anything like last time to go by she'd have pounced on the poor guy on the dance floor and then asked his name.

When we push for who the guy is, after a little delving it only turns out to be Danny from the packing department. Just when we thought we couldn't top Roxanne, out pops Jerry ready to claim the limelight. Of course telling us was completely the wrong thing. Because we all fall about laughing not quite believing our ears. Can you imagine how embarrassing it is coming into work and seeing a familiar face in a haze across at the coffee machine. And thinking now where have I seem him before. This is priceless. We can hardly let this one pass by now can we. Surely we have to carry this one on a little. Gertie finally comes round to our humour for once and joins in the banter. Tony from the warehouse had dropped off the daily sheets ready to be invoiced. He goes over to our board drawing a picture of Danny.

Gertie draws a brick wall behind Danny asking does this make him look more familiar. Then Tony remembers he has a photo of Danny at last year's office party. After a few minutes he returns armed with photos. We rifle through them until we find a picture of Danny. In a fit of giggles we run back to the board holding up the photo against the drawing of the brick wall asking 'Does he look more familiar now.' Jenny sits in her hot seat trying to look offended but can't take us seriously. Tears are rolling down my face. I hear my phone ringing but I can't answer it because my sides are hurting from laughing so much. Jerry is convinced it's him but begs us not to say anything.

When we hear footsteps approaching the door we try to stop and contain ourselves for a moment. But all they can hear is the raucous behaviour from our department they decide to walk on by. Gertie really enjoyed the banter for a change. Olive thinks we are childish and is the only one working. In fact her face is like a crab apple, Lawrence thinks it's hormonal and Sebastian wonders what on earth it is. And Larry, well its Larry King night so we won't see him until Monday. Which is probably a good thing, because we don't want to hear about his fictitious antics with his lady friend.

We ask has anyone else got something they need to share with the office before the hot seat is put away. After all we do have work to be getting on with, and I don't think we can take much more of this. Jenifer decides to finish off the days antics with her story. She sympathises with Jerry saying how easily it could happen, then goes into great detail of how many guys she thinks she's slept with. Admitting she'd need a few pairs of hands just to count how many as many of them were one night stands, or weekend flings. Shocked at her brazenness we thought this was Jerry's forte.

Teasing her I walk past the hot seat waving my hands up and

down whilst pretending to do the Charleston indicating how many partners Jerry had. Jenifer had to laugh she knew we'd have to take the mickey at some point, might as well get it over and done with now. The entertainment value at work is classic, almost as good as Coronation Street. I think I should apply to become a script writer for Corrie I'm sure some of our stories could match their storylines. Jenifer must have felt her sharing to be therapeutic because she went on telling us about going to the Costa Del Sol with her ex. They were invited to a party by a bloke they'd only just met.

Oh dear this sounds like the Sebastian scenario all over again. It was supposed to be a pool party, but everyone left the pool and disappeared into the house. Thinking they were alone Jenifer and the ex got a little amorous in the pool. Only to realise the bloke they had just met started taking photographs of them in the pool. They both jumped out of the pool and ran into the house. Then one of the other guys invited her into the other room. Looking around to what was going on it was then it dawned on them they were at a swinging party. They do a runner to the nearest bar realising what a lucky escape they had.

To top it off from the description she gave of this bloke he sounded like a right minger. We had visions of this dirty old man hovering around looking for young couples to join his party. Was the raincoat not a dead giveaway. It's putting me off wanting to go swimming now, who the hell would have been in the pool before me. Upon reflection I think I must have led a very sheltered life, but then again thankful that I had. Before we go home we draw lots of hand prints on the board for Jenifer's benefit, just a little reminder. For a while after we drew around our hands and put the pictures around her computer. She couldn't really complain because what would be the point of telling us if we couldn't have fun with it.

A few weeks later flu did the rounds at work leaving us short staffed again. Olive and Gertie were up to their old tricks again and Antonio is on holiday. Thankfully the phones are unusually quiet. Jerry is back from her course tomorrow so hopefully there will be more of us back in tomorrow. We get through what work we can between us. When I finally get time for a quick break I grab some lunch and go down to get some coffee's from the machine. I finally get time for a quick break and grab some lunch. I've been told to play down the absences from our 'international managers' we don't want to alarm them. Plus they'd only come into the office interfering. It's best to keep away from them for as long as possible.

At the coffee machine I've only got one of the managers in front of me. I try being discrete not making eye contact and hopes he will talk to somebody else. Unfortunately he spots me enquiring how customer services are going. I tell him it's really quiet this morning, thinking if it's quiet we can cope better with the workload between us. He looks at me alarmed at why we are not busy. Damn now what have I said. Not thinking I try to diffuse the situation telling him it's a good thing we are quiet as there are only two of us in this morning.

But it was one of those moments that made a bigger hole for myself because he looks at me even more alarmed than before. Oh God, can the ground not open up and swallow me please! Maybe I'll speak with your boss' he mutters walking away. Sheepishly I head back to the office knowing the others will probably kill me for dropping us in it. Trudy was full of germs and not feeling at all well, had dragged herself into work when she should be in bed. Knowing others are off with convenient ailments she couldn't bear the thought of her job not being done properly. I decide to keep quiet about bumping into the manager. He might forget if something more pressing keeps him occupied. Well I can hope can't I. But before I can speak the phones start to ring, jolting out like alarm bells. Oh well back to the grindstone. Oh the thought of giving it all up to go travelling.

The next day we are almost back to a full office. I decide its best to casually inform them of my encounter at the coffee machine before our boss gets in there first. Of course they take it as well as expected. They look at me open mouthed they can't believe I've told the boss. 'You've told tweedle dum, bloody hell Ang if he didn't have a reason to keep on our backs before he certainly does now. Jenifer asks what planet was I on yesterday.

Getting her own back Jerry pipes up I was on planet Ang! True to form tweedle dum and tweedle dee started popping in more often that usual for a while after.

A charity letter circulates work asking people to raise money for people terminally ill with Cancer. They don't mind doing the fund raising but nobody wants to put their name down for the event. Curious I ask why is it a sponsored run or something. When the letter reaches me I realise why. They want people to abseil 100 feet down a high rise building in Manchester. Come to think of it I'm not very good with heights. But there are some Royal Marines helping you which make it sound interesting. I suppose with your safe with a strapping marine to train you. I figured they'd train you in the morning then do the absail in the afternoon. I presume you don't do it alone so for a mad moment I think to myself I could do that. I'm sure I'd be safe with a marine. Its only 100 feet high Jenifer asks why don't I do it before someone wants to push me off. Her sense of humour is so sharp these days.

Getting giddy with myself I put my name down. The others don't believe me asking 'what your actually going to do it' Yes I tell them grinning to myself I will do this. I haven't figured out how I'll get over the fear of height thing yet, a minor detail I'm sure I can overcome after all it is for a good cause. I can't stand near the edge of high buildings so I'm not so sure how on earth I'll get through this one. Just to keep up the goodwill and me being generous and all I don't want to hog the limelight all by myself I put my friends name down on the list too. Besides we've been friends for many years so I'm sure she won't mind. Or she'll learn to forgive me, eventually I try telling myself unconvincingly.

I return the application form with anticipation. Holding my fingers crossed that I get through this or I will be shown up in front of everybody. I call round to Sadie's to break the news after all it would be a good idea to tell her before hand. Come to think of it I've never heard her say she doesn't like heights so I hope for the best. Right on cue I get a nervous laugh and tell her I'm doing an abseil to monitor her reaction. Of course her reaction is I must be mad. Grinning, I add 'by the way I've put your name down too.' Both of us start laughing. Then her face stops laughing as it registered what I've said. Now I feel a trauma coming on. She can't believe what I've done, but neither can I for that matter. Worried this will harm our long standing friendship I try warming her to the idea it's raising money for charity. Before she gets annoyed I let slip 'Did I mention that Royal Marines will be training you.' Funnily enough this managed to persuade her.

It wasn't until I was on my way home that it dawned on me the Royal Marines might be women. Then I'd be laughed at. I send my sponsorship form around work, I'm thankful some guys from the warehouse and manufacturing offer to sponsor me. This is really good of them after all I don't know them, in fact I don't think I've met hardly any of them as they work night shifts. All the office staff sponsor me even the management, well on their wages I should hope so too. Some ask if I have abseiled before and a little surprised that I haven't until they see the fear written all over my face.

As the day draws nearer I can feel myself bottling out. But everyone has been so supportive. In fact they have been too encouraging. This worries me a little. Do they want to see me achieve or is it more to do with they want to see me hanging from the top of a 100ft building. The jury is out on that one. I best not ask Gertie or she'll have her voodoo doll out. Trying to collect the sponsorship money was another thing. Most people who didn't have the change on them were really good bringing the money into work over the next few days. However, one member of management was another matter. In fact he became a real pain. He never seemed to have the money on him at any time. At the beginning of the week, the end of the week, the end of the month.

And there's me thinking only Royalty never carried money on them. Some colleagues say they'll show there backsides if I get any money out of him. Apparently he was known for it. Promising sponsorship in front of other managers then never paying up. When I mentioned it he always came up with an excuse, even when the sponsorship had to be paid by me. They others laugh that the wife doesn't give him spending money. Either that or he's a tight git. I think the latter is more accurate.

When the day of the abseil arrives, oddly, I feel okay. Quite confident in fact. Stan drives Ayeisha and me to the abseil. Sadie is there already. Thank god she's still up for it. We managed to get lost on route. Being a Sunday there isn't anybody around to ask for directions. When we finally find the building we notice an ambulance on standby. Stan found this hilarious telling me that's for those who miss the rope. I don't find this funny at all! I tell myself not to be stupid the ambulance have to be here for safety reasons. And to make me feel even worse I've missed my time slot. Luckily, there are so many people doing the abseil somebody else goes in my time slot. Looking up I see these little bodies scaling down the building with great ease.

I gasp, realising they are descending alone! I try reassuring myself stupid girl, obviously some of them must be experts. I try calming myself down but can only wonder what the hell I'm doing here. I feel my throat going dry. I try gulping but my throat seems tight and sticks even more. I tell myself to take deep breaths I'll be fine, repeating it over and over. I'll feel better with training, so stop worrying I'll be alright. I register and sign a liability form relinquishing them of any responsibility should I fall. I'm told to take the lift to the top floor, somebody will show me what to do. I'm feeling very unsure and my legs are shaking.

More deep breaths I tell myself but the others in the lift look just as terrified as me. Thank god I'm not alone you can tell it's their first time too. This gives me some relief. Its one thing making a Pratt of yourself alone in front of people. But if you all make Pratts of yourself well that's okay I can cope with that. We try making light of it and tell jokes to cheer each other up. One guy says pretend we are in Mission Impossible scaling down a building. Another says start humming the tune to Mission Impossible if you get nervous. We all start humming Mission Impossible then burst into laughter. Looking up I catch a glimpse of my face in the lift. My God I look like I'm on drugs. My eyes are so wide open I look like I've just seen a ghost. Get a grip girl I shout at myself.

Reaching the top floor I try walking forward but my legs won't move. I hear a voice in my head telling me to stay in the lift go back down, run, anything but go out on the roof. If you've ever been on the roof of a high rise building you'll know it's horrible. You can feel how high up you are because your legs start shaking. Your hands start to numb and your head goes light headed. I felt a breeze of cold air flow through the doorway to the activity outside. I remind myself to breathe in deep be confident. Though it doesn't do me any good, my panting is getting louder.

The six in our group are ready to go out to the roof for our training and try mumbling small talk to each other. Before I know it some guy grabs hold of me, whips a safety harness around me in a second telling me I'll be okay. Sorry but I'm not okay and I can feel a trauma coming on. I've convinced myself the safety harness around my waist is loose, of which I promptly tell him. Only for him to reply it's alright the leg harness will hold me in position. What! 'How can I be safe if the waistband is not tight? If I tip upside down whilst dangling over the side of the building, then I can fall out of the bloody thing can't I.'

He now looks at me like I'm a raving lunatic. 'I know you're only petite but your quite safe this is secure, I am used to teaching all ages, even children'. Now I feel really embarrassed. I don't think the children he's worked with has performed as much. Am I panicking unduly I ask myself,? I know I'm over reacting but can't stop myself. Come on deep breaths and you'll be ok I tell myself again. Then the guy gives me one minute of guidance of what to do when going down the rope. How to hold my hands and feed the rope through the hoop, don't worry there will be somebody at the top if you get into difficulty.

I'm puzzled, what does he mean *at the top*. Shouldn't he be saying there will be somebody at the side of you. He then says about gently bounce your feet against the wall as if doing small steps. And worst of all the hardest part which happens to be the most vital bit is the start of the decent. He wants me to stand on the edge of the building, be strapped to the post, lean backwards as far over the edge of the building as possible with shoulders pressed back. Yeh right, just lean backwards a 100ft in the air whilst dangling over the edge, I don't think so somehow. Trying to be rational I thought to myself I could sit on the top and just lower myself over the edge. I know damn well there is no way I could lean myself backwards.

If somebody goes over the edge with me then I'll be alright. Speaking of which where's my damn Marine. Out onto the roof top waiting for my turn I see the people from the lift lowering themselves over the ledge. With a bloke at the top of the building speaking to them coaxing them over. Although he doesn't look like he's ready to go over with any of them, and I know they weren't experts. I look at them puzzled when it dawns on me, Christ they're going over the edge alone and on their first go. Smiling he beckons me over I feel my legs go numb. I walk towards him not being able to speak. Feeding the rope through my harness he laughs 'Right it's your turn, I need you to climb onto the edge, face me and hold onto the barrier, perch on the edge and lean back'. I hear him but it's all swirling around in my head. There are some occasions when you feel you are near to death and this is one of those occasions.

I don't feel confident, quite weak in fact. The horror of what I have to do is now reality. No more 'Are you really going to do it' from the office or 'Good luck.' I'm ready to dangle myself over the edge what on earth was I thinking about. I could run away not do it but I'd have to face everybody. Tell them I was pathetic and I didn't even have a go. I somehow manage to clamber onto the ledge, although I'm gripping the barrier for dear life. I hear when your ready lean back and let go of the barrier. Hello, I don't think so. My legs are caving in my throat feels like I've swallowed glue. Like a frightened rabbit I ask who is going down with me. 'You are.'

Seeing the fear of God in my face he grins reassuring me I'll be alright. I don't like heights I mumble. 'It's a bit late for that love, whatever you do love don't look down' he laughs. I'm still gripped to the barrier and not budged an inch. When I try feeling where my feet are my foot stumbles off the ledge. I feel this is the time to say goodbye to everyone I know. I can't let go of the barrier and find myself squatting on the ledge. I hadn't noticed any noise before it seemed like a haze, then from the distance I can hear people shouting at the bottom. I can't distinguish what's said but did hear my name shouted. Still in squat position I feel my heart beating faster and faster. Someone tries to talking to me. The guy who fixed my harness appears too. They are mouthing me to lean backwards and to go.

My heart feels like its about to burst with pressure. I start panting trying to calm myself but feel tears well up in my eyes. I hear 'Don't look down…. deep breaths, deep breaths then realise I'm holding my breath. I hear more shouts from below snapping me out of it. I find the willpower, in my mind going down the wall is okay. I'm strapped in and I'm in control I tell myself, find the courage to lean back. Finally I make a move if I don't go now I never will. I sort of crawl over the ledge bunched up like a ball. So it's not quite the dignified entrance that I'd like to have made, its more on a par with a Mr Bean impression. I lean back about two inches and start to scale down the wall hearing a big cheer.

It was Stan and Ayeisha cheering below that spurred me to make a move. The descent seemed to go on forever but halfway down I thought I can do this, it isn't so bad after all. My main concern was the wind and hoped it doesn't blow me sideways. I'd be swung around like a rag doll. Overall its wasn't as bad as I thought. Apart for the ledge bit, I'm not sure I would ever get over that trauma. When my feet touch the ground I almost wobble over with the nerves.

Stan rushed over giving me a big hug. 'I might have bloody known it had to be you' he laughed. Hurt I ask what he meant. He laughed 'It had to be you sat on that ledge for ten minutes, you were up there that long I thought you were having a brew. Loads of people went whilst you were up there sat on the top, I didn't think you'd do it after that performance.' He asks if I heard him shouting. I could hear my name shouted. They were all laughing at me shouting cut the rope I'd taken so long. Stan then delights in telling me how he thought I'd get hysterical and bottle out. I don't believe it there I was having a panic attack and all he could do was shout cut the bloody rope. He laughs telling me you did it though didn't you. I'm sure the guys at work have taken bets that I wouldn't do it. But I did, and I can't help smiling to myself.

Back in work they ask whether I went through with it. I tell them of course I did although I was a tad scared at first. It was the truth, and without going into great detail I play down the length of time I faffed around. A few managers drop by to ask how I got on and to congratulate me. I proudly show off my certificate. They tell me I was really brave and that they couldn't have done it. One asks if it was easy and would I do it again. I admit to panicking a little at first but thought now I'm up here I have to do it. If I did it again then I'd like to enjoy it next time. They congratulate me again and leave in good spirits. The manager who hasn't paid yet, the one the others said I wouldn't get my money, still hasn't shown his face. The money I had to pay in out of my own pocket I might add. Can you believe a manager who earns far more than I still won't pay his dues. You wouldn't embarrass yourself would you.

We decide to put his name at the top of our special board after all he earned it. They nickname him Basil because he resembles Basil Fawlty. False and full of himself. You know the type, one who bends over backwards for people in high places. Always agreeing with the hierarchy and never going against them. Only ever saying what they want to hear just to please them. I've always thought a good manager should be a strong character, friendly and most of all a good leader. Then it dawned on me, the only reason he agreed to sponsor me was because the other managers was putting their names down. Why do I always get the pain in the arses? Is it me, had I been so horrid in a former life?

I decide to send an email reminding him of the sponsor money. I copy a few others in pretending they owe money too. That way it looks official. A few days later and no response, I send another. After the third reminder I get a reply: No money on me I'll bring it in. It's only a couple of pounds for Gods sake. He's very well paid, he has money to go fishing and golfing doesn't he. The guys have upped the bets saying they'll run naked through the streets if I get money out off him. This is really embarrassing now. I couldn't look people in the face if that was me, I'd be more embarrassed of what others would say about me. It just goes to show what sort of person they really are underneath all that pomp, two faced and greedy. I hope he never asks for sponsorship money for his daughter's school, I'd love to humiliate him in front of his managers. The whole office spent the next few weeks laughing and doing impressions of Basil Fawlty. We pretend Basil's playing cricket or golf and going really over the top trying to impress people. Oh if only the managers could see us now.

If our numbers come up on our lottery syndicate we laugh that we'll all move on his street just to annoy him. We'd buy tacky cars and put our names on the windscreen 'Angie & Stan.' We decide he should have *the rat* on his. We laugh who could get the most ridiculous car horns then we could beep him in the mornings. We'd have parties on the weekends inviting our loudest friends who like a drink. Oh well that means everybody I know. Of course our cars would get the sickliest colour paintwork that we can find, and maybe put tacky stripes down the side too. Oh and we'd have to have the furry dice dangling. We'd let him know how posh his neighbourhood is. And just to make sure he really gets the hint we'll join his fishing and golfing clubs. I'm sure he's a member of both. He's probably wangled free membership by being on the committee. We'd make sure he couldn't find peace their either.

Aren't we horrid. I never realised he was so popular. Right now he's as popular as influenza around here. I think the whole office took it badly because it was taking money from a charity which is something you don't do. Oh what fun we'd have winding him up. We all take great delight seeing who could make him squirm the most. Even Gertie and Olive join in this one. I've never seen either of them smile so much. We're not mean for the sake of it, he brings it on himself being such a snob. Apart from thinking he's better than everyone else, although we cannot see it, he's so arrogant and chauvinistic. Now we can add tight fisted git to his list of attributes. It's legendary that at Christmas when customers send gifts to him he arranges them around his office. And then invites staff in to see how popular he is. We enjoy winding him up by trying to take some chocolates before he shouts at us not to open them. He explains he's only showing them and refuses to hand any of them out. A customer once sent him bottles of wine.

He thought it wasn't a nice wine and sent them to his fishing club. Leaving remainder to be shared out at work to his grateful staff, pretended he'd bought it.

Another time he received expensive chocolates and gave them to another boss and his wife for entertaining him to dinner. And pretended he'd bought them, can you believe it. When I was told he was the original scrooge I never believed it. At first I felt the stories were somewhat exaggerated. After my dealings with him how wrong could I be. I wouldn't say we were evil, but we wasn't content to leaving it there and decide to carry on the banter. Laughing that if he was in a shipwreck he would be standing on your shoulders to get out, and certainly wouldn't be helping to save anyone. We laugh in hysterics when Trudy says you wouldn't hear him shouting for help because he would have his head so far up the Senior Management's backside. It would be like Mr Bean and the turkey episode, only it would be the top boss bobbling about on his shoulders. Oh, if only he knew how his colleagues thought of him.

A big customer of ours is holding a golf tournament against our company. Other customers play in the opposition team too. Usually only people who know how to play join the team. Most of them are managers. During our banter that you can hear from down the corridor we are told anyone from the company can join the team. Anyone I ask, now there's a thought. Anyone that can hold a club is the rule. Well I know what a club is, after all I have played crazy golf before. That's a start isn't it. I ask the girls to join the team with me, just to pee my sponsor mate off. As much as the thought entertains us none of the girls are up for it. But I so wanted to make him cringe.

We need six days off work. I suppose our office can't spare that time off really. And I won't join on my own as all the other teams are blokes. But could you just imagine his face when we walk across the grass. Not one of us know how to play golf and I wouldn't even know the difference between a club and a shot put. The look of sheer horror on his face would be worth it. Not only can we not play, we are all female he would be so embarrassed he'd rather die of shock than let the girls in. Especially whilst he's hob-knobbing with management. The thought of him squirming keeps us going for days, we heavily underline Basil on the board. Even other departments say our caricature of him is so true. But he has done that one all by himself.

~ Chapter Nine ~ **Back at the office and Jip's adventure**

Just when I think it can't get any worse Stan arrives home with a box full of holes punched through the side. He tells me it's for Ayeisha. Now this means one thing, whatever is in the box is alive. Otherwise why would it need air holes. Bash runs straight up to the box grinning away. Awww she says and pulls out a chocolate coloured squeaking thing. Then Stan puts his hand inside and pulls out a pale coloured one. He's only brought home a pair guinea pigs. He better not be thinking of keeping them inside the house. Thankfully he says he'll build a big hutch big outside for them and we name them Coco & Chanel. Why guinea pigs I have no idea. They are cute but not as cute as rabbits. But if it keeps Stan entertained that's the main thing.

I didn't think we needed more pets, and he fusses round them so much Bash doesn't get a look in. He thinks they're really cute but I beg to differ. He tells me I'll soon come round. As if I need to come round, so long as he feeds and cleans them then I suppose I don't mind.

A few days later Sadie called round. After a while we wonder where Stan and Ayeisha have got to. He said he wouldn't be long, its been a couple of hours, and its getting dark. When he eventually strolls up the path with her its worse still he's holding another box. Sadie laughs her head off asking whats he carrying more guinea pigs. Oh God, this box looks heavier than the last one I mumble. What has he brought back this time. I shout if there's anything alive in that box its going straight back. He just laughs along with Ayeisha thinking I've said something funny.

Their reaction said it all it is something alive. We don't have time for looking after more animals I moan. She has enough rabbits and guinea pigs I plead. Bash laughs her head off but I don't get the joke. 'I ask is it a rabbit'. No. 'Is it more guinea pigs because I'm telling you now were not breeding them.' He answers no. Is it a dog? No. A cat? No. Then Stan opens the box. Sadie and I stare in the box in disbelief. What the hell is it she shrieks. I can't believe my eyes, and neither can Sadie. My God the thing is huge, has a beak and has feet that resemble a baby dinosaur. The poor thing has what looks like strips of plastic looking things hanging from its wings which I'm told is where feathers should be. Its feet have got to be the biggest I've ever seen. In fact it looks like a plucked turkey with monstrous eyes and fluffy bits all along its legs. What ever it is it isn't staying. I shout at Stan that it has got to go. Ayeisha and Stan both stand their laughing at me. Don't you think it's cute he asks. Sadie laughs not quite knowing where to look.

Stan laughs and asks if I know what it is. How the hell should I know. The last time I saw feet like that was in Jurassic Park. He asks isn't it lovely. Lovely, what on earth is he looking at, and what is it. 'Its an owl a European Eagle Owl actually.' Oh well that's alright I think to myself sarcastically, if he'd said that in the first place it would have made all the difference. What do we want with an owl aren't we busy enough looking after guinea pigs and the damn rabbits. We have nowhere to put it and nothing to feed it. I don't suppose it lives on worms.

What does an owl eat anyway. For a moment a horrible thought crossed my mind, that the guinea pigs could be food for it. He ignores me and tries to get Ayeisha on his side. 'Look isn't it cute' he asks. Of course she stands their grinning back at the thing. I don't believe it, yet another toy for him. But what happens if he's bored of it. I'm sure it takes a little more looking after than a rabbit. The poor thing can't even stand up or sit upright on its own. Stan finds a towel, wrapping it in a circle like a little nest and says at least it can lean against it like it's a nest. He doesn't want it to go outside either because it's too cold for it. So what is he saying he wants it in the house. The whole time the poor thing stares at us. I can't help but feel sorry for it. It shouldn't be here it's not right, and it's far too young to be separated from its mother. Stan recons it's too late to take it back the mother she won't accept it now. So there it is we are stuck with it. Sadie makes her excuses and leaves, I think she could sense a row coming on. We'll speak later and arrange to go out. After all I may need a few drinks to calm me down.

She laughs heading back to her car waving. I cringe, she'll go straight home and laugh you'll never believe what Stan's done this time. I'll be the laughing stock again. With nowhere to put it and nothing to feed it on he's lost his marbles for sure. He says it has to eat raw meat, chicks. 'Chicks' I ask surprised. They have to be ordered from a farm. And he has to pick up a deep freezer because they deliver in bulk. Unless you want them in your fridge he asked sarcastically. I must be mad allowing this. Stan goes to find a box from the garage. Cutting part of it open he puts a dish inside with the towel and makes sure its okay. Honestly, you'd think he was looking after a baby. He thinks this will make a good nest if it can sit upright in this it will be fine. He rifles through the fridge for meat but the only meat we have is fillet steak. Surely he won't feed it fillet steak. Sure enough he stands their slicing it into tiny pieces then pops it into the microwave. Flabbergasted I ask 'It needs it cooking as well.' Stan laughs that it's a little too cold from the fridge, it just needs a tad warming up. Oh for Gods sake what next give it my double bed!

We don't have a name for it yet. Stan suggests a few names but nothing that suits. Ayeisha asks if we can call it Jip. She remembered a book she had read at school about a cat called Jip. She smiles at Stan trying to work him, they seem to agree it suits. I just hope it doesn't give us any Jip. Although its beak is huge and feet seem monstrous I am getting a little used to it. I suppose the fluff around its legs does make it look ridiculously cute. The more you looked at it you couldn't help but like it. With orange eyes so big they are lovely, they look like they stare right through you. And if you look close enough they look almost watery.

Of course Stan's priority is not work but spending the next few days building an aviary for it! He decides to build a box that looks like a ridiculous monstrous bird box almost as large as the shed. He's even built a little roof on top. I look at him bewildered. He tells me it's for Jip to sit inside for shelter. But that won't be for some time because Jip can't even stand yet. He recons whilst it's still young its best to stay in the house with us. Why not, in fact I'm sure we've room for a rhinoceros if we put our minds too it. I suppose we're stuck with Jip for a while then. Back in work it's the usual scenario, me being the source of entertainment. Of course they think the new edition to our household is hilarious. And all say there is no way they'd allow these random pets into their house, or into the garden for that matter. But then again I'll be surprised if they have anything more exciting than cats and goldfish. And most of them don't live for long. None of them even have a dog or budgie. Although I've always liked animals I just never envisaged them all living with me. I don't mind really it's just the looking after them that worries me. At least our house won't be a boring house. That would be an understatement wouldn't it.

I don't suppose any of Ayeisha's friends can say my owl is bigger than your owl. Her teacher tells me she's been talking about an owl. I told her it's the new edition to the family. She laughed because some of the children spin a few yarns whilst in the classroom. She wasn't sure if Ayeisha was telling the truth. But did say she would have been surprised at Ayeisha telling fibs. A slight exaggeration maybe, but fibs that's so unlike her. She asked if we'd bring Jip into school one day the children would love to see an owl. I can imagine Bash saying keep away Jip's my owl.

Jip's getting bigger almost by the day now Stan feeds her day old chicks. I'm quite squeamish, and I don't eat meat so don't like to watch, but I understand the need. Stan asks if I'd rather Jip hunt the rabbits around the garden. I suppose he has a point. Over the next few weeks Jip is sitting upright on her own and will soon be walking. It's almost like looking after a baby. I've found myself cooing over her already. She has the most ridiculous looking legs you have ever seen. They're like stringy turkey legs with fluff around her thighs making it look like its wearing jodhpurs. It's really funny to watch her taking her steps forward. Because her feet are so big she started waddling forward whilst lifting huge claws along the ground. Which looks like they belong to Tyrannosaurus Rex. If like me, you haven't been around birds of prey before this is quite entertaining to watch.

Ayeisha's friends come by to have a look at Jip. Then friends of her friends come to look at Jip. Before long all the local kids come knocking our door asking to take a look. Then neighbours ask, and when their families come to visit they call in for a look too. She's become quite popular to say the least. We should charged an entrance fee at the gate we'd make a small fortune. Stan is currently doting on his little pet, feeding her chicks and quails. Quails! Isn't that a delicacy in some parts? He moans at my shopping bills and when I spend on myself. Yet spares no expense when it comes feeding Jip. Just let him moan again the cheeky bleeder.

Jip's taken to sprawling on her tummy and resting her chin along the back of the settee. You can imagine when people come into the house not expecting her there. Almost looking like a teddy until she starts moving, then they jump out of their skin quite shocked, it's hilarious. Jip soon got too big for our house and its time she went in her own. Stan's tried getting her used to being in the garden. Hoping she'll settle in the newly built aviary, with her newly built house to go inside. Along with the plants and logs. It's not like he's gone to any trouble or anything. She is so big now he's built the aviary along the back fence. When I say big she's already got a wing span of five feet. And she'll get bigger. The mess she makes in the kitchen is awful. We advise friends not to stand behind her, or be prepared to get sprayed with a bucket full of mess. It will be a pleasure not having to carry a sheet around for the mess. It's quite gross really.

Stan became quite popular around our way from taking Jip everywhere with him. And I mean everywhere. She sits in the van perches on top of his seat. Which is quite funny to us. But probably isn't funny when your driving along side and glance up, it looks like Jip's perched on his shoulder. People do double takes almost crashing their car. It's not as if she is the size of a budgie she is about a foot tall. Stan even takes her fishing, bloody fishing for god sake. I think he's become attached to her like others do with a dog. He tethers her to a little bungee that's attached to a perch and she jumps down when she wants to or sits on her perch. What's even more ridiculous is she's very content with it.
She likes people looking at her so long as they don't crowd her. Stan makes sure they don't get too close in case they might scare her. Scare her, I thought it was the other way round, I know nobody wants her claws to grip them.

One night Stan decided to take Jip fishing with him as you do. It was pitch black you couldn't see a thing, and so quiet it was eerie. Stan was on the bank getting his fishing tackle ready. Jip was on a perch at the side of him. A guy came down the path not expecting anyone to be there. Suddenly a Doberman dog raced past the guy right towards Jip. The guy tried to shout the dog back but it caught sight of Jip at the last minute. Ignoring the owner it starting snarled at Jip. Jip reacted straight away opening her wings and hunched herself into what looked like a huge ball and hissed back at the dog. The Doberman stops in its tracks yelps then legs it back hiding behind its owner. Stan quite seriously explained its okay he doesn't think his dog scared her. The owner snapped back 'I was more worried for my dog actually.' Stan burst out laughing because he sees Jip as his little baby, and thinks everyone should see her as a baby too, bless.

The neighbourhood kids are fascinated by Jip, but they are becoming a pain. The brats have now taken to climbing up the back fence against the aviary, all trying to get a good look at Jip. Every time I'm at the kitchen window I'm constantly shouting at them to get down. Worse still they are poking sticks through the fence trying to get her attention. Eventually we think reasoning with them could work, it might stop them climbing if they come and have a look at her. So again we traipse them all through the garden to her aviary and let them crowd round her. She delights them by flying towards Stan squawking away. They're all amazed shouting wow. And now they've seen her this better stop them climbing up. If that fails then I resort to putting them in the aviary with her. I'm sure that'll stop the little gits.

Work finds it hilarious that nothing goes right for our house. In work we all eat snacks at our desks. I'm usually found munching a packet of shortbread biscuits mid morning just to tide me over until lunchtime as you do. I try keeping to fruit in my desk but having snacks in the tuck shop makes life so difficult. You just can't resist them when they're in front of you. Coffee tastes so much nicer with a biscuit. When I get them Olive's face drops. Not impressed she comments 'another packet' and tutts under her breath. I presume this means Olive is not impressed with me. I suppose she wants me to eat nothing all day just to make her happy. It makes me wonder if other people have this to put up with this from their work colleagues.

When I came back into the office Gertie took one look at me and stomped off through the office in a right mood. I'm not sure if this is for my attention or if someone has upset her. We seem to have the habit of doing that just by being there. This time it can't be me, after all I haven't done anything except walk into the room. She'll let us know what's wrong, eventually. On her way back Gertie shouts down the office 'If I even look at shortbread I put on two stone, its not fair' then points directly at me saying 'she snacks at her desk all day long' then stomps back to her desk. I look around in disbelief trying to contain myself. Staring ahead I desperately try to hold my fury. If I say anything I know I will erupt. The others are stunned at her outburst today. Something's bothered her. Today it looks like my turn today to bear the brunt. I feel like telling her if I eat twenty packets of shortbread then I will put pounds on too.

I can't say anything or I will end up giving her a few home truths she doesn't want to hear. That and I'll probably have a few machetes in my back by the end of the day. I must applaud her though because it does make Olive quiet. She doesn't mutter another word because she felt my fury ripple across the room. I wouldn't have minded if Gertie had said it laughingly but she was spitting venom about it. What on earth did I do to warrant such an outburst. To my defence Trudy shouts 'If I could eat what she eats and stay slim I'd eat shortbread too.' Gertie chooses to ignore her stomping across to the fax machine.

Oh well another fun day at the office. I shout to Lawrence 'Mmm this shortbread tastes so good' and I give him a big grin. He laughs 'You bitch.' He'd love to have a bitch fight with her, he says she needs to be put in her place because she is so nasty. If me eating bothers her why the outburst? She has the problem with it not me. I'd understand if I was eating garlic bread all day and stinking the office out. But its biscuits for Gods sake. But then again she doesn't need a reason. Any excuse for her moods will do.

Jerry wants to know if other offices are like this one. I whisper a Gertie and Olive exist in every office. She bursts into the most outrageous laugh and tells me only the ones that I frequent. If the truths is known she's probably right. Could it be there's Gertie and Olive loitering away in every company. Sat waiting with abated breath for the rustle of a crisp packet or the smell of a biscuit. It might give them a purpose for living. It gives them an excuse to rage at colleagues. Anything to create a scene ensuring they are centre of attention. All because they have a problem you're eating food.

Maybe they join forces emailing each other. That way they retain their 'normality', then outbursts are not an issue because they're all doing it. Stan laughs and says it's my fault, that I'm awful eating in front of them. But they eat too! I sulk. You'd think I was doing drugs in the office the way they behave. What a perfect solution I have, each office should employ an Ang. An Ang who they can make voodoo dolls of and take pins home to enjoy at their leisure. An Ang who they think can eat what they want, and when they want. But what they don't realise is I don't eat what I want. If I have something naughty I balance it with a healthy meal. Well most of the time I do.

Good God to be so wrapped up in someone else's life then surely it's a sign to get a life of ones own. But how do you say that to the Gertie's of the world. You'd look like the bitch from hell. I'm tempted to buy the biggest bag of chocolates I can find and sit eating them all day every day. Sadie wants me to sit the largest bag of chocolates on the edge of my desk. And keep rustling the paper, just to see how many times Gertie and Olive can resist looking. But then this will please the Gertie because I couldn't put my hand in the bag and leave empty handed. I'd get fatter and probably turn into Gertie.

Oh God, the voodoo dolls are working, its time to slap my face and snap out of this. Get on with your work and ignore her, let her go home as unhappy as she came into work. If only Gertie knew I have friends who are large and even consider themselves obese. They have had problems dieting for years, but are lovely people who I like and who like me. They wouldn't dream of being nasty to me for being slim, nor I be nasty to them for being large. Gertie would love to say I dislike her because of her weight. But I dislike her for being her. I had thought of going to night school to learn about human behaviour. Then again who needs night school when you can learn human behaviour in our office first hand. That reminds me I must write a adaptation of The Office, I think I'll call it 'The Culture of Weirdo's and Lunatics.' Because where ever I go, they always seem to be around me. It is sure to be a best seller. I think I need to call at my friend Lucy's for a caffeine fix and let off some steam. We can have a good bitch putting the world to rights as you do.

At Lucy's house, I'd not been there long, just enough to catch up on the latest when Stan ran past her garden. He was legging it down the street with a plastic dish in his hand, and looks like he's shouting something towards the roof. Wondering what's going on we jump to the window taking a better look. We see half a dozen kids run past and look like their chasing him. We both look at each other puzzled thinking did we see what we think we've just seen. Lucy asks 'That was Stan running past with kids chasing him looking like the pied piper wasn't it.' We both burst out laughing put our coffee's down and run outside to find out what the hell is going on. He's already down the bottom of the street and almost around the corner. We jump in my car following them down the road.

What on earth has he done now. And why is he watching the roof. As we approach the corner there is a crowd forming around Stan. The kids are revelling in the excitement and a few adults have joined in too. I look up to see what all the commotion is about. Its only bloody Jip perched on rooftop staring down at all the faces. And all the faces just as bewildered are staring back at her. Oh no, how embarrassing. Stan tried shouting Jip desperately trying to coax her down. Jip chirps back at him, ignores his plea's and sits there quite content. She doesn't look fazed or frightened in the slightest. In fact she looks like she is enjoying all the attention and plumps her feathers up as if she is settling in for the night. I must admit it does look funny to see her up on the roof, especially when you're used to seeing her in your back garden.

Stan is not amused and tries again to coax her down. This time with food, dead chicks cut up into little pieces. All the kids scream Eeewww in unison. He's actually got pieces of chick legs dangling from the bowl. I can hear some of the children saying they feel a bit sick looking at the dead feet dangling. They were after all fluffy little yellow things running around a few days ago, I hope they don't go home traumered. I can see some of the houses nearby, their curtains have started twitching. They're wondering what all the activity is outside. At least they don't know its anything to do with me.

Stan starts to wave the dead chicks around franticly trying to catch Jip's attention. Who in return is snubbing him. If anything she's getting irritated with all the attention now, she looks like she wants to be left alone to perch there for the night. Suddenly with no warning she opens her wings and effortlessly floats across a few houses. Again Stan chases her, with the kids, neighbours and now a motorbike in tow. Passing cars stop to take a look at what's going on. She ups and floats off again this time she flew over the other side of the houses. We jump into the car trying to follow her, I shout over to Stan to get in the car but he doesn't hear. He carries on running around like a headless chicken, no pun intended.

This is ridiculous how the hell did she get out of her aviary. Around the corner Jip settles herself on another roof. How the owners don't come out with all the commotion going on is beyond me. Stan parades around their gardens and climbs up a shed as if it's his own. I stand in the road pretending to be an innocent bystander. That was until one of the brats shouts to me isn't that your bird Mrs! If that wasn't enough the brat shouts to his friend 'That's Ayeisha's Mum.' I shrink into my shoulders whilst everyone turns around taking a good look at me. Lucy of course pretends she's not with me. I've never been so shown up in all my life. I look away trying a forced smile whilst sheepishly taking a step backwards. Mumbling under my breath 'You little git.' Again this is one of those many moments in my life when I cringe with total embarrassment. I suppose I should be grateful for small mercies and thank God that it's getting dark.

By now most people have closed there curtains or else the whole damn street would be out. Sure enough Jip gets bored and flies off again. We can see her in the distance across the roof tops. Stan saw me and runs over. He shouts for the keys to the car. Then launches himself into the car and throws the bowl and dead chicks across my passenger seat. I gasp in horror, bits of dead bird and blood are now on my seat! I mean its one thing to take my car but throw little dead bits across my seat is another. There had better not be any blood or gunge on my seats when he gets back.

There's nothing more I can do here besides wallow in the embarrassment piled on me yet again. Lucy and I retreat back to mine for a coffee. I'd have a drink. I think occasions like this warrants one, except I have to pick Ayeisha up shortly. After an hour or two of chasing all over Audenshaw Stan returns home empty handed, and definitely not in a good mood. He phones the RSPCA and RSPCB hoping somebody might have phoned with a sighting of Jip. They take details and will contact us should they get any sightings. After a restless night and a few more calls to the RSPCB, still no news. The next morning I have to go in work and yes I'm sure they'll love this one.

Stan on the other hand takes the day off to sit by the phone. Being self-employed he has the luxury of taking time off when he wants to. Funny though I didn't see the same enthusiasm in keeping his woman happy when a certain Springsteen concert warranted the day off. But for his bird it's no problem, even staying up all night for her. At least I know where I come in the pecking order… after his bird, the rabbits, guinea pigs and below next door's cat. He'd better clean the mess off my seats. If he thinks I'm driving with that crap in the car there will be trouble.

In the office everyone chats about what they watched on TV the night before and ask if I saw any of the programmes. I tell them I didn't get to watch TV because I was too busy chasing around the damn streets looking for Jip. Of course they find this most amusing. So much so they draw a picture of a bird. Well it somewhat resembles a bird, and put a wanted note underneath. *Bounty for lost Jip, 10 pence reward, a dead rat and some chicks thrown in for free.* 'Very funny' I reply sarcastically.

They'd better not turn it into the dead cat scenario, I won't find it funny. Stan phones through out the morning letting me know he's still heard nothing. We're really worried. We had hoped for some sightings when it became daylight, people are up early walking their dogs. Stan's concerned about kids on their way to school. If they see her they might frighten her whilst trying to get a closer look, she could fly further away. You know what kids can be like, little gits at times.

We keep our fingers crossed she is alright. Another phone call from Stan, this time saying the RSPCA advised him to get in touch with the Manchester Evening Newspaper (M.E.N.). They think people might phone in saying they've spotted a large owl. Anything is worth a try and gives them a call. The M.E.N. return his call shortly after. They think Granada Reports might want to do a news report on Jip being missing saying they will be in touch soon. A short time later they ring back saying they want to send a TV Crew over. They're concerned people should watch out for their pets as Jip might be hungry and attack a pet. Of course I got the updated phone calls from Stan he sounded devastated. Soon after the M.E.N. ring again advising Stan that Jip's been sighted ten miles away and she has flown off with someone's dog.

Stan had been worried sick thinking he might not get her back because she's not used to fending for herself. Plus other birds would hound her out of the way thinking she might attack their own nests. And now they think Jip's savaged a pet, this is terrible. Stan races to the sighting. Luckily traffic was clear, he makes it in no time. He phones the M.E.N. asking where Jip was sighted because he can't find her anywhere. Nobody around has seen her either. They ask if Stan can wait there, they want to send a photographer to take Stan's picture. Will he wear his glove he uses when he flies her, and can he hold some of the dead chicks, and he needs to show a sad face. He didn't want publicity, but if it gets her back I suppose it has to be worth it.

I know what he's like cringing with embarrassment having his photo taken. He is contemplating it when he hears laughter in the background of the phone call. It registers what all this has been about. It's all been a hoax. Having a laugh at his expense knowing he is worried sick. Damn, why didn't I think of that one. It probably wasn't even the M.E.N. phoning him, or it could have been one of their sales team wanting to have a laugh and cheer the office up. I've known sales teams do that before. Either way he was furious, Jip could be near home and he is wasting time miles away.

But to his defence we have seen articles like this before. Pets have gone missing and their owners are photographed looking sad in the local paper. I got more of the updates from Stan, poor thing he was devastated. The guys in the office took great delight in the events. Cutting up pictures of little birds and yellow chicks pinning them to pieces of string, bouncing around like wind chimes. They are loving every minute of this. The reward has been upped from a ten pence, a dead rat and a few chicks to couple of fish fingers, twenty five pence and a bowl full of dog food! They are absolute b*****ds, have they no thought or what. Obviously not.

I suppose you have to laugh at their humour. And if it was happening to one of them then I would find them hilarious. This is one of those days when we say you have to have drunk the water here to understand their humour. Most people would think this bad taste and insensitive. But this banter is what keeps the office going. When it's all going mad around you even at work you need to keep your head above water. It actually chills the office out and in a way that brings them together because whilst their laughing at your misfortunes they are not squabbling amongst themselves. It makes sense in an unfortunate way. If you took it personally you wouldn't last long in the office because they can be cruel, funny but cruel. Timely our boss walks in sees what is going on shakes his head and walks out again. He looked like its one of those things that he wouldn't know where to start if he tried. At least I'm keeping the troops entertained, again. Trouble is its getting to be a bit of a habit now.

That night we get a phone call from the RSPCB. A woman has spotted Jip in her garden. Thank God she reported it. Stan raced down to find her. The woman had said she was stood at her kitchen window when it all went dark, she knew something dropped on the roof of her extension. It was as if a dark cloud had hovered above her window. When she went out to investigate and saw jip sat on the roof of her extension. Jip perched there quite happily watching the world go by. Stan raced there as quickly as he could, worried she'd take off again before he got there. She was only five miles away. We should have known that she would have taken off in the direction of the wind. When he arrived a little crowd formed around Jip. Luckily but they were being quiet so didn't frighten her off. Jip squawked when she saw Stan, probably grateful for a familiar face. She was really good this time, it didn't take long to coax her down. I suppose with the sight of dead chicks and rat's tails was enough. Jip's adventure was over. We were so glad to get her back home, enough excitement for one day. I look forward to a quite time, no trauma's no excitement. Surely it is somebody else's turn for excitement.

~ Chapter Ten ~ **The Tooth Brush**

For a while now Stan had been complaining of sore gums. When he wasn't moaning about something else that is. I'd put it down to the new toothbrush, it was probably too hard. So I bought him another one. This time with softer bristles on the outside thinking this should do the trick. I put his new brush into the holder with the others, not giving it a second thought. A while later I decided to clean the bathroom. Especially as this week's gripe from Stan is the mess we leave in there. We, I suppose that means me & Ayeisha. It couldn't possibly be him now could it. What does he expect, we both work full time and have a daughter that's like having three teenagers in the house.

He soon forgets he's a builder and makes most of the mess, it drops from his trousers. Soil and dirt causes dust everywhere. It's a daily task of trying to keep up with it all. And I really don't have the time or patience to keep up with it. Today I decide to make the effort. As he has a nice new toothbrush I've been using his old one. I saw a great tip on TV for cleaning, use an old toothbrush to clean the bathroom. Its great for getting in the nicks and cranny's such as in the middle of tiles and around the bottom of the taps. It best for a used toothbrush which is slightly worn it will be soft enough to use without scratching. It's also practical to use around the toilet too, for the hinges of the seat where it gets really grubby. So, for a few weeks I tried it, it worked a treat. You can't get a cloth around the tap properly and tissue breaks up, it usually takes forever so this really is a quick fix. I don't have the time to be Mary bloody Poppins... the perfect house-keeper or mother figure. No I need a quick wiz over, a minutes scrub and done, perfect! Just let him moan now. I'll swap his new toothbrush for his old one ha ha, only joking.

He has a few toothbrushes to use from the new pack. But where can I put the used brush so he doesn't mistake it for his new toothbrush. If I put it in the cupboard he's bound to throw it in the bin, or even worse use it. I know I can put it behind the sink stand, surely they won't notice it there. It's not as if either of them clean the bathroom so it won't be noticed. A few weeks had gone by and Stan was still having sore gums. Poor thing he's worried to death his teeth are falling out. I moan he has to visit the dentist, even though he doesn't like going to the dentist. He thinks they all have a vendetta against him, all revelling in giving him pain. But that's only the ones I've paid... only joking.

Finally, he gives in and pays the dentist a visit. The dentist can't understand why it's started for no particular reason. He eats a fairly good diet. All fish, chicken, pasta. He doesn't eat much processed foods full of additives and colours. Nor does he eat chocolate or biscuits like me. The dentist advised him to use a sensitive toothpaste and a softer brush, combined with some mouthwash. Mouthwash they give you for gingivitis he whinges. He's to call back if he still has problems. For the next week or so he gives this a try. But I find Ayeisha and Stan winding me up every day. Every time I go into the bathroom they have moved the old toothbrush. I keep finding it on the side of the sink. I keep putting it back behind the sink and out it comes again. I'm beginning to get annoyed with this. If I catch them at it I'll swing for them. They can't blame me if it gets mistaken for his toothbrush when they carry on like this.

Poor Stan, he's taking extra care in the bathroom, scrubbing his teeth for ages, in fact he smells like a walking bottle of antiseptic. The gingivitis mouthwash smells horrid I won't go near him. You can actually smell him coming from ten yards away. It's that strong I'm beginning to wonder if the dentist told him to use this instead of using aftershave. This goes on for a few more weeks. This particular morning I didn't realise he was already in the bathroom. He usually has the tap running whilst cleaning his teeth. He knows this bothers me big time. I have a real problem with people keeping the tap running whilst cleaning their teeth. I think its such a waste of water, why not fill up a cup of water to use. Its not that I've ever had a water clock, its the sheer waste of water that bothers me.

When I didn't notice the tap running I walked straight into the bathroom. Stan scrubbing his teeth only something is different. It takes a moment for it to dawn on me. It doesn't look like his toothbrush. In fact it looks nothing like his new toothbrush.... any of the new ones. I can't help but stare at him, not quite taking in what I am looking at. He shouts 'For Gods Sake can't I have a minute's privacy before you invade my space.' Again I stare ahead at him, still not taking it in. In fact I feel quite odd, I have all this nervous energy is building up inside of me. I step back and close the door. I can feel a hot flush coming on, oh I feel quite queasy.

Taking a deep breath I get ready to open the door again. I could be mistaken. I might not have seen what I think I've seen but I need to make sure. Slowly I open to door again. 'What's wrong with you now' he asks. As calmly as I possibly could I ask why he isn't using the new toothbrush. 'Why' he replies scrubbing at his teeth again. I can't help but stare, all I can see is the brush going up and down in slow motion... Oh My God I mumble staring at him. I can feel a trauma coming on and think I'm going to faint.

He asks why I'm staring and why the sudden interest. 'Next you'll be telling me you've used it to scrub the bloody bath with.' At this point all the nervous energy building up is getting uncontrollable. I try stepping back to close the door but burst out laughing. So much so, I'm almost doubled up with laughter and my ribs are hurting. I know it's not funny but when I'm nervous or embarrassed and its serious I get the nervous laugh. I can't help it. It's always happened for as long I can remember. Today is one of those unfortunate days. Stan is not amused, in fact he's getting a little annoyed.

'What's so funny have you used it to clean the bath' he asks. 'No' I answer, which technically is true I didn't go near the bath, but in a minute you'll be wishing I had I think to myself. 'What are you laughing at then' he shouts. Doubled up with pain and laughter I try to tell him its nothing but he's not falling for it. He knows something's wrong but he can't work out why. 'Angie' he shouts annoyed 'What have you done with my toothbrush.' I tell him nothing but can't keep my face straight. 'Well what is the problem, have you scrubbed the sink with it.' Again I tell him no desperately trying to look like I've done nothing wrong. Which again, he would be grateful if it was only the sink I'd cleaned.

I look at the toilet but no words come out. He sort of looks at me and wondering what I'm looking at. At first it doesn't register then all of a sudden he erupts 'You've gotta be bleedin' jokin' He bawls. 'Please tell me you haven't been using it for the toilet' He looks at me pleadingly in a kind if childish way, almost begging me to say no. Its one of those moments you wish the ground could swallow you up and it be all over when you return. I can't answer him the words just won't come out. I tried summoning words but only manage to gulp in despair. My throat dried up into a spasm, feeling a cactus is stuck down there. I try to find suitable words but none surface.

Staring at him I wonder how I'm going to explain this one. I ask where he got the toothbrush from. He told me some idiot keeps dropping it behind the sink. I try diffusing the situation asking him why he's not using the new ones. 'They're too hard' he moans, 'My gums are really sore, the new ones aggravate. And every time I look for my old one I find it at the back of bloody sink.' I can't look him in the eyes now. I feel myself blinking at the floor, the walls, anywhere but direct to his face. He isn't going to make this easy for me, so I try to telling him but still lost for words. Still he stares at me waiting for an explanation. Making me feel even more nervous than before, if that's possible. It's kind of like the calm before the storm. The nerves get the better of me and double over again laughing. And not because I find it funny but more like I feel that bubbling feeling of a volcano ready to blow.

You can feel the tension getting stronger. The stronger it gets the worse the attack of nerves get. I try holding it in so much that tears prick my eyes. 'He just stares again saying, please tell me you haven't Ang' But I can't answer. Even louder this time he shouts 'PLEASE TELL ME YOU HAVEN'T USED IT ON THE TOILET? I can't even deny it. I wish I could lie to him about it but I can't. Mustering all the strength in me and manage to blurt 'I didn't know you were using it.' He replies 'So you have used it' and steps back in shock. Not knowing whether to laugh or cry I sort of nod. 'And you've used it on the bath' I nod, looking up at his face saying 'Well sort of.' Which I suppose is true it wasn't exactly the bath but he taps I'd used it on.

He looks at me like I have just told him he is going to die. Flabbergasted he asks 'You've used it on the sink too.' 'Sort of' I groan, he then starts to rant 'I can't believe it.' Then even louder 'I can't bloody believe it. Well that's alright then.' He looks at me again pleadingly, hoping I'll say it's all a big joke. His face starts to distort, his eyes ready for bulging out of his head. He's holding his breath waiting for the answer. I can't help but giggling with nerves knowing its going to cause a row, not just any row but the mother of all rows. I go on the defensive saying 'How am I suppose to be a mind reader, how am I supposed to know your still using it, I bought you two new ones.' Like that's going to help me now. No it's not going well, no this is not going well at all.

In disbelief he moans 'All this time I've been having trouble with my gums, and all this time and you've been scrubbing the God Damn Toilet with it.' Well, so far so good, he hasn't tried to throttle me yet. But then he repeats it again but this time ten times louder. Then he paces around the landing screaming 'I've had bleeding gums, worried my teeth are falling out and your scrubbing the f***ing toilet with my toothbrush. Because he's so serious I want to laugh again. For gods sake don't start again now. Hold it in, choke if you have to just don't laugh.

'Are you for real, are you trying to kill me or something' he bawls. I plead that it was an accident, a genuine accident. 'That's right' he shouts 'It's an accident that all the men in Britain are rushing to the dentist because their Mrs are all scrubbing the toilet with their god dam toothbrush. Why didn't I think of that one. And here's me telling the dentist I don't know why it's started. There's him telling me I could have gingi-bleedin-vitis and all this bleeding time its you'... at this point he stops and stares at the toilet. Not knowing whether to laugh or cry, he storms past me puts the full tube of toothpaste in his mouth trying to swill it out. Then he gets the antiseptic mouthwash and shouts to me 'I suppose I'll be needing this for a while wont I.'

I stomp off downstairs leaving him be. 'It's not my fault, anybody would think I did this on purpose' I shout up to him.

Trying to justify it I mumble to myself after all it was me trying to help by buying him the new ones in the first place. And it was me telling him to see his bloody dentist. I was worried about him, I was the one caring. If anything he should feel sorry for me, I pout. I hear him coming downstairs. What! He says flying through the door. 'I should feel sorry for you! How d'u work that one out then.' I try offering a morsel of guilt.

I know this is definitely the wrong time, but I still try explaining myself. 'I genuinely didn't know you were using it' I plead 'I kept putting behind the sink so nobody would mix it up. I wondered why I kept finding it on the side of the sink, I thought you two were winding me up, for gods sake I have been worried about you.' 'Oh well that's all right then' he shouts sarcastically. 'I'll remind my dentist of that the next time he's treating me for gum disease... by the way not to worry Mr Richards, it was all a mistake. It was only the Mrs using my toothbrush to scrub the toilet, How about that then. Hey, I bet you've not heard that one before? But she says she sorry bless! He rants staring at me. 'I'm sure he'd understand!

What could I say to this, no amount of grovelling is going to get me out of this one. I know it was a mistake, but god what a mistake to make. All that time I used it to clean the toilet. The chemicals I'd used. I bet it was burning his gums! Not to mention the germs! Oh what have I done. I could have been poisoning him and not been any the wiser. I feel really bad, I look up at him ready to cry but I get no sympathy there. All he can say is you can forget looking at me with them eyes because its not going to wash this time! Oh dear... I think eating humble pie for the rest of the year is called for. I bet now he's going to tell his family. I ask him not to tell anyone, begging and pleading with him not to. I couldn't cope with the embarrassment. I just can't believe what you've done, he keeps repeating to himself over and over. He's still in shock, he's hardly going to forget this one in a hurry. He's going to enjoy holding this one over me, for forever and a day no doubt.

I try avoiding conversations about mouths, teeth, dentists and toilets, anything that reminds him really. Otherwise he won't let it drop. He threatens to use my toothbrush in revenge. Hot sweats are over me for a while. I know he wouldn't do that on purpose, surely? A few weeks later we were having dinner at his mother's house. I'm just about to get stuck into a plate of spaghetti when he pipes up 'I've been to the dentist' Oh God I feel a trauma coming on! I can't lift my head up to look at anyone. I hold my breath as my heart starts racing. Only for him to announce 'All that trouble and all I needed to do was change my toothbrush' and looks directly at me. I hold my breath in feeling my face start to flush.

He smiles across the table. Yes he's enjoying this one, he's holding this one over me and loving every cringing moment! His brother laughs out loud. I don't believe it he's already bloody told him hasn't he. Suddenly I've lost my appetite. The food sticks in my throat like a spiked apple when I try forcing it down. He just looks at me smiling, revelling in me squirming, keeping me dangling, waiting for him to spout it out. His mum looks over knowing something is going on but not sure what. She probably thinks we'd had an argument over buying a new toothbrush or something silly. If only she knew!

~ Chapter Eleven ~ **Chocolate - Make The Damn Call**

For some time now, well for as long as I can remember I have always been a chocolate lover. Some days I can take it or leave it, but most days I have to have something or other chocolaty. Stan moans about this all the time. He has this strange way of thinking that if you like something you should limit yourself. Limit yourself I ask you. Why on earth would you limit something you like. If I was eating bars by the shovel load then point taken but a bar of chocolate here and there, whats the big deal.

There's something about chocolate melting in your mouth that just hits the spot. And it has to be milk chocolate. I don't know about these guru's who tell you you eat it because you are missing something in your life. Personally I think they talk a load of crap. You eat chocolate because it's nice and tasty. The problem is one bite isn't enough. I suppose some people have problems, gorge themselves and maybe comfort eat. But for me it's purely for enjoyment. Although I'm much better than I used to be. There were times I would have eaten a bar for breakfast then another in the evening. I suppose twice a day is a bit much.

Stan moans it's just sheer greed. If he sees me going to the cupboard he moans 'Are you eating crap again, why don't you get yourself some fruit.' Well yes I could but this tastes nicer. My God, what would it be like if I was around him all day, working together like some couples do. Can you imagine every time I went to get a cup of tea and biscuits all day I would get do you know how many calories are in that. Now I could please him and say I know I shouldn't eat it, yes Stan of course I'll put it back. But then who am I pleasing. I'm certainly not pleasing myself because my tea doesn't taste the same once you've got the idea of a biscuit with it in your head. Of course he would be pleased, but really, do I need to please him just because he's obsessive with healthy eating and I'm not. Just because he's able to restrict himself to one chocolate bar a week or even a month. Yes a month! Now that's just not natural is it? That's not restraint that's outright denial. If you eat healthy you should have treats without the guilt trip.

It wasn't enough I have colleagues at work jumping on the band wagon getting wound up saying I eat what I want without piling pounds on. The truth is I'm fat free, I do have wobbly bits and the odd cellulite here and there. Just not enough to say no more chocolate and start starving myself.

I know women who are successful yoyo dieters. Starve yourself today and feel slim when on the 'all the air you can eat diet' then moan they pile it back on when they do eat instead of eating a balanced diet. I've worked at more companies than I can remember where it's indoctrinated that they have the Monday morning diet. That lasts until Tuesday. A few colleagues genuinely wanted to be good, and again every Monday morning 'I'm going on the healthy no more treats diet today.' They're on the scales with good intentions and their will power is amazing, they have such enthusiasm you can't help but will them along. But sure enough there are always those few like Olive and Gertie who mock saying it won't last long once you stop your diet you'll pile it back on. The Olive's and Gertie's of this world are jealous of them succeeding. It's like they have a genetic make-up to be angry at those who succeed. Then they'll have a go at me saying it's all right for you as if I'm eating pies, chips and pizza all the time. What Olive doesn't realise don't realise is I healthy meals, and I know a treat isn't the whole bloody fridge full.

I suppose I don't help myself though, I'm always shoving chocolate wrappers in the ashtray of my car, as you do. Except this particular day Stan leant over putting something in the ashtray. Only for all my bloody chocolate wrappers to be on show. It wasn't one or two, as he opened the ashtray they almost sprang out like being in a jack-in-a-box there were so many wrappers in it. I wanted something to swallow me up as I could feel a rant coming on. So many were squashed in he couldn't have fitted a matchstick in between them if he tried.

It was one of those 'Oh God, I've been caught again' moments. I'm really lazy and can never be bothered to clean the car out. I certainly wished I had now. Almost surreal I could actually feel myself thinking he might not notice. Yeah right. I burst out laughing feeling like a naughty child who's just got caught stealing sweets.

But Stan didn't laugh, he stared in disbelief then pulled them out one by one... 2 packets of buttons...1 crunchy... flake...cream egg...a couple of flytes and 2 packet of chocolate cookies! 'For Gods sake how much crap are you eating' he asks. And me trying to justify it spout 'but they've been in there for ages, you must have noticed before.' Now I feel like an alcoholic who has to say if they've had a drink they'll be sent to alcoholics anonymous. Is it me that has a problem, or is it him and he's so obsessed with other peoples pleasure.

Are other people made to feel like this, having to answer to partners because they've had a snack. Or made to feel they have to sign up to eating anonymous classes. If I was eating this many a night then sure he's got a point. Although looking at the evidence in front of me it is a little hard to justify. I look across staring at him like I've been caught with my fingers in the pie. I try turning my face towards the window hiding the guilt, but it feels more like a sulking pout than a guilt trip.

I try not laughing desperate to hold it in. But, as he's trying to stare me out it's a little difficult. Oh well I best just take the rant...which means every time he sees a woman with big backside I'll get the 'You'll be fitting in her clothes soon! I try ignoring it thinking he'll stop soon enough. But oh no, a few days went by and he's still doing it thinking it will put me off my treats. He's even upped the tempo now commenting when someone large is on the TV. Realising this wasn't working on me it transcended into someone on TV with a great body he tells me 'Just think you could look like that if you stopped eating *all* that crap and worked out occasionally. Of which I retort back 'But Jim doesn't like working out! Hardly appropriate I know, but it's the only thing I could think of at the time without sounding like a sulking child. Then its the 'you'll be sorry on the beach... you'll be sorry when you can't fit into your clothes.

Stan is equally obsessive when it comes to grocery shopping. When he goes shopping he buys foods which 1) He enjoys 2) Is good for you. Which is okay let him think healthy for us. But he refuses point blank to get any treats. No crisps, chocolates anything. I'm not asking for barrels of biscuits just a little something to nibble on. Yet, he does manage to squeeze a trifle in the basket for himself. Trifle he tells me not to buy or he'll eat it. But brings a trifle back when he shops. Can you believe the cheek of it. When I ask what else he's bought thinking there'll be something else for me surely. He says chicken, rice, mince, pasta and salad, weetabix and shredded wheat.

'Okay but what's for me' I ask. He looks puzzled then answers there's some cottage cheese. 'I didn't get you any crap because that just encourages you.' I don't believe it, now he's bloody rationing me. I can feel a row coming on but it's not worth it. But then this is me and I can't keep my gob shut can I. 'Who made you Colonel' I shout flouncing out of the room. 'Well someone has to monitor what crap you eat or you'll be joining the bleedin go-lightlies' he shouts back. Yep we have the row. Not just because I am angry he's on the 'eat healthy' crap but because of his damn arrogance about it.

You know the type of row, the one that gets louder and louder. And everything over at least the last five years gets dragged into it. Even the things you didn't realise you remembered. I rant that I don't need telling what I am and am not supposed to be eating. The row gets bigger than what it was originally about. The row stops being about snacks or crap as he puts it. It now becomes some senseless argument that isn't even relevant. Then we are that pee'd off about the new row we end up bawling at each other even more. He then shouts ' You're nothing without me, in fact you'll fall flat on your face without me there to wipe your backside for you.' Raging I shout back ' You'll need me before I need you' then off I stomp grabbing my bag and car keys.

I don't know where I'm going but I'll know when I get there, anywhere, just to calm down before Ayeisha comes back and sees us like this. Off I go driving around blasting music at top note, in goes the CD… straight onto Springsteen's 'Born to Run' how apt! After calming down from driving around for a while I feel a little peckish and pull over at a shop. I'll have some chocolate I think and maybe a little bottle of something nice and fizzy too. When I get back to my car I say out loud 'Hah I'll take a picture and send it to you' obviously meaning Stan.

This amuses me, I'm sat there grinning to myself when I realise that the music is on still. I usually always turn it off but then my head wasn't really with it. When I turn the key in the ignition the music cuts out slightly making a pathetic weak groaning sound just before it cut out completely. I hope it's not ruined the cd. I turn the key again, but it cuts out on me again. Oh no, panicking I try turning the key again only for it to cut out again making some awful choking sound. Oh no, this is all I need, don't conk out on me now. I take a deep breath give it a minute and start again. Anxiously I turn the key. But no, it's not having bloody none of it.

Almost in tears I sink back into my seat. Now reality kicks in, the car is broken down. And me in my infinite wisdom had decided that I didn't need to pay extra for breakdown cover. I only drive local so I didn't think I would need. Besides, Stan is always around if there is something wrong. I now have a choice, I can sit here until some stranger decides to take pity on me and helps me out. But then again with my luck he could be some maniac and I'd have my bonnet up with no means to escape. Then Stan would go ballistic I didn't phone him.

My other choice is I phone a breakdown company and have them tow me home. This would cost a fortune and I still have the luxury of having to be towed back to the garage and then the cost of fixing it. And suffer watching *his* face glow seeing my car being towed. God No, I couldn't bear it. Every night I'd shut my eyes going to sleep I would see his face laughing at me, haunting me. No bloody chance! I'd rather walk home and leave the car here until the garage can pick it up tomorrow. But chances are I won't have any wheels left on my car in the morning, and it's due to go dark soon. Or I make the call. I sit sulking for a few more minutes then try the key again.

I could make the call. I hold my mobile for a minute or two longer, should I make the call. Ten more minutes pass, which seems like an eternity. I have to make the call, reluctantly and begrudgingly I have to make the call. This is going to hurt. As the phone rings I am trying to plan my request. Damn he's answered already. 'Hello' I hear at the other end. 'Hiya' I reply sheepishly.

'So your ready to apologise then' he says? 'What' I reply stunned at his arrogance.

He revels in saying 'Going bloody stupid and causing a row for nothing, again.' I bite my tongue, and take a deep breath. 'Well no actually' I reply. 'So what are you phoning for, are you expecting me to apologise? At this point I want to shout *obviously* and whilst you're at it you can fix my car as compensation. But this may not be the right time, so I take it delicately, embarrassingly delicately 'well I've just nipped out to the shop.' 'You mean you stomped off' he says almost gloating. 'I just decided to get some air' I reply playing it cool. 'So your coming home now you've calmed down' he asks. 'Err yes' there's just a small problem I splutter. 'What problem exactly' he asks intrigued.' 'It's my car it wont start' there I've said it, now that didn't hurt much did it. I hold my breath waiting for the reaction but it goes silent at the other end. Eventually in a very stunned voice he asks 'What.' I reply 'My car won't start.' Silence for a moment then starts the laughter. I hold the phone away from my ear, because now it's beginning to hurt. Then he quietens down a little.

'When are you coming home then' he asks just to stick the knife in a little more, make me cringe or beg more to the point. I won't beg, I absolutely refuse to beg. If he won't offer to help then that's it! I think to myself letting out a big sigh. I can't believe he is going to make me beg for help. Well I can that's just bloody like him. I go quiet because now I'm almost ready to burst into tears. I'd rather pay a bloody fortune and pay a mobile mechanic than ask him to help me.

When he says 'Do you want me to come and take a look at it then.' 'Only if you want to' I reply feeling very, very sorry for myself. In fact if I pout any more I could lift the car up with my lip. Then he decides to add 'But I thought you wouldn't need me before I'd need you' with a laughing sadistic tone. This is hurting a lot now and I'm ready to rant 'Well if you don't want to help' I shout. But he cuts in 'Where are you' with a weary tone. Well, I didn't ask him to help did I, he did offer.

When he pulls up he gives me the 'You know you need me' look. Well yes I do but I don't have to act grateful now do I. He asks what's wrong with it. 'I don't know you probably pulled a wire out on purpose.' Not helping the situation I know, but he knows how difficult it was to phone him. 'Now Now, he says sarcastically, you'll need me before I'll need you' At this point I feel like taking that bloody spanner to his knees. But no, I have to bite my tongue.

It would have been really funny if I wasn't so angry and upset. But now is not the time to find this funny. I stare ahead refusing to look at him. 'You'll *need me* to open the bonnet for you' he says. I know exactly what he is doing. Trying to get as many 'You'll need me' comments in as he can. But I refuse to take the bait or I'll blow my top. Finally the engine starts. I am grateful but the devil in me wants to say 'Ha sucker, who's laughing now.' But he'd probably take my tyres off and put the car on bricks and cut up all my shoes up just to spite me, or rather to get his own back. So I don't say a word just half smile. I am very grateful but it would probably kill me to show it. He says 'a thank you wouldn't go amiss.' I mumble thanks with all the drained energy I can muster.

As I'm ready to drive back home he says *'Now tell me you need me, you can't do without me... tell me your nothing without me'* whilst laughing in my face. He knows I'm fuming and likely to run him over. He's absolutely revelling and taking great delight in this one. I refuse to feed his ego and sit there sulking. Then the sod tells me 'I've just come out to fix your car, and now you are going to eat humble pie.' I moan under my breath Bloody Git. I glance at the passenger seat at my part eaten chocolate bar which doesn't look as tempting now. Back home he tells me I can apologise if I want. Flabbergasted I stare in disbelief. Surely he means I will allow him to apologise. Humble Pie for the car yes I'll accept I will have to be nice. Well polite at least, but apologise, Christ I'm going weak at the thought. If I remember rightly he distinctly started the row trying to ration me. For my humble pie I make us a cup of tea, well it's a start isn't it.

He tells Ayeisha 'You can tell your Mum I'll have some of that humble pie with my brew now' I respond by saying 'You can tell your father he's eaten all the humble pie he's gonna get, and if there was any more he'd choke on it.' How big does he think this pie is anyway Desperate Dan size. She doesn't know why but she knows we are being sarcastic. 'Now now' he laughs 'you'll need me before I need you! I look at him with a 'say that again look and you'll be sleeping in the shed.' After the strop he says 'With your amateur dramatics you should be on stage.' I reply 'There ain't nothin amateur about my dramatics' and smile back sarcastically. I tell they guys at work the next day of which they find hysterical. Antonio said he wouldn't come home for two weeks. I laugh that it had crossed my mind.

~ Chapter Twelve ~ **Another The Night Out**

We were supposed to be booking our Sri Lanka trip. Now Stan's moaning the work he's taken on is taking longer than he thought to finish. Because he's taken on too much work there is no time to fit it all in. My reaction is tell me your joking, I feel so annoyed and disheartened. After all the trouble I went to trying to get the time off now he tells me he can't spare the time. I think I'm going to explode. He tells me to calm down and compromise, we can book another trip for maybe he could spare a week or ten days. Or we wait until Christmas. What and pay twice as going at Christmas. How great is that.

I'm absolutely furious, and now he wants me to go in work and show myself up after last times performance. We can't even swap the dates and go in a few weeks because others have booked their time off. And I've stopped people taking time off in the three weeks we would have been away. They are going to curse me, I'll never live this one down. I dreaded going into work to tell them. To be fair they go easy on me because I'm so upset about it. Thankfully nobody takes the mickey, but say for Gods sake Ang I'd go without him. But now is not the time to go into it. My boss stands their in silence shaking his head, stunned and goes back into his office. Thankfully he'd rather keep the door shut than say something he'll regret. We decide on a night out to cheer us up and seeing that the office has settled down for a week or two, now seems to be as good a time as ever.

Trudy asks where shall we go. We don't want to go near work because the pubs there can get a bit rowdy. Antonio mentions Denton but Denton only has a few pubs, it's not quite as thriving as it was a few years ago. Ashton is heaving we won't be able to keep together. I mention town it's usually a good night there, its quite central and easy for everyone to get to. Most seem up for Manchester. I mention we could go over to the Village but Jenifer stares at me. What? 'I ask, it's really good at the village. Its safe, has lots of pubs and wine bars. The atmosphere is great, and whilst we have some nice weather people stand outside near the canal.' Again still she stares at me. 'What's wrong have you been to the village before and somebody upset you' I ask. She shakes her head saying she has no wish to go to the village in a sulkily attitude. I ask why not bemused by her reaction.

Has she been barred for being too loud or has she upset some lesbians I ask myself. It's just not somewhere I'd feel comfortable she told me. Now I'm really intrigued and push why not. 'Ang do I have to spell it out for you' she says in a surprised tone. I'm still not getting this one so I ask her to spell it out. 'It's full of gay people' she replies. Stunned I reply of course it's full of Gay people it's the Gay Village. 'You work with gay people, you have gay friends so why on earth would it bother you.' She looks away really embarrassed. I don't know whats frightening her she's usually bubbly and more up for a laugh. Oh well, you can't please everybody. If she has been there before and didn't like it then fair enough, but don't judge if you haven't been. I don't know anyone who has been and didn't like it. Even Stan came with me one night and had a lovely meal there. It has great music and a great atmosphere. It's the only place I know where women can walk about have a good laugh and a dance, and not have guys letching over you thinking you're on the pull. 'Yes' she replies 'Exactly, no guys letching over you.' I laugh 'is that your problem that the guys won't be interested in you.'

The others over hear and find this very funny and are as intrigued as I am now. 'No' she says stubbornly and looking rather worried. She pleads with the others to go somewhere else but they are definitely up for it. I've never seen her like this before. Lucky for her Sebastian hasn't arrived yet and Lawrence hasn't popped in the office. 'Do you think some girls are going to try it on with you or something' I laugh at her. She looks directly at me all flustered.

'For gods sake Jenifer, believe me they won't be interested in you, and if you feel the need to then take someone to the toilet with you anyway.' She looks really embarrassed because she now looks like a homophobic and she knows it. She says it's not that she minds gay people she'd feel uncomfortable in the village. I tell her there is nothing to be worried about because the girls won't be interested in her in the slightest. I think they'll work out who are gay and who are not. If she's really that bothered I ask the others if they prefer to stay around Deansgate. Trudy asked them but they still want to go to the Village. Getting annoyed with her and not knowing her reasons why Trudy tells her she don't have to come if she doesn't want to. As the night out draws nearer Jenifer started coming up with all sorts of excuses why she might not be able to come. The others are not amused telling her she wanted to have a night out and now she's dropping out. Jenifer recons its just awkward timing.

Okay then lets change the night out for when it is convenient for Jen. Let's watch her squirm out of this one Lawrence says, considerably annoyed, but still no idea why. Now she's slightly cornered Jen says she'll sort it. Poor thing she's looking tense and says she won't stay late, she'll be driving so will be on soft drinks anyway. I've never known her to go out and not get tipsy yet. I know she'd enjoy herself if only she'd relaxed. We don't want anyone to go and not enjoy themselves. It's quite funny to watch her squirming, because she's usually fun and bubbly.

They're all asking what's wrong, why all the excuses under the sun. I tell Jenifer we're going to trendy wine bars not some dirty hovel where you'll get groped or attacked. Besides the men are gay so they certainly won't be trying it on. The others click on to her being scared of lesbians. Sebastian says we'll have to take her in a bar where all the bar staff are transvestites, lets see if she notices. What a wicked sense of humour he has, just on my wave length really. With the exception of Jen we're all really looking forward to a night out. Busy discussing who's wearing what, as you do. Lawrence makes more fuss of his clothes than any of us put together. Saying clothes say a lot about a personality. Lawrence says he likes a guy who makes an effort he has to look groomed, and takes care of himself.

We find this amusing, it's usually one of us girls saying what she likes in a guy, not a guy saying it to us. He parades around the office getting into the party mode already. Trudy says she hopes we are not going to be in competition here. Lawrence claimed there won't be a guy in town that will be interested in any of us. We burst out laughing which takes the tension out of the air. Well for everyone except Jenifer. Unfortunately Antonio was called to a meeting in Europe and phoned to say he's sorry that he won't make it back in time. Arranging to meet at eight o'clock we remind Jenifer to make sure she wears trousers. We thought it was funny, however she does not. Oh well tonight should be fun, if only for watching Jenifer all night acting like a frightened rabbit scared to cross the road. We shouldn't laugh I suppose. But she is making a storm out of a tea-cup. Let's hope the bubbly Jenifer returns to us soon.

Everyone arrives in dribs and drabs. Lawrence, already on the tipple, is in good spirits. Sebastian hopes to bump into someone he knows. What encounter this might be I dread to ask. Trudy is on top form being very giddy because she's out with us all again. She's a stickler in work but loves a good night out to let her hair down. Olive had phoned in sick today so probably won't be coming, no surprise there then. Gertie surprisingly is out, and appears to be in a good mood this time. I was unsure she'd come after the last time.

We had an open invitation for a select few who we sometimes come on our nights out. Jenifer arrived looking rather nervous and asks for a soft drink. We can't help but look at each other and laugh, she's usually first one on the dance floor and first to get drunk. As usual after a few drinks the atmosphere in our crowd gets a little rowdy. We had the cheek to be worried about rowdy pubs and now this lot is the rowdiest. We couldn't help it when Charlie from the Accounts Department arrived. Trudy shouted 'I'm glad you've come out then.' We all burst into laughter because Charlie has a pair of three quarter length pants on. Matched with the tightest tango orange crop top you could find and glitter in his hair. Charlie then announced he's gay and probably always have been. Gertie asked didn't he have a girlfriend a couple of months ago. Brazenly he said he did but it didn't feel right, then started coming out in Manchester and one night it just felt right. I asked 'What, you walked in held your arms out open shouting I'm Home.'

More laughter follows. Some think he's only doing this for a wind up. I'm not so sure, he looks like he's pretty content and he's enjoying himself far too much. 'Any more announcements to make' I ask looking at Jenifer. She smiles sarcastically knowing were only having fun on her account. She seems to have calmed down a little now and even has a drink. The atmosphere is good, the music great, we all end up on the dance floor. Charlie, however is in the centre of us shouting 'It's my party and I'll come out if I want to' totally camping it up. This is hysterical and it's only nine thirty, what more can happen. It's a lovely warm night, too hot to be inside, we all end up outside on Canal Street enjoying the atmosphere. Everyone is relaxed and enjoying themselves. We decide which bar to go to next. On route Sebastian keeps trailing behind talking to friends. I wonder what he's up to.

We decide on the Mancunian Bar where bar staff are transvestites. We've got to send Jenifer to the bar, let's see if she figures it out. She's finally got over her fears. So much so, she is asking the transvestites how they keep their figures trim, how they keep in there ahem 'outfits' without 'falling out' as it were. After all the outfits are rather skimpy. 'It's a secret' they flounce back at her waving a feather boa in her face. They probably get this interest all the time. Jenifer can't believe what fantastic figures they have for men. 'Look he has a better figure than me' she laughs. At least she's enjoying herself now.

Lawrence thinks this is hysterical Jenifer making friends with the 'the gays.' She gets on great with Lawrence but told him she is frightened of lesbians. Lawrence laughs 'Does she think they all want to pounce on her.' Tonight she realises that they haven't even looked at her. She has even gone to the ladies toilets on her own, in fact she's chatting to everyone she meets. Jenifer's was supposed to be meeting a friend, but her friend rang to say she's running late. She'd got caught up at the other end of town. Trudy laughed saying Jenifer probably needed some backup in case the lesbians swamped her. Trudy is getting louder and louder, and Lawrence is encouraging her.

As the music gets louder Jen takes to the dance floor with Gertie and Lawrence. Gertie spends her time following Sebastian around the dance floor. There has never been any love loss here and he starts to cringe. We find this hilarious, poor Sebastian hounded by Gertie. Maybe she wants to turn him straight. She dances very provocatively around Sebastian, waving her scarf at him and being very flirty. Over comes Jenifer to join in. She pretends to pole dance around him. If you can call it pole dancing, it looks more like she's drunkenly staggering around him. If Sebastian's friend can see him now he will lose all credibility and tries to make a sharp exit.

Charlie is acting queen of the dance floor with all the young boys around him. Lawrence then somehow ends up getting sandwiched between Trudy, Gertrude and Jenifer who are all trying to do a dance off with each other. Trudy straddles her legs around Lawrence, she's shouting along to the music. Drunk he starts bouncing her around to the music. How he doesn't fall over I'll never know, he's had so much to drink. Trudy then decides to swing herself to the floor whilst still attached to Lawrence's waist. She lunges herself backwards arms bent over her shoulders and leans down to touch the floor. Lawrence still tries bouncing her around his waist. How he didn't break her back I'll never know. At one point I thought he was dropping her on her head. If you didn't know them you would think that they were trying out a new mating call on the dance floor. Not content with this Trudy decides she wants Lawrence to lift her onto his shoulders. Gertie is not impressed Trudy's getting all the attention and parades around Lawrence. He is so drunk that he wobbles about with Trudy still on his shoulders. Then Lawrence crashes to the floor dragging Gertie and Trudy with him. Trudy grabbed hold of Jenifer trying to break her fall but she ended on top of them. How they didn't break their necks is a miracle.

Trudy's legs are akimbo in the air. You couldn't tell which arm belongs with which body they are that mingled on the floor. Even stranger was everybody else ignoring them like it's a regular occurrence. Gertie crawling about on her hands and knees on the floor tries steadying herself on Trudy. But ends up pulling her back onto the floor. Trudy had a lovely lemon coloured blouse on that is now splattered with grey and black blotches. Lawrence can't get up for laughing and Gertie half sits on him sat on the floor pretending to do the eighty's dance to Oops Ups Side Your Head. Jenifer clambers off the dance floor heading towards us shouting 'It's great here, I don't know what I was worried about' then disappears off towards the bar.

I'm embarrassed that we have lowered the tone yet again when I notice Jenifer's friend Melissa arrived just in time to see the end of the display on the dance floor. Looking stunned Melissa asks 'Isn't that Trudy on her back.' Yes it certainly is! We have met Melissa before on nights out. She is really nice in fact she is very quiet, the complete opposite to Jenifer. Looking bemused at the display and hoping nobody else we know is in, we try to find Jenifer with her. She's not at the bar, nor back on the dance floor either, that leaves the ladies loo.

To say she was scared of coming to the Village she seems rather fond of it now. Sebastian comes over for a moment then disappears yet again with friends. Nobody would know he was with us at this rate. But then again who would admit to being with us. Its getting rather crowded in here, we eventually find our way to the ladies. Opening the door to the ladies we see a few girls waiting in the queue but no Jenifer. Then over the chatter we hear can Jenifer's voice. Intrigued we peep around the corner, only to find Jenifer with tissues in hand consoling a transvestite who is in tears from a row with his/her boyfriend.

He/she is giving Jenifer the full sob story of how his/her boyfriend has dumped him/her and is now flirting with his/her best friend. Jen is giving advice on how all men are b******s and we are better off without them. 'I know' he/she says and looks up at our faces peering in which stops him/her in his/her tracks. The poor thing has mascara running all down his/her cheeks. Jenifer looks up shouting these are my friends Ang & Melissa, on top note and not in the slightest bit fazed. Ang wanted to come here for a night out, she said it was great. I didn't want to come and now I can't believe what a great time were having and can't wait to come again.

I can't help but laugh. Isn't this the person I said would enjoy herself, and she was frightened to death. Now here she is sat with a transvestite having a 'Trisha' moment. The next thing we hear is someone throwing the remnants of her stomach up in the next toilet and starts shouting for someone to pass her some tissues. The thought of seeing or hearing someone makes me eave. My stomach starts to churn I have to get out of there.

As I pass the cubicle with the horrendous noise, the door swings open and there crouched on the floor kneeling over the toilet is Gertie oblivious to the world. I cringe with embarrassment for her. Pretending I don't know her I leave Jenifer to do the Mother Theresa act. Why drink until you feel sick, what on earth possesses someone to drink so they can't remember who or where they are. She must have been downing some concoctions. Oh what a night! Here's until the next one.

On Monday morning Trudy keeps pretty quiet about her antics. Lawrence complains of the lack of talent out that night, so had to put up with us lot. The cheeky bleeder. Sebastian said he wasn't complaining, and found plenty of interesting people to talk to. Well, he did end up leaving with a few 'friends'. We ask Trudy if she enjoyed the floor show. She looks at us enquiringly. 'You do remember don't you, your acrobatics' we ask her. She groans 'I remember saying I can do the twist and maybe a few other moves, somebody asked for a demonstration, but other than that no.' We just burst out laughing. We asked her if the demonstration was from Lawrence's shoulders. She claimed she remembers very little of that night and had spent most of the night with her head in a bowl. How convenient.

~ Chapter Thirteen ~ **The Bloody Dog**

Just when I think my life will now become quiet and resemble some sort of normality we arrive home only to find we had been burgled. They've broken into the garage stealing some of Stan's tools and fishing tackle. He's absolutely furious, definitely more angry than upset. He starts ranting that's it were getting a dog. But I don't want a dog; we don't have time for a dog. So many jobs at home need finishing and Stan still doesn't have time to do them so the last thing we need is a dog. I make my feelings clear telling Stan there is no way we are getting a dog.

The next day Stan's late home from work, yet he knew I was finishing early today. I have no idea where he is. Because his job is never nine to five, some days he's finished at three o'clock other days it can be six o'clock. Tonight its nearly seven and still no sign of him. I could have made plans tonight for all he knows. He can't even be bothered to let me know when he'll be home. At this rate we'll end up having a row when he does get home. I don't mind him going anywhere but just let me know where at least. Eventually the phone rings. Its Stan letting me know he's had his phone switched his phone off. He tells me their isn't much battery left on his phone but he is on his way home. I try asking where he's been but the phone goes off, conveniently. When he finally arrives I notice he has something in the passenger seat. This particular something happens to be moving. I don't believe it. This had better not be another pet.

Staring through the window trying to make out what it is. At least it's not another bird or it would be in a box I'm sure. What the hell is it then. Stan climbs out of the van walks to the passenger side and lifts 'it' out. I don't believe it. It's a bloody dog. After all I've said, he still ignores me and goes out and gets one. I might as well be speaking to the damn wall. How irresponsible can he get, how god damn irresponsible. When he comes through the door I am ready to go into rant mode, or ready to explode. In he walks bold as brass with dog in tow, smiling away. Smiling, can you believe it. Then has the cheek to say look what I've got for us. It's a big golden brown dog with big brown eyes. Its looks fully grown, most certainly not a puppy.

Ayeisha's at her club, thank God she hasn't seen the dog yet. At least we have time to send it back. He asks isn't it cute. Cute! I think it's bloody awful 'That's not a dog it's a horse' I shout. You can't bring a fully grown dog home, it doesn't know us and more to the point we don't know it. 'But it's only a puppy it isn't fully grown yet' he says grinning away. He sees my face does not look amused, and tries to win me over. 'Stop it Stan, it isn't staying and how can you say it's not a puppy it's fully grown' I snap. But he insists it's only five months old and couldn't resist it. He sits there cuddling the thing, and lets it wander around the room. 'Just to get its bearings. Let it get used to new surroundings' he laughs. 'Stan, I thought I made my feelings perfectly clear' I shout back but might as well be talking to myself.

Off it wanders around the house sniffing everything, the furniture, carpet, the kitchen, us. I ask Stan what he thinks he's doing and insist its not staying. It has nowhere to sleep, we don't have a collar or lead, no dishes for it, no bedding. It's far too big for the house it's the size of a fully grown dog, and we don't know what its temperament is like. Off I rant but he just ignores me being quite smitten with this thing. But I don't like dogs I never have. I've never really been around one, although tried to stroke one once. It belonged to a friend of mine. She told me it was really soft and never bites, don't worry give it a stroke. Stupidly I did, but when I went to stroke it, it bloody went for me. So no I'm not really a dog lover.

I only like puppies, and even then I like to give them back. But still he doesn't get it. All he can say is she's only a puppy, look she's got a baby face they called her Bonnie. Baby face is not what I'd call it, nor Bonnie. She's huge, but baby no I don't think so. It's the size of a Labrador to me, a fully grown one, not a puppy. A puppy you can hold in your hands. This thing I couldn't hold with two arms if I tried. After wandering around for half an hour the dog settles in front of the fire. Look! He says 'she likes it here.'

I try telling him he doesn't get it, it's not staying and he'd better take it back. He moans it took an hour to get there and then couldn't find the place so she won't be going back tonight. I try explaining it's not a puppy. It's only because she's a big dog he tries telling me, so obviously she'll be a big puppy. 'What, you mean it's going to get bigger' I shout flabbergasted. Stan looks at me grinning then says not as big has her brother. Her brother I ask. 'Yes Clyde' he says glowing 'He was twice the size as Bonnie but he's already been picked by another couple.' I gasp at the thought of a dog bigger. Bonnie & Clyde I don't believe it. I'm only just getting over the shock of Jip arriving. It could only happen to me couldn't it.

Yes, he said it's a good job Clyde had been sold already, or I would have picked Clyde, or even worse brought both of them back. More worryingly he wasn't joking. I don't believe what I'm hearing. I stare at him in disbelief. We must be on different planets, surely. We don't want any dogs. What about all the jobs that need finishing on the house. He's still in the middle of building Jip's aviary bigger. He wants her to have an enclosed part now. Where in the hell is he going to find time to fly Jip, house train a dog and find time to walk the dog. That's without the cost of feeding the thing. Bonnie looks like she could get through some food. Bonnie looks up at me with her huge brown eyes, looking all lost and in need of some comfort. I suppose she is cute. But she's so big. I need to think about this some more.

It's time to collect Ayeisha from her club. I need to calm down and think rationally. The drive will do me good, blast music in the car and clear my mind. What good it did me I have no idea. Because as soon as we walk through the front door Bash sees the dog. Of course she is all over Bonnie stroking and cuddling it. Worse still, Bonnie loves the attention lavished on her and runs around the room giddy for more. Which of course gets Bonnie more fussing and attention. Ayeisha bursts with excitement and wants to keep her. I explain Bonnie has to go back we don't have enough room for her. Stan of course tells her if she wants Bonnie to stay she can keep her.

I glare at him because he knows damn well he is using her to manipulate the situation, the little git. For the rest of the night Bonnie lies in front of the fire being pampered. She looks quite comfy next to Ayeisha, too comfy in fact. Stan tries telling me I'll get used to her soon enough. But that's the whole point I don't want to get used to another pet, especially a dog. I must admit she settles down really well. He says lets keep her, just for a few days and see how it goes. I suppose it wouldn't be fair on Bash to send Bonnie straight back. Only a few days we agree on.

Ayeisha tells anyone who will listen we have yet another addition to the family. All the kids in the neighbourhood come by for a look. Right on queue Bonnie jumps up getting giddy wagging her tail. If anything she's a little too giddy almost knocking the kids over. Her temperament seems okay she hasn't tried eating any of the kids yet, so that's a good sign. Then we get confident letting her out in the front garden. Big mistake, she's barking at anything that moves past the garden. She growls at strangers, refuses to let anyone up the path, anyone except Ayeisha that is. Well at least we know she's protective. I think she's loud and embarrassing, Stan on the other hand thinks this is great saying at least she'll keep people away.

The neighbours comment that's some dog you've got. Stan takes great pleasure in telling them she's only a baby, she'll grow twice as big. Stan's enjoying this, he laughs that at least it will keep mythering neighbours away too. I'm cringing, Bonnie is making such a racket she can be heard right down the street. Worse still, when Bonnie sees she's getting a reaction she goes even louder. I moan 'Stan for god's sake put her in the back garden, we can't have this racket every day.' We think this might be because she needs to settle and know it's her home, she'll calm down soon enough. Bonnie has a good sniff around the back garden, conveniently seeking out Jip's aviary. She gets rather brave walking right up to the edge of the aviary. She ponders nearer sniffing at the mesh, then spots Jip perched inside.

At first Jip looks really dignified ignoring her. And then the barking started. On and on, louder and louder, echoing right round the garden. She seems to revel in the noise she is making, hearing herself louder it frenzies her up even more. It's so loud I cringe, Christ the neighbours are going to have a field day with this one. No matter how we try she won't quieten down. In the end I tell Stan that she has to go, there's no way we can have this racket. Haven't we been shown up enough in front of the neighbours over Jip. He insists on letting them get used to each other saying they'll soon settle down, Bonnie is just trying to mark her territory that's all. Yes but at what consequence I ask myself. Scaring Jip is bad enough but what if he turns his back and all that's left are feathers scattered. I plead with him to take Bonnie inside but instead he decides to watch like an onlooker enjoying the circus. At this rate we are turning into the circus. Jip continues to ignore Bonnie refusing to take the bait, which of course makes Bonnie worse.

The barking gains pace getting louder and louder. All of a sudden Jip swoops down to the bottom of the aviary stopping right in front of Bonnie. Bonnie retaliates by jumping up on the mesh barking trying to get at her. By this time Jip has had enough of her and needs to show her whose boss. She ruffles all her body up fanning her wings around like a circle around her. This makes Jip look huge and it's enough to make Bonnie back off anyway. Stan grins at me as if he knew it would happen 'See Jip isn't bothered in the slightest she won the battle, next time Bonnie will think twice before starting.' I'm stumped for words. For a while Bonnie tried in vein to stand her ground standing near the aviary to have a little bark enough to show off but decides to leave Jip well alone. Settling down, they appear to tolerate each other.

Whilst we're both at work we think its best to keep Bonnie in the kitchen. We don't want a mess left for us. And besides she seems keen on chewing anything. Stan hasn't fixed the door leading into the kitchen yet and it doesn't shut properly. I moan at Stan for another job not finished, he tells me just put a weight in front of the door for now he'll finish it at weekend. Telling me to stop nagging he can only do one thing at a time. Yet this is exactly what I meant by not having a dog yet. All these jobs need finishing quickly with a dog around.

Of course the guys at work find our new addition to the family hilarious. They can't believe that Stan has brought yet another pet home unannounced. Jerry says that Jip would have been pigeon pie by now. They advise me to tell Stan that Bonnie got off her lead but really take her to a dog's home. They have a wicked sense of humour, and we are laughing now but it may come to that if she doesn't settle down. No matter how guilty I'd feel for Ayeisha.

The next morning I woke to hear Bonnie barking like mad and pouncing at the front window. I wonder what on earth all the racket is, it sounds like somebody is breaking into the house. But no, the racket is for the benefit of the milkman coming down the path. The noise was horrendous and she didn't stop until the milkman had gone at least a few doors down. This is ridiculous, but Stan knows I'm going off ready to rant so he laughs and hides under the duvet. Later while I'm trying to get ready for work she starts the barking again. Trust Stan to have gone already. I knew he'd let her out for a drink before leaving, so what is it this time.

I look out the window to see the postman coming down the path. By this time Bonnie not content with just barking is now savaging at the window. She's stood upright frothing at the mouth and pouncing on the window with her front paws so hard that the glass is bouncing. It looks like the glass is going to break through the window frame. Christ, I wouldn't like to be on the receiving end of her wrath. As the postman walks past the window towards the front door the she follows him all along the window. All of her fur on the back of her neck is standing on end. Trying to shout at Bonnie to get down only adds to the frenzy. As the postman walks back past the window she follows him all the way back, but knocks over my vase in the process. What could I do besides cringe with embarrassment. The whole neighbourhood *must* have been woken up by the racket. Even if they had the radio on they would have heard it. I'm sure we're going to get complaints. Yet once the postman has gone past she shuts up instantly and looks at me to say I saw him off. This is getting ridiculous, I'll be glad to get back into work for some peace and quiet.

I finish off getting ready when the police called by to take a statement about the break in. Apparently there have been other thefts in the area. Trust Stan to have nipped out and not arrived back yet so I let them in. Unusually, I hear her in the living room making a noise, she isn't aware of the police at the door. I thought she'd have made a right din. When I walked into the living room I saw why. All my net curtains are lying in a crumpled mess all over the floor. That bloody dog has ripped the curtains and the rail off the wall. Screws and all. I stand there cringing with embarrassment yet again, as the two coppers come inside. I splutter 'I'm sorry but you'll have to excuse the dog' as we look at all the mess on the floor. The damn dog runs in circles dragging the curtains with her thinking it's a game. I'm so embarrassed I don't know where to look. Where the hell is Stan when I need him.

Bonnie almost bursts with excitement at the two strange men. She can't believe her luck, not one but two strangers to target. And they come inside, not carry on walking past the window like the rest of the strangers she's tried to savage so far. She starts bouncing around at their feet jumping from one to the other. They try ignoring her and talk to me, but it's not happening. Giddily she charges at them and slavers all down their nice clean pressed uniforms. They stand their trying to be dignified and desperate to keep her at bay. I try grabbing hold of her to get her in the kitchen but she hasn't got her collar on. Because Stan with hindsight thought she looked cute without her collar on so took it off whilst she was in the house. Now I can't bloody get hold of her. The more I try and grab her the giddier she gets and runs rings around the three of us. One of the officers tried to be helpful and make a grab for her, but she runs through his legs almost pushing him over.

The other tries but realises she is just getting giddier and decides its best to ignore her. 'Let's just take the details' he said rushing to get out. The first policeman sits down on the settee and gets his folder out, at least to try and get the statement started. I stand near the kitchen door hoping the damn dog will go in. As I do Bonnie runs towards me and goes into the kitchen, thank God! Just as I rush to close the door behind her she turns around before I can get there. Worse still she bounds back towards me. I try to hold the door back but she flew straight past the door like a bouncing rubber ball picking up speed. She takes a leap across the floor and from the middle of the floor springs her onto the settee next to the officer. The sheer weight and speed of the jump bounces the settee crashing it back against the wall a few inches behind before the settee bangs back onto the floor with said officer in tow.

I burst out laughing with nerves and the second officer still stood up bursts out laughing in disbelief at his colleague. The poor guy just sits there pretending none of it was happening and surely wishing he was somewhere else. He was probably worried what more can happen. I mean how much more embarrassment is one supposed to endure in a day or worse still ten minutes. Just when I thought things couldn't get any worse Bonnie decides she's not quite satisfied with her delightful puppy performance so far. And decides to pounce on the poor guy and clamps her jaws around the back of the nice policeman's neck. I freeze not quite knowing what to do, well short of owning a shotgun that is. I've never had a dog before, I don't know their nature or what to expect from them. Thankfully she's playing, luckily the nice policeman realises this and decides its best to keep still and not antagonise her for a moment. Trying to keep his composure and some dignity he gently pushes her off him with his free arm not holding paperwork. I try grabbing her off him whilst desperately trying not to laugh. The other officer however is not able to hold his laughter, and makes his colleague feel even more undignified. He tried to grab the bloody dog but gives up in hysterics.

I, of course cringe with even more embarrassment if that's at all possible. He says maybe its best if I walk into the kitchen hopefully the dog might follow you. Embarrassed I try shouting Bonnie towards the kitchen and look at the poor officer sat on the settee waiting for her to move. He's sat there trying to wipe all the slaver from Bonnie off the back of his neck and shoulders. I can't make eye contact with him, I am utterly lost for words. What apologies could I offer that would make the slightest bit of difference. Once inside the kitchen the damn dog runs to the door and jumps back circling again. The weight behind the door isn't enough to hold it and she pushes her way back through. This time the officer has to stand in the kitchen hoping she will follow him.

Finally there is a God, she follows him into the kitchen. He quickly jumps back through the door before she bounces through. If Stan walks through the door now they'll be arresting me for murder, because I'm going to kill him when he gets back. To top if off I can't shut the door properly because Stan hasn't fixing the bloody door. He took the handle back off because it didn't fit right. You know the job he was supposed to fix straight away. And now I have the pleasure of seeing my curtains ripped from the wall in a neat little pile around the copper's feet. My dog is parading round like it's on speed, and the officer is full of slaver. If I even think about what's going on I will surely die. I have the delightful pleasure of standing at the door with a couple of Stan's weights wedged behind the door and me trying to hold the door shut whilst she bounces at the door trying to play with the policemen.

Well this is just one of my wonderful moments. Moments of which are getting far too frequent of late. I wonder what I've done to deserve this, is it my lot in life to go around embarrassed at all the carnage around me. I am willing Stan to show his face. He needs to feel the embarrassment that I am feeling. And not swan around the place in his van trying to look busy. The officer sits on the settee still wiping his hand from across his neck and onto his trousers, which are of course now full of dog hair. 'I'm really sorry' I blurt out. But knowing damn well it makes no difference to him, the damage is done. He tells me it's alright trying to be polite. Adding he's surprised anyone would try to break in with a dog that size, she does seem rather alert; you'd think she would frighten them off.

Cringing yet again I tell him we've only just got her. As if to trying to redeem some sort of dignity saying its not our fault she's completely unruly and non house trained. They take the details down, hastily I might add. Because whilst they are doing so Bonnie is convinced she's being ignored. Thus trying to bounce her way through the door, jumping and barking at it the whole time. She knows she is getting attention even through the door. It's a shame its glass otherwise she wouldn't be able to see us and might have quietened down. The dog's home is looking very appealing at this moment in time. The officers rush through the details not being able to get out of the house fast enough. I stand at the door watching them walk and almost breaking into a sprint down the path.

Even though they have their backs to me, I'm convinced they can still feel the burning sensation on my cheeks. This is farcical, one of those moments when you pray for the ground to open and swallow you up. Yet the moment they are gone Bonnie is in baby mode again wanting to settle by the fireplace. Is this the same dog that I had ten minutes before? Then out of nowhere she bounces up with excitement wagging her tail because Stan arrives home. She looks all full of innocence as if nothing has happened. He walks through the door saying she's such a cutie she has to stay now. I stare at him not quite believing what I am hearing. He's obviously not noticed my face like thunder and the steam coming from my ears. Then he looks up realising him definitely not amused. He has the cheek to ask what's wrong.

Within three seconds I go into rant mode. 'What's wrong, I'll tell you what's bloody wrong, that dog has to go. I have never been so ashamed in all my life. First she bounces at the window trying to savage the milkman, and then tries getting the post man. And then police come, she yanks all the net curtains from the wall. When they come in the house she pounces on them. That's what's bloody wrong.' Taking a small breath I rant 'Not only that she slavers all over them, grabs one of them by the neck, slavers all over his neck then bounces at the door. Why didn't you put her outside' he asks like I'd not thought of that one. 'Because she's got no bloody collar on is why not, have you tried getting hold of her when she's on a frenzy, you put her outside. Other than that everything is hunky bloody dory.' Just when I think he gets the message he replies 'I got back at the right time then eh Bon' and starts laughing. Bonnie gets giddy again because she's getting more attention.

Is it me, am I in a horrendous dream, is this all a test or something, ready for something better to come? Maybe this is when I wake up and laugh it was all a horrible nightmare. But reality hits as I look at them and he's laughing telling her she's only a baby, could they not handle you Bon.' 'It isn't funny, do you know how embarrassing it was' I shout furious that he's not taking it serious. Then has the cheek to say they were right when they said no one would break in with Bonnie here. I'm ready to froth at the mouth and he's laughing at me so much tears well up in his eyes. I give up!

This one keeps the troupes at work entertained yet again, and spends their time wondering what on earth is coming next. They take bets on if my life will be event free until Christmas. They're giving me a hundred to one that it stays event free. It's like the bad dream keeps on going, picking up momentum like a steam train. Driving home today I saw a van today with a sticker 'what the world needs is more Laurel & Hardy, and if I keep watching them my wife is gonna leave me... I'm sure gonna miss my wife.' How apt this is the only thing to bring a smile to my face.

Of course Bonnie still tries to savage the postman. It has become her aim in life to take out both the postie and the milkman. The milkman has started calling earlier in the morning, knowing she is in the kitchen and can't jump up at the window. The postie on the other hand isn't that lucky he has his rounds to do at a set time each morning. And Bonnie makes the most of it. We thought she'd get used to people coming down the path and hoped this helped to socialise her. Instead it fed her frenzy even more. It's like a timer set each morning when the postie walks down the path.

This particular morning Stan shouts quick I've got an idea. He runs into the kitchen grabbing something from the cupboard and rushes to the front door. Just as postie approaches the gate Stan shouts wait a minute and shuts the front door behind him. Postie kindly stops thinking Stan is about to ask of a delivery he's expecting or apologise for the dogs behaviour even. When Stan says 'I just want to introduce my dog to you.' Of all the people to choose he chooses the softest guy in town to pick on. The poor guy freezes in shock. Walking towards him Stan says 'I think it will help my dog settle in' and goes to put a dog biscuit in Postie's hand. The poor guy stands rigid with fear. He obviously thought he was safe because Bonnie was always on the other side of the window. Stan had to prize his hand open to give him the biscuit, whilst he stood there open mouthed. The colour slowly drained away from the guys face and starts to go a sickly pale grey. He's so scared he can't even run. He just mumbles something about being scared of dogs. Only for Stan tell him don't worry she's only a baby.

Postie looks towards the window at Bonnie barking aggressively. She's bouncing on the window and frothing at the mouth. She looks like she's ready to crash through the window and head straight for him. Stan grabs Bonnie's lead and walks her out the front door saying be nice. At which Bonnie takes the 'be nice' command to charge straight across the grass dragging Stan behind her whilst hanging onto the end of the lead. Petrified postie shouts out aaarrgghh thinking he's going to be eaten alive. He then goes an even paler colour if that's possible.

I think he stopped breathing because he went all quiet, even his eyes didn't blink. Bonnie jumps up against him almost knocking him over. She thinks its frenzied playtime, only this time she doesn't get a bone she gets postie. She must have thought all her Christmases had come at once. Stan shouts to the postie 'its alright she's is no threat as he wants to take control of the situation. He shouts get down to Bonnie letting her know whose boss. Postie is still froze rigid, frightened of moving a muscle. Stan then has the cheek to tell him its okay, it'll be better next time because she'll have chance to get used to you. Funny that, because he never did our round again.

For a while after life became somewhat unbearable at home. Because Bonnie was still not fully house trained. We tried getting her to do her business outside but some mornings we wake up to a nice little mess in the kitchen. I always know when, because I hear Stan ranting and raving. If he wants to keep the dog he gets the pleasure of her mess. Although other than the mess, we are getting used to her being in the house. You can't help but feel safe whilst she's in the house. People don't even have to walk down the path. They can be walking past the garden and she acts like they're breaking into the house.

People have started walking on the other side of the road. I

151

can't think for the life of me why. Stan finds this hilarious as usual. Friends and neighbours don't call anymore. Stan doesn't have time or patience for neighbours anyway, so it's done him a favour really. Stan is what you'd call an 'unsociable git.' He can't be doing with the neighbourly thing popping into each other's houses for a coffee or a few beers. He calls this s invading your space and mythering. I, on the other hand can sit quite happily with friends having a coffee and a good gossip. Although I couldn't be doing with it everyday. I suppose the difference is they are friends you've chosen not just neighbours who happen to live nearby.

~ Chapter Fourteen ~ **Phone on a Cheat**

Stan has always enjoyed fishing, day or night fishing. This time his van was in the garage and he decides to hire a van. Which is alright but when you hire a van it's generally required to give it back in the same condition it was taken. 'I'm going fishing with our kid' he announces, they are going fishing for the weekend yet again. Its okay with me I'll have peace and quiet. And I have Bonnie in the house so I don't mind. He tells me they'll behave. I give him a sarcastic look because the last time they went fishing, Stan decided it would be a good idea for his brother George, yes his brother not him, to swim out to the middle of the reservoir. All because they couldn't get the bait in the right area they wanted. Bearing in mind it was getting dark as night time was drawing in, and was freezing cold. Neither of them had waterproofs with them, only thick socks, jeans and heavy boots.

It would have been slightly funny, but for the fact that George wasn't even half way back when he started to struggle. His head kept bobbing underneath the water. Stan was worried to death and kept shouting at George to hurry and keep his head up, whilst trying not to panic him. But Stan did worry as George almost didn't make it back to the bank. Although they both laughed after as Stan still didn't go as far as getting his own kit off to try saving him.

On this fishing trip Stan had a brilliant idea and decides to fish near a marshy area. As they approached, the road became small and winding, and then got very bumpy. Whilst trying to get over bumps the back of the van drops down in between the lower part of the bumps. As they tried to manoeuvre out it gets stuck on the bump. The middle of the van is balanced on one hump with the wheels on either side not being able to move. If they try moving it could break the chassis of the van. As if this wasn't enough incentive that maybe they shouldn't be there.

They decide to struggle on and prize the van free then keep on going. Yes, keep on going closer into the marsh. They've had one scare after all, why not have more because that might not have been enough fun. Anybody else would come straight back. But getting closer to the marsh is all that counts. I mean, they don't want to carry their fishing tackle far now do they. Oh no, especially when it is much easier to take the van right to the edge of the water. Than have to carry all the heavy tackle back to the van.

So, they move the van closer driving as near to the edge of the marsh as they can. And, in doing so Stan in his wisdom misjudges the depth in the next bend in the lane. The van drops into a ditch full of water then pounces forward almost toppling into the water. Then Stan has an idea and wants George to open the door and hang out. Of course why didn't George think of that, after all he did nearly die on their last fishing escapade. Stan hopes the weight of George will balance the van back onto the road. They are desperate to stop the van from dropping into the water at any cost.

Stan shouts for George to open the passenger door. Telling him to lean as far out of the van as he possibly can whilst hanging from the door. After a few scary moments, a near heart attack and an urgent need to go to the toilet, they managed to reverse the van back out of the ditch and out of danger. I suppose any other sane person would have turned back and parked in a safer place. They, on the other hand thought it best to carry on. After all they've come this far. It isn't as if they are only half an hour from home, they have a few hours drive back. So they fish for a while but don't seem to be lucky.

To make matters worse once there they're messing with water fishing tackle worms and dead fish. Before you know it they're delving through their lunch and munching the sandwiches. After about half an hour they realised their hands are all grubby with fish slime, and neither of them had washed their hands. Ugh, the thought makes me feel sick. I can't believe them at times. Imagine taking the keys back to the rental company… adding we couldn't bring the van back as it's at the bottom of a marsh! The fish seem to be avoiding them today.

Of course Stan's excuse would be the temperature wasn't right. It couldn't possibly be their fishing skills now could it. Stan hates the thought of match fishing saying its not real fishing trying catching as many little sprats as you can to make a decent weight. He prefers to spend days and nights catching nothing for the mere chance of catching the big one. It's all about the quality he waffles. But to me there has to be something wrong with staring at the water for hours. Even days on end waiting for a ripple. It isn't normal is it. I could understand if he said it's just to get away from me, get some peace and quiet. But to him sitting for hours watching nothing is exciting.

Apparently, the conditions weren't right this time. Mmm, how convenient. Driving home they laugh at what a near miss they had. Both them and the van almost ending up in the water. How would they explain that one to the hire company. I didn't think driving into lakes was covered on the insurance. Yet they laugh it off as if it were nothing. Whereas I can't help but wonder should they be allowed out alone.

When I arrive back from the supermarket Stan's van is already home. I walk down the path to see Stan and George staring through the window. I can't make out what is going on. From the looks on their faces they can't believe their eyes. George is laughing so much he is holding his stomach with pain. Intrigued and a little worried I take a look at what's so funny. But stand dumbfounded not believing what I'm seeing. The sofa is in the centre of the living room yet when I left I distinctly remember it was against the wall. All my cushions are scattered all over the floor. The stuffing from the settee is strewn about the place looking like confetti. To top it off the damn dog is contently chewing one of the heels of my shoe. If that damn dog doesn't go to the dogs home by the end of the day it will be a miracle. Stan goes into the house ranting 'for God's sake Bonnie.' Obviously unsure of whether I'm going to kill him first or the dog he's trying to diffuse the situation.

I dump my shopping, get my handbag and walk back down the path and straight to the shops for some retail therapy for me. If I stay home I will surely kill one of them. It's in their best interests that I stay out of the way. I decide its best to spend on clothes and shoes with the full knowledge that for once Stan can't moan. He won't be able to ask why have you bought that when you already have one. Or why have you bought that when there's already a shop full in your wardrobe…blah blah blah. No I don't need any of that today. I feel the delight of the oh so lovely credit card being swiped, ahh bliss.

Stan never quite grasped that my shopping wasn't for the sake of spending. It's if I see something I like then I will buy it. Where as Stan on the other hand replaces want with need, and us females know it's not always a case of need. We see something nice we feel we need it. Granted I may have a few things in the wardrobe that I maybe didn't need to buy. But at the time I thought it a good idea. And I know in my wardrobe there maybe one or two things still with the price tags on. Of which I had every intention of taking them back but left it too long. Or not too sure if it suited me and left the price tag on just in case. Stan however, never understood this concept. He just sees it as clothes in my wardrobe for months. Well okay, maybe a year or so that I haven't worn yet.

Sometimes I debate whether to take the items back. Then think I might have an occasion that warrants wearing it. Occasionally they need alterations that I never get around to doing. It's a female thing which the male species do not understand. Rather than explain myself and then have a row over it, its best if they just 'butt out.' Don't look in our wardrobes and don't ever ask why have we not worn this yet. Even when the price tag is still attached because it only leads to rows. If you don't want a row then just don't ask. You see Stan in his wisdom once thought it might be a good idea to 'tidy' my wardrobe. Yes Tidy! The thought alone makes me gasp.

Any girl in her right mind knows this is no go area. I don't need my things tidying up because I know where everything is. Except when I'm going out and need that one particular item. You know that one that you were convinced you knew where it was, but couldn't find it to save your life. I came home one day to see Stan folding tops into tops pile, skirts into skirts pile and pants into pants pile. I nearly had a cardiac arrest, I really could feel my heart physically slow down. I think grabbed for the smelling salts it took me by such a shock. What right did he have to be even be looking in my wardrobe, let alone tidy it for god's sake.

I asked what on earth he thought he was doing. Only to be told 'I was looking for something and half your bloody wardrobe nearly fell out on me.' Really, 'exactly what was you looking for in *my* wardrobe a drill maybe, a lump hammer' I shout sarcastically. He rants 'Looking for the hairbrush and could I find one, could I hell as like.' That was until he found three brushes and two hairdryers at the bottom of my wardrobe. One of the hairdryers is broken but it does my hair nice, and haven't had time to fix it, in the mean time had to buy a new one. Well that makes sense to me but won't do me any good at this moment. 'Underneath the eight pairs of shoes' he adds. 'Only eight pairs I must be slacking' I say wryly. But he wasn't amused by it at all.

Now I know it needs a little tidying up, but I don't need to hear it do I. I feel a major row coming on but try to calm the situation, I have to bite my tongue because he is folding my clothes in rather an aggressive manner. Maybe now isn't a good time. 'How many God damn pairs of shoes do you need' he shouts and stressing the God damn. 'It's not as if you wear any of them anyway.' 'None of your bloody business, and anyway some things only go with certain outfits, *and* a couple of them are boots' I shout back like that's going to get me out of it. I stare at the bed, at piles and piles of stuff...clothes, shoes, belts, skirts... Then he holds up one blouse asking 'When did you ever wear this I've never even seen it before.' That's it he's pushed me too far now, I'm ready for world war III. I scream 'I can sort my own god damn wardrobe out and I don't need you interfering, like you should be in a woman's wardrobe anyway.'

He bawls 'In your wardrobe that's not a wardrobe, that's got to be storage for Oxfam or something, I'm sure even they don't have any where near that amount of clothes in their shops.' I try a little justification saying 'It isn't that I buy a lot, I just don't like throwing anything away. Why he asks me. Well, I don't know why, I suppose because I like throwing some stuff away and feeling cleansed for getting rid of rubbish. But this isn't rubbish its clothes. At some point in time it will become necessary, and I know as soon as I bin it I *will* need it. You know what it's like, that item that you *know* will come in handy. I know there may be a little too much here. But don't need to hear it from him. After all who likes to tell their partner yes your right. Yeh right, I think I'd rather choke.

Sometimes in a girls life we need space. And my space is my wardrobe or wardrobes. And that goes for my drawers and my side of the bed too. At no stage is it necessary for a guy to enter into these parts. On any occasion unless specifically requested and approved by us should they go into our space. This is not one of them occasions. It's like being invaded for god's sake, a guy pawing through your clothes thinking he's being helpful. But believe me, it is definitely not helpful. If we were married this would be grounds of divorce. He doesn't understand the concept of 'space' and 'no go area.' Oh no he insists he's being helpful. I wonder if he would think the same if I start messing with his fishing tackle, sort them out clean his rods, repacking his tackle box after he's spent the week rearranging. Would he thank me for being helpful. The only difference being I wouldn't be so bloody delicate with them. I take over ranting I'll sort the damn clothes out. I put my clothes back, all of them, and then take deep breaths to calm myself.

I refuse to talk about it and we both think we're right. We will probably row until the cows come home on this one. Stan takes the hint, realises he's not welcome, and stomps off downstairs. What a surprise, he puts his music on full blast. What is it today Screaming Jay Hawkins, Robert Gordon or Gene Vincent. Which ever it is the volume is on far too high. Which isn't difficult really, seeing his speakers are roughly a metre high each. You know when he flicks the boost button you feel floorboards start to vibrate.

It's a good job our neighbours are practically deaf on either side of us or they'd be complaining everyday. Once Ayeisha was down the street and could hear a humming and thumping sound. The nearer home she got the louder it went. When she was a few doors away she realised it was coming from our house. Her friend asked where's that racket coming from. All she could do was laugh in complete embarrassment. She asks is this what it comes to, parents embarrassing you. Which is bad enough if your out with them at least you have chance to hide. But when it's from your own house, then its bad as you have nowhere to hide.

Of course the office yet again think the latest outburst is hilarious. I've started to come into work for my sanity, how bad is that. Olive said if anybody ever went in her wardrobe she'd break their arms. This I could well believe because she has arms like a shot-putter anyway. I mean, what brave man would dare to enter the realms of her wardrobe. Jenifer can't believe what my problem is. And Trudy said she often asks her partner to sort her things out. Especially as they're getting bigger wardrobes anyway. She'd love him to get things organised for when she gets home. Am I hearing right, they don't mind! Jerry would be offended if her partner went through her things. What worries me more is I'm on a par with Jerry! Olive and Trudy spend their whole life organising and planning for next year, or even the year after. Lawrence lives for today, and Sebastian says enjoy today. Gertie on the other hand doesn't want to enjoy today or any day.

The thought of planning years ahead frightens me to death. Knowing what you're going to be doing next year or the year after is mind boggling to me. It's not like they're planning to do something wild that needs planning. Just general jobs around the house. Jenifer says she wants to put double glazing in her house this year. Next year she might do a patio and fencing and the year after they will add an extension onto the house, it will be a sunroom. I understand if you've moved and need to plan the work. I ask what if it didn't go to plan, what would happen if something came up that prevented their plans running smoothly.

The look she swung me was enough to kill, but I really didn't mean it sarcastic. I meant what would happen if they don't get what they want, would their world collapse. Are plans so set in stone. Would they not love something different to happen. Even if it meant not keeping to the schedule but be daring. Christ if I have to hear this mind boggling monotony any more I think I'll top myself. I don't want to know what I'm going to be doing in six months let alone next year. Especially if it's the same old crap I'm doing now. I feel like going round to their houses and sorting their wardrobes, mixing the colour coded items up, and separating the socks. Then maybe put crazy paving in horrendous lime green or ultra blue on their beautifully paved drives. Could you imagine their faces, I suppose this isn't a nice thing to think, but it does keep me sane just thinking I could do that.

Stan and I do have plans that involve travelling or doing something with our lives. It's not practical whilst Ayeisha is at school. Somehow teachers mind you taking your children out of school. They think if your child isn't in school and on a production line controlling their way of thinking then you're a failed parent. Worse still a parent that doesn't care. Our only option left other than the education authorities taking your child away from you is wait until your child finishes school.

Personally I don't see a problem with Ayeisha taking a year out and catching up when we return. The office finds this traumatic for me. Almost to the point of telling me I'm a bad mother taking her out of school. But she'll learn far more from travelling and seeing different cultures than reading about them. The snag is to afford this we'll have to work a little more, because we need money behind us to come back to. Or it would be traumatic starting again.

The girls think I've lost my marbles, but Lawrence and Sebastian agree with me. It worries me that I'm on their wave length. Making plans that aren't going to happen in the next six months surely depresses me. I'd rather be spontaneous and say lets get packing were going next month. But because it's in the future its like it's not tangible yet. I'm sure work thinks I'm talking crap just talking the talk. You know one of those people who make up stories to get attention. I think they're already calling me Pinocchio because I can't even take a few weeks off with Stan let alone a couple of months.

But with Stan there are no ground rules. Last month he wanted to look at properties in France. This month it's Scotland. At least France it's warm most of the time. But Scotland, for a holiday home maybe but to live up there its freezing seventy percent of the year. Does he honestly think I'm going to do the wellies and fishing thing....for the rest of my life, I don't think so. For a year or so I could maybe do that. So the best thing I can do is encourage him to think of warmer climates. Like Australia, Goa, Italy. After a while he thinks he's come up with the warmer climate idea. It looks promising, he's actually looked on the internet for properties but guess where he comes up, with Tasmania! I suppose I asked for that. If I leave him long enough no doubt he'll be looking elsewhere again.

For the past few days I'd been feeling unwell. At first I thought it was the stress of that damn dog. Or even Stan driving me mental, but it's a bug that's going round. It isn't like me to not go in work but I feel terrible. It's that bad I haven't even put my lipstick on or washed my hair so I must be ill. I've gone a horrid grey colour, and my mouth feels like its blistering with ulcers. My whole body felt like it had been punched all over. Which ever angle I lie at I feel bruised from head to toe. So I do what I do best, feel really sorry for myself. Especially as there is nobody at home to look after me.

Before Stan leaves for work he asks if I wanted a brew. I don't think my taste buds are working because it tastes like dirty water. I moan I feel like crap, everywhere hurts. And he's just going to leave me all alone to wither away. Hoping the sympathy tact might work, he comes over and kisses me gently on my forehead then tells me he thinks I need a bath. 'Thanks! But I need some sympathy I'm not well' I whine. Stan says sorry but he has to go to work, I'll be alright and he'll try to get home early. Then buggers off to work. I can't believe it, he's just left me. I'm not often sick, when I am I do expect some looking after. It even aches when I try lifting the remote control.

I look a right mess. No make-up on. Hair all over the place. And I've got the oldest grubbiest tracksuit on I can find. But it's my comfy tracksuit. And all I can do is doss about on the settee sleeping. After a few more days I did feel a little better. Enough to get up and make some soup trying to get something down me. The aching isn't quite as bad as the day before so I think I'll try to perk myself up a little and have a bath. Before I get chance to, there's a knock at the door. I know I'm not expecting anyone because we're usually at work. A thought flashes through my mind, it better not be work checking up on me. After all the time Olive and Gertie take between themselves I'll go ballistic. I'm getting myself all psyched up before I answer the door. But when I do open the door to my surprise there's a nurse standing there. I have a puzzled look on my face thinking is this a wind-up from Stan or work. After all work would pull a stunt like that.

She is a genuine nurse though, calling on a neighbour over the road but couldn't get in. She asks if I know anyone who has a key. I'm sure the neighbour next door to him has one. I think his mother might be at a day care centre, although I'm unsure where. Nobody is home next door to him she'd already tried there. Wondering why she needs access I asked if the bloke is in. But she thinks he's collapsed, he's sat on the floor and can't get up. She tried shouting for him to open the door but he's just sat looking at her. I tell her Stan is due home, he could try to break the door down. But she's reluctant to let him. I knew the guy hadn't been in good health. He never looked healthy and didn't go out often. He hid behind his curtains watching the world go by.

I rushed home to ring Stan but he's not answering. He won't be impressed either because he had never liked the guy. He was strange though, he was the sort of guy who couldn't look you in the eye. When I passed him in the street he'd hide his face away really obvious. Oh dear is that somebody else I've upset. I seem to be making a habit of this. Oddly, the guy did the same to Stan too. And Stan never hid the fact he disliked him intensely either. Always saying there was something strange him. The nurse asks if I know the family, but I only know them to say hello to. The man lived with his mother. His brothers called but didn't live their. I didn't tell the nurse we never liked the son. As she asked luckily Stan pulled up in his van.

Before he'd even climbed out of the van I'm asking him if he'd break the door down. But he gives me a look, well more of a stare. Fortunately the nurse was stood back and didn't notice. I ask him why shocked. Bluntly he says No. I explain the man is on the floor unable to get up. Stan said its best to call the police or knock for another neighbour. This really isn't like Stan at all. I've known him to help a person even if he didn't like them. The nurse was getting worried as he lived alone with his mother. His brothers called often but didn't live there.

I knew Stan was annoyed because I've seen him get out of his van in the pouring rain to help push a stranger's car, whilst everybody else passed by and watched. Another time an elderly neighbour's dog got run over. The poor thing was stuck under a car. It was Stan who went out to console the guy and helped get his dog free. Again, whilst everyone else stood by watching.

As much as he's moody he always helps so this was really out of character. I knew Stan was usually a good judge of character. So I let him be. But this outburst came as a shock.

Even though I never liked the bloke I still felt obliged to help. Still feeling like crap I grab for my phone. The nurse was eager to assist him. We walked towards the house checking if a key had been left under a plant pot. But we couldn't find one. We went round the back of the house in case a window was open. But they were all locked. When we get back to the front window I see him sat on the floor without any clothes on and still unable to move. All he has is a pot towel to save his dignity. The nurse can't wait for the family to come home any longer and needs to get inside.

I pass her my phone, she thinks its best to phone the authorities and get advice. Thankfully the police arrive within minutes taking all of two seconds to break the door down. She asks if I can help to get in touch with his family, if I could try to find the phone number for his brothers. I know he has two brothers and a son but I only know their first names. I'm not sure where they work. The police check for anybody else in the house and that he hasn't been hurt by anyone. But he seems to have fallen whilst getting ready.

He is awake but quite cold. He must have been sat there for a couple of hours. Thinking he might have caught hypothermia we phone for an ambulance. The nurse grabs a blanket to cover him up. The policeman rubs his arms and legs trying to get a little bit of circulation going. The poor guy is sat on the floor looking really embarrassed and helpless. I almost feel sorry for him. The nurse asks him if he's alright but doesn't answer. He just looks helpless and holds his hands out as if to say I don't know. I feel quite bad knowing that we never liked him, we could have misjudged him.

I notice an address book by the phone. I flick through looking for familiar names, hoping there would be emergency numbers there. I thought emergency numbers would be at the front of the phone book. I can't find the numbers at all when all of a sudden I turn the over page. But there in black and white is my name staring right back at me. I'm stunned, my name and my address! I try to figure out why he has these in his private address book when we've never exchanged more than a hello is worrying. As it is registering I notice not only does it say my name and address but the words Phone-On-A-Cheat underneath and a 0800 number with it.

Even more flabbergasted I read it again thinking I'm seeing things. It must be the tablets I've been taking, am I hallucinating. I stare at the book again trying to take it in. No I'm not hallucinating its definitely there. What I can't comprehend is why I'm seeing it, what is he trying to say. I glare at him sat there, next to nothing on looking helpless and pathetic. He has everyone fussing around him and I'm livid. The 0800 number written underneath is for people to phone anonymously. To report people they know are working and claiming benefits.

I've always worked from leaving school and even before I left school I worked my weekends. The only time I didn't was when Ayeisha was born and whilst I was at college. I've always been employed full time. And that horrible poor excuse of a man has the god damn cheek to put my name in his phone book for the purpose of reporting me. It's me that works to pay for him to be sat at home all day the b*****d. And I won't even be eligible for a pension when I retire, I have to provide my own private pension.

I feel tears start to prick my eyes but I'm still too angry to cry. I refuse to show him my tears. I glare at him, I'm almost ready to go storm over to him and slap his ugly face. I can feel my heart racing and the hairs on my are neck stood on end. My illness seems miles away now, I don't feel an ounce of pain. I look at him again sat there in his pathetic state hoping, praying he can read my mind. What puzzled me more was how on earth he knew how to spell my name. Nobody gets my name right, even people who know me and work with me still say how do you spell your name. Is it Nawas or Nowas but never do they put Nawaz. And there in black and white staring right back at me is Phone on a Cheat with my name and address with the phone number.

My blood is boiling. I turn round to look at him again and glare at him until he looks at me. I hold the phone book up to show I'm reading it. I want him to know I that I know whilst holding this precious phone book. I feel my throat tighten and want to scream at him. But still he sits there looking pathetic hoping for sympathy. Well he won't get any here. I tell the nurse I can't find the phone numbers and there is nothing more I can do. How they didn't see my face full of fury I'll never know. I head for the door. As I'm walking through the door I could hear the nurse thanking me for my help. Can you believe it, thanking me for the helping that thing. I walk out the door closing it behind me and storm down the path.

I thank God I'm out of that house. I felt I couldn't breathe for the last few moments. I stomp across the street to home and slam the door as I go through. 'What's wrong' Stan asks. 'What's wrong, that b*****d is what's wrong' I shriek. Stan looks at me shocked. He can't believe my outburst and asks whats the matter and has he said something to me. 'What's he said' I shout angrily 'It's what he didn't have the guts to say and what he's done is the matter.' Stan looks at me even more confused. I sit down with tears filling my eyes. 'What's the matter, what has he done' he asks again worried wondering what on earth it could be. Why had I gone over to help him. I can't believe it and explain he had my name and address in his phone book. He looks at me even more startled than before. I add 'With Phone on a Cheat and a free phone number next to it. Now Stan looks as shocked as I.

Still not getting it out of my system I rant on 'He's had my name in his phone book to report me. Me that's working to pay for him to be at home. Me that tried to help when he collapsed, even though I didn't like him, but I felt it was the right thing to do. Me that helped his mother when she forgot where she lived when suffering with dementia. Me that gave his wife lifts home from shopping when I saw her struggling whilst he was sat at home. I'm telling you now, you had better speak to his brothers when you see them. Because if I see them I'll give them a bloody mouth full.'

Stan frowns and says he'll speak to them. He sits beside me and puts his arms round me. He asks if I've calmed down yet and do I want a cup of tea. But I'm too busy feeling sorry for myself. Then I realise I didn't manage to clean myself up after all. I must look a right state, my hair all over the place, pasty looking skin and in tears. But he still gives me a hug. Now I feel even more sorry for myself than before if that's at all possible, still not quite believing what just happened. Why just my name and not Stan's name in the book. I can't understand how the hell did he know how to spell my name. Then it dawned on me my post must have been delivered to his house at some point or how else would he know. We were always having post delivered to the wrong address.

Stan said 'Leave it now Ang, I'll have a word, its not going to change anything is it.' Still feeling really sorry for myself I sulk drinking my tea when Stan starts laughing. 'What are you laughing at' I sniffle. 'You should have seen your face when you come home' he laughs. Somehow I don't find it funny. 'I know' he chuckles 'But your face, I told you I didn't want to help, let the police deal with it but oh no you have to be the good neighbour, and now look where its got you. Did I say I always had a feeling about that guy' we see the ambulance leave for the hospital. I wonder what he'll say when he sees me I think to myself. I bet he wouldn't have the guts to speak to my face, because that's to sort of thing he does behave like a coward behind closed doors. Just you wait I'll give you a few choice words when I do see you.

Later that week neighbours are talking about the collapse and that he's still in hospital. I didn't tell them I knew already. I really didn't want to go into it. Days later Stan came storming through the door looking quite shaken. Before I could speak he said 'don't you ever ask me to do your bleedin' dirty work again, you git' and stared at me. Bewildered about his outburst I ask what's wrong now. 'Go and have a word you said, oh yes ME to go and have a word' he rants. And? I ask eagerly. 'I've just seen his brother I asked could I have a word like you said. I told him his brother upset my Mrs, that she came over to help when he collapsed and tried to find your phone number. Instead she saw her name and address in the book saying Phone on a Cheat. She's really upset and wants to tell him what for.' And...I ask? 'He said he's really sorry and it won't happen again. So I told him you were going to see him but he tells me it definitely won't happen again because he died last night.' Aww my God I gasp looking at Stan's face.

I'm not sure if Stan looks more shocked or annoyed. 'What did you say to that. He fumes 'What could I say, there isn't much you can say to that besides cringe and wish the ground would open up thanks to you. I told him I'm sorry for hassling him and walked away.' Now I'm in hysterics all I can picture is the look on Stan's face being told, wanting the ground to open and wishing he could strangle me. Going through my mind is thank God it was Stan who confronted him and not me. I wouldn't have known what to say. And Gods knows what I'd have done if it was me. I'd probably have started laughing with nerves for sure.

Although I can't but wonder why I should have seen that phone book just before he died. Was it fate? Did God or whoever is up above want me to see it? I know next time I won't be so trusting. In fact I'm hoping their won't be a next time. Of course everyone at work yet again thinks it's hilarious. After all I shouldn't have been there I would normally have been in work. And the only few days I am off sick I'm dragged into something yet again. They have upped the stakes of the bet on me for no more incidents to happen before the years out. I have a thousand to one that nothing else will happen before the year is out. I think I may take to my bed for the remainder of the year and hope it's a better one next year.

~ Chapter Fifteen ~ **Back in the office**

Oh well a chapter closes and another one is sure to open. So many trauma's, so many laughs, but what is our destiny. I sometimes wonder why we are here. All going to work, every day, every week. The last week's events have made me think of it even more. I wonder why people leave their homes at eight in the morning. We all go to work like little ants. I imagine what we must look like from the sky, what would aliens think of us, that we are all busy little bees.

Is there something else out there? I question why we work nine to five, five days a week. Why not three or four days a week. Why are we conditioned to work forty hours a week minimum. Why must leave for work in the dark and return home in the dark. I'm sure God gave us daylight for a reason, and that it should be enjoyed. I dread to think I'll still be doing a nine to five job until I am sixty five. I don't mind working, just not five days a week. And a structured rigid job that dictates you sit at a desk for eight hours a day. People say change your job and choose work that isn't structured. But how do you get a job without the experience. Tell a company to take you on and by the way you bring no experience to the job you just don't want to work in a nine to five. Yes I'm sure they'll be beating down my door to join them. In fact I can hear their feet running up my path!

Unfortunately I have to work, well I don't have to, I suppose I choose to. I could work part time and take a pay cut or stay at home, let Stan can support us. But then reality sinks in. If I want to treat Bash I'd have to ask for money. Even worse every time I needed a lipstick I'd have to ask Stan for money. Can you imagine after the wardrobe scenario I then ask for money to buy lipstick or clothes... Heaven Forbid. Yes I can see him now being in his element monitoring what I bought, then checking my wardrobe to see if I really do need it. It would make his day telling me I don't need it.

The thought of depending on somebody totally, for everything, it sends a shiver down my spine. I think it would actually feed

Stan like a drug, he'd be on cloud nine telling me 'Is it a want or is it a need.' Not to mention the 'What have I done with my day, did the washing get done.. you haven't done much cleaning today' Oh no, I definitely need to work if only for my sanity. Unless Stan gave me a wage to stay at home, no questions asked, no moans allowed. But somehow I don't see that happening.

Back in work I look up to see Olive having her weekly I don't feel well days. Oh what a surprise its Thursday and this is for our benefit, for us to see she won't be in tomorrow. Another long weekend for her. Gertie is vying for the attention too. God forbid we give Olive attention and not her. Gertie is going for the 'Grunt' today. In other words most of us can say good morning but she offers a grunt. Even if you ask a question you get is a grunt. Now the grunt is interpreted in many ways… 1. it is a sign that I don't feel well so ask me why 2. It's a sign that I'm in a mood 3. It's a sign that I have too much work to do 4. It is a sign that its all of the above. And today is not one of them days where I feel like pandering to her attention. I keep my head down and work through the files my desk. Being off sick I have a lovely backlog of work to get through. I really don't feel in a mood for either of them today.

I try to think of nice things to keep me going throughout the day. Like Australia, Goa, France or Italy. What would it take to up sticks and go. I day dream off into my own world. Just as I'm deciding whether to go with or without the swimming pool and if it will have three or four bedrooms, I hear a voice in the background.. Ang…Ang. Then I realise its Tony from the warehouse. How dare he interrupt my daydreaming, just when it was getting interesting. What? I reply flustered, hearing his voice going louder and louder and becoming rather irritating.

Tony needs new paperwork because the stock I've allocated isn't in the warehouse. I ask the warehouse to check again, but still they can't find it. To make matters worse its for an urgent airfreight that needs to go out today. Tony asks me to stop what I'm doing, of which I was in the middle of some important daydreaming, and redo the paperwork. Re-work I can do without. I'm already playing catch up without having to do catch up twice.

I really don't have time for this. I've got orders to process, paperwork to print and faxes to send. Ang he whines, I look up and his face is pleading as if to say Now. 'And I need to use the stock for another order so if you could do it asap' he adds. I suppose so I sulk, knowing he does do me plenty of favours.

'You'll have to get me a' but just I'm saying it he puts a drink of hot chocolate on my desk. I have to stop what I'm doing, go into the order, de-allocate stock, re-allocate stock and print all the paperwork again. Three bloody times. Once for my copy, once for the customer copy and once for them to go with the goods. People had better leave me alone today or I'm not getting my work caught up. I'm still not feeling 100% but its back to rushing through paperwork and no time for a break.

There is one consolation there's no time to watch those two wallowing in self pity. Gertie announces she needs to go home, she's not well poor thing. Obviously needing to outdo Olive as last time Olive beat her to it going home first. This is ridiculous when I am off sick I am ill. These two feel like throwing a sickie when ever their mood warrants one. To add insult to injury, Gertie's been seen calling at the supermarket on her way home. This is five minutes after claiming she was dying. We wouldn't mind if it was for necessities, or a ready cooked meal. Because nobody likes cooking when not feeling well. Oh no, her basket was full of crisps, chocolate cake and biscuits. Essentials obviously. You can appreciate how this winds everybody up. Unfortunately, we have to pull together when they're on a sickie and do their work.

The next phone call is a customer of Gertie's demanding an immediate answer. And it's my lucky day to cover her job, on top of the catch up with the re-work and new orders piling in. Yes I'm in a lovely mood. Okay, I still feel like I'm running on two cylinders and maybe feeling just a little sorry for myself over the Phone on a Cheat thing. All I have to think about is the look on Stan's face when talking to the brother, which is horrid I know but seems to put a smile back on my face. Not to be mean I assure you, just still thanking God it wasn't me. Again I stop what I'm doing to find where Gertie's order is up to. Find where the driver is, bearing in mind it's a French driver and he'll probably have his phone switched off. And they could be at lunch being ahead of us, time wise that is. Yes its one of those days I can do without. I see my in try of files getting higher and higher. I can't see my desk for paperwork and have no idea how I'll catch up. And yes the French driver has his phone switched off and Gertie's customer is getting irate.

I start to feel down, its times like this I feel I could turn to drink. It's a good job I don't like getting drunk, or every day at work would be enough to tip me over the edge. Then Tony appears looking rather worried. Sheepishly he asks the others if I'm okay. They tell him today is not a good day to hassle Ang, unless it's urgent I'd leave it till tomorrow if I was you. It is urgent he stresses. Trudy tells him 'the blockades are going up.' Meaning it's our office joke of a row is about to erupt and you want to keep out of it.

The blockade idea came in to play when French lorry drivers put blockades up at the ports, for any reason they see fit. Unusual I know. News reports showed irate drivers on either side ranting about the other. We feel it represents our office on many occasions. If any of us are in a fowl mood, or one of us is ready to rant, we shout the blockades are going up. I use the phrase to say keep me out of the row. Everyone wonders what he's about to ask when he disappears from the office. I didn't notice why because my phone rang, again. I'm too busy trying to pacify Gertie's customer. Smiling through gritted teeth saying of course we are doing everything, immediately, now, yesterday, then apologise saying I'll have to put her on hold I have another call coming through and stress it could be the driver.

Whilst on hold I pretend to yawn saying 'Yeh right, driver my arse.' The driver is unlikely to be on the phone. You've more chance of getting through to Elvis than getting hold of the driver. He's more likely to be on his two hour lunch break. And this customer will be on hold the whole time. If the customer had been pleasant but worried, then I would have had genuine sympathy, but she is not. So I will be 'officially helpful with a smile on my face, saying yes I'm here to help you, missing you already' but can't really be bothered. Then Tony appears in front of me smiling. If he's smiling he must need something, and that something must be from me. Not today I really don't need this. As he approaches I shout to him I'm too busy, trying to keep France quiet, trying to get my orders on the system, trying to take phone calls, and shove a brush up my backside at the same time.

Tony looks at me with an anxious smile. He leans over my desk places a bar of chocolate down. Normally I'd be thanking him but today I'm worried. He's doing this because he needs me to do something that he knows will make me angry. 'Ang sorry to hassle but you know that paperwork you did? I ask him if he means the first amended lot or the second. 'The second' he replies. 'What about the paperwork' I snap 'and don't tell me is wrong because I've just done what you asked me to, because the lads couldn't find the bloody stock, if I remember rightly.'

He continues standing there with the worried look, then puts a coffee on my desk. Normally I'd milk this for some more bars of chocolate but I'm really not having the best of days. 'For Gods sake, what d'you need now' I ask. The others start laughing in unison, laughing at my horrendous day, laughing at me about to have a nervous break down. 'Well it's the stock that you've allocated' he moans. 'What problem exactly you can't find this stock either' I ask sarcastically. 'Well that's the problem' he says holding his papers in front of his face. One to hide his laughter and two to stop me throwing something at him. 'Tony you've got to be joking, you can't find the stock again.' He moans that it was right the first time but couldn't find the stock. The second time it was wrong because the lads realised this stock was at the back of the warehouse, it would take them a few hours to move the front stock out of the way. In between time the original stock has been found and loaded on to a truck for another order, so it needs to be changed again.

He shoves papers in front of me telling me which stock to allocate. That needs to be done now because my driver is here. I feel like screaming. Then the phone rings, what a surprise it's the French customer again. I think I'm ready to kill someone. The order has to have labels attaching to each item but no labels are in the cupboard. Everyone turns their heads away when asked where they are. 'Please tell me you didn't use the last ones, I ordered that stock before I went off sick.' Again everyone chooses to ignore me.

Tony holds his papers up in front of his face trying not to laugh. You've got to be joking they can't have all gone. Sebastian explains they delivered the wrong ones. What, nobody could be bothered to phone up and ask them for the correct ones to be sent, bloody great! What am I expected to do pritt stick them on or what I shout sarcastically. I'm now feeling even more depressed than before and munch on chocolate, then gulp my coffee hoping the caffeine will do me good.

I start printing my paperwork. No I'll rephrase that. I try printing my paperwork, only the computer stops working. And for a moment I think someone has pulled the wires out of my keyboard. But nobody has been near my computer except Tony. He is one for practical jokes but no even he wouldn't dare with the mood I'm in. We try messing with it, pulling at wires, but nothing happens. I phone the IT department up but no one can help for the next hour at least. I stress it's an emergency but they still can't come for half an hour. I ring Evan begging it's an emergency, we have drivers waiting and need to get the stock out, pleeaase.. Alright he sighs, I'll come up anything to keep you quiet. Great he's willing to help. He's only supposed to cover for IT when their department are out it isn't his proper job. He's one of those gadget guys forever messing around with computers and always buying the latest gadgets. I should have rang him first.

Evan wanders into the office saying it's all my fault. But I haven't done anything except look at it, exactly he grins. Now is not the time for frivolities it's really important. I ask him to hurry. He has a mess around with the computer but its not having any of it. When was the last time you cleaned this thing anyway? He asks wiping his finger across the computer. Does it matter when I last cleaned it, I need it to work not look pretty. Jenifer laughs saying that's what us girls are for. It was rather funny but he didn't think so. Just look at that keyboard you dirty thing he shouts at me. I do use a telephone wipe on my keyboard so it can't be that dirty.

But looking down taking a peek through the keys it does look pretty shabby. In fact it looks down right minging. I wouldn't be surprised if this thing has stuff growing down there he mocks at me staring at the keyboard. Just to embarrass me he unplugs the keyboard and giving it a good shake. Oh dear he says as crumbs drop out. Then he jiggles the keyboard around only for more for crumbs and bits to drop out. 'I can't believe the crap in there' he shouts trying to embarrass me further. He picks at the crumbs of shortbread and crisps and holds bits of the crap on the end of his pen. Look at this he says waving it in the air. The proceeds to take it around the office showing everyone.

We all squirm ewww! If you had a piece of paper down on the carpet you'd have thought he was emptying a bin with the crap there. I'm too embarrassed to take a closer look, and choose instead to cringe behind my computer. We all burst out laughing when Evan starts to dance shaking the keyboard about. The laugher gets louder when he swings the keyboard around his head with the lead. He'll get sacked if his boss catches him doing this with company property which makes all of us laugh even more.

Next he drops the keyboard on to the floor starts tapping it with his foot shouting 'that's the way to do it.' We're all in hysterics, because he's camping it up all the time. We can't help but get louder and louder. Then starts stamping on the thing just as another manager opens the door. Probably because the noise can be heard at the other end of the building. We are all rolling about with laughter. Tears roll down my face and I'm laughing so much my stomach hurts. Who's keyboard is that? Asks the manager. They all point at me. Bloody typical. I can't say anything for laughing, the poor guy goes back out closing the door behind him.

I feel much better now Evan has cheered me up. Jerry wanders through and she's not amused. She must have spoken to the manager on route. She can be bossy when she wants to be, and doesn't like to upset management. Oh well, who asked her to join in the party anyway. You could say we are known as the loudest office. I suppose you wouldn't get away with this racket at other companies. With us as long as the job gets finished then its okay.

Our boss is usually fine so long as we don't take it too far. I suppose we did go a little too far this afternoon. But in our defence we needed a hell of a pick me up. Okay, I needed a hell of a pick me up.

We decide to put France on our 'special customer pain in arse' list. After all they do excel themselves today. Just when I think it's going to settle down, the phone rings. What a surprise it's Gerties customer, again. I've already advised the driver will be with them by 4.00pm, of which they say it is 4.00 there. Damn, I forgot the time difference. I put my forehead on my desk and start to bang it. What can I do. Can I physically grab the driver, go pick up his truck and deliver them myself. If he gets stuck in traffic then what can I do. This earache should be given to Gertie not me. But oh no she'll be sat at home with her feet up watching Richard & Judy. I could pacify them, or even better pretend they've got through to an answer phone saying the office is now closed. Although it's tempting it's not worth losing my job over.

As we are in stupidly giddy moods we might as well finish off the day as we started. We say we'll hold our pretend draw for the car tomorrow with the incentive to be in work to win it. We still find this hysterical, I mean come on, our lot in the running to win a car. Can you imagine Gertie, Olive and Larry having to work a full week. A whole week without moaning, a week without migraines. Without a 'need' to go early because the childminder is on half day. The cat got out, the budgie escaped, the tap was left on, we've got mice. Olive did try to go home with a splinter once even though we had a needle to pick it out. It was so small you couldn't see it with the human eye. Olive claimed she was scared of needles. We wouldn't mind but the needle was smaller that the splinter. Jenifer offered to pull it out for her, with gritted teeth I might add. And we had to keep Jenifer away from Olive as she wanted to use a blunt knife from the canteen on Olive's finger.

The next day we all discuss what model car we shall have. More to the point which of us gets the car. Sebastian was standing by the side of me measuring labels he needed when Gertie walks down the office. She declares she should get the car for being such a good worker. Hello have I missed something here. Yes all that time she buggered off home must have been an hallucination. Silly me, she must have been sat there the whole time. Sebastian wants to hit her over the head with his ruler. We're all stunned at her cheek. Trudy's annoyed about dragging herself into work whilst ill and ready to hit her as Gertie claims she wants a people carrier for her and the kids. Sebastian laughs 'she won't need room for the husband then.' Then adds 'she should have a black one to match her moods.' Meow, put them claws back. We have to laugh because he was on top form today.

Larry is laid back as ever saying he'd be grateful just to be put into the draw. Maybe he'd get the old style Mini if he could. Shouldn't he be thinking on the same lines as Gertie, and go for the people carrier. After all if the 'relationship' thing works out he'll be needing the extra space in the car. Antonio decides his will be a Ferrari, nothing less will do. Trust him. Trudy wants a Vaultswaggon, it has to be sturdy. I don't know I'm thinking of a little convertible for myself, in metallic blue. Yes I can picture myself with roof down on a sunny day, except its crap for the hair, unless I drive at two miles an hour. I'm already picturing what I will look like in it when Olive decides the car is hers. Shouldn't she be thinking more on the lines of 'Am I eligible to be in the draw.' Next thing you know she'll be thinking should she get a house to park the car in.

Sebastian wants a red Subaru with tinted windows. Isn't that usually a boy racer come part time drug dealer's car? He thinks it will be a red hot pulling power passion car. Jen wants a BMW. Lawrence wants any car that's an injection. And he reminds me I can have the steering wheel to help me practice missing the cats in the road, bloody git. Trudy says she'd like a Mitsubishi shogun, something with a bit of umph to it. Jerry wants a big black Mercedes, we ask if it has to have a big back seat. She wasn't amused. Just when were starting to have some fun. We are warned to be on our best behaviour because visitors are on site. Which is a subtle hint to get rid of any filing or crap from off our desks. If we don't have time to file it, we pile it neatly onto a tray hiding the crap. That way it always looks like ongoing work. We'll have to be quiet or at least act like professionals.

Gertie says she's over her illness today. What a surprise it's all in a miraculous one day recovery. Or more like fifteen hour recovery because she didn't leave until mid morning yesterday. Today Olive is in a good mood for some strange reason. I must admit when she is in a good mood she can be really funny. Unfortunately with Olive its chalk and cheese days. It's like she's a different person each day, each of her personalities do not mix.

Some days you feel you've walked into a party atmosphere other days into hell. When she's on a good day you can have such a good laugh with her, her jokes were so humorous. But when the bad mood sets in she'll be itching to start an argument or get you into trouble. I could never work out if it was for attention to make herself look better, or just out of pure malice. Either way she will do it with venom. Today it backfired ever so sweetly.

Olive announced we've had complaints from other offices about the racket we made yesterday. We were only larking about, I mean god forbid we enjoy ourselves at work. Strangely, when we asked who complained she wouldn't say. She claimed they'd confided in her yet asked her not to say anything. This sounded ridiculous because all departments know how loud we are. But they also know how hard we do work and the extra time we put into our job. Well most of us anyway. We were furious. Trudy demands to know who said it but she still won't say who. Just as it's about to kick off the door opens. We are supposed to be looking busy at our desks. Instead we look like we're all on a coffee break as Antonio walks through the door with his customer.

Luckily, Trudy has some pieces of paper in her hand. She instinctively reads from the paper, pretending she's half way through a pep talk about the computer system. Phew, that quick thinking got us out of a hole. Looking rather flustered and knowing something is wrong Antonio introduces Pierre. He explains to Pierre who's who and who does what and explaining a little background of us all. Pierre's a small guy, greying a little and very polite. I cover Pierre's orders when Antonio is out of the office. Antonio takes Pierre to see our boss for an update on his orders, and talks over any problems he may have.

As Pierre was leaving he asked who will be taking care of his account whilst Antonio is on vacation. Antonio points over to me saying Angie will look after your account. At which point the little guy looks at me, smiles and stands there giving a big over the top wave at the door. As Antonio and Pierre walk out the door we all burst out laughing. It was so obvious he didn't even look at anyone else to say goodbye. He was only interested in who was going to take care of his business. We give them five minutes to get out of hearing distance before Jenifer shouts at Olive 'Right who's been complaining.' Olive repeated they've asked me not to mention it anything. We all take deep interest and a few have crowded around wanting some entertainment.

Jerry showing no mercy won't let it drop. Getting annoyed she shouts 'Well you have mentioned it now so you can tell us who complained.' Olive going bright red gets very flustered. Jerry insists on getting it out of her, eventually she says it was Ernie. But begs her not to say anything to him. Ernie works a few offices away I wouldn't like to be in his shoes right now. But it's so unlike him, if he thought we made too much noise he would pop his head through the door and ask us to keep it a bit quieter. Jerry storms out of the door with Jenifer and Trudy in tow. Then everyone else follows. We wouldn't miss this action for all the tea in China but we can't all pile into his office so a few of us linger behind. Jerry storms into Ernie's office, half knocking half pushing her way in. When Jerry is on one she is certainly on one. It's just a shame Ernie is in her way. The mood Jerry is in she is ready to spill blood. The rest of us hover around outside his door.

Taking one look at Jerry's face the poor guy looked ready to jump through the nearest window. Jenifer jumps in first abruptly asking if he complained about the noise yesterday saying his it was a racket. His face looks quite shocked at the outburst. 'No' he replies slightly embarrassed by it all 'although I did walk past your office and heard the noise, I commented that it sounded like you were having a party in there, but not in a complaining way just commenting. To let Ernie know where it came from Jenifer turns round to Olive shouting 'Where did you get that he complained Olive.' Olive's face was burning wishing the ground would swallow her up. Looking so embarrassed she must have misheard him. Jerry triumphantly tells her 'Yes, you certainly did get it wrong this time, didn't you.' Jerry apologises for the misunderstanding.

Returning to the office Jenny repeated he didn't complain at all did he, it was just a misunderstanding. Olive didn't take kindly to being show up for being a liar. She retreated into one of her moods for about three weeks, refusing to speak to any of us. She has this fantastic knack of making you feel like it was all your fault, like we told her to lie and be malicious. It made our day to let her know we knew of her blatant lying. There really was no denying her ability to stir things up, and here it was for us all to see. Oh well another incident over. Lets see what tomorrow brings, hoping things might settle down.

Later that day I arrive home to hear a right racket. It seemed to be coming from our house. I can hear it over the music in my car. It's a loud barking noise that seems to echo down the street. The decibels seemed to go higher the closer I get to my gate. As I enter my garden I can see Bonnie in the window, literally. She's stood lengthways across the windowsill acting like a peacock showing off her feathers. I'm cringing with embarrassment praying that the neighbours haven't noticed, hoping they are working, shopping anything but witnessing her latest performance. When I left this morning there was a vase in the window, what the hell has she done with it.

I open the front door quickly and bellow at the top of my voice for her get down. She jumps straight from the windowsill bounces onto the chair beneath then onto the floor. She stands in front of me wagging her tail, looking all proud of herself. But when you think of 60lbs of dog on stood on all fours in your window, she hardly looks like a delicate Chihuahua. Oh no, my lovely vase is smashed to pieces on the floor. Depressed I look at my armchair to see chunks of it missing. She's only gone and chewed through the wood edging all around the top. Using it like it was a damn bone. The dog's home is coming decidedly closer by the minute. I can't find the energy to phone Stan. I dread to think what next week may bring.

I'm beginning to wonder if all this happening around me is my fault. Was I a bad person in a previous life? They do say it comes back to haunt you. Maybe I was bad as a child and its my karma? I know events can affect from when you're a child, we can carry this baggage into adulthood. I vividly remember a teacher ripping up my art work whilst at school. Our teacher hadn't arrived for the lesson, I thought I might as well finish my art work rather until the teacher arrived. The teacher obviously thought different and walked straight into the room, saw me with my head down and made a beeline for me. Walked straight by my desk picked up my work and tore it up in front of the class. Then shouted 'you don't do that in my lesson.' Because the teacher was in an arsy mood felt it appropriate to humiliate me. That's what good teachers do don't' they. I suppose it was too big a thing for the teacher to say put that away.

I was speaking to a friend of mine about when you're young and events that humiliate you stay with you for life, even being traumered by it. She remembered when she was around eight or nine years old her family was quite poor bringing their children up on a low wage. She was in trouble with her teacher by forgetting her dinner. The teacher dragged her off to the headmistress, who asked her what she had for tea the night before. Feeling really chuffed with herself because they'd had meat the night before, she said meat and potatoes. But the teacher turned to the headmistress and said 'See no vegetables' and looked down her nose at my friend. She said to this day she can still remember and feel the embarrassment felt on that day. And how awful it was that she was made to feel ashamed. Even for things out of her control, and as a child she had no means of understanding why they thought the way they did.

Even when I complained about my teacher I wasn't really believed. I don't know why, I wasn't lying. Maybe they thought I was. Obviously in those days the teachers word was taken for granted against a pupils. It's funny how things turn out really because my teacher left school shortly after. Apparently wanting to set up a computer centre and wanted to borrow computer equipment from school. They very kindly offered some computers but needed them back obviously. The school never did get their computer equipment back and the teacher had left the country soon after. Oh dear, isn't that stealing. Maybe the school should have said borrowed means it is to be returned. I wonder if those teachers I complained to remember our incident, well they've seen straight through this one now.

Another time I remember being traumered in my youth was when I heard my brother and my cousin in my Mum's bedroom. Being nosey I went in to see what they were doing. My brother laughed and pointed to above her bed and betted me I couldn't touch the ceiling. Dangling from the ceiling I could see a wire hanging down. It had no light attached just the bare wire. Of course I can I told him climbing onto the bed. I tried to reach it but it was too high. They walked towards the door and stood by the light switch laughing. As I jumped up and down on the bed trying to reach the wire my brother switched the light on. This time I jumped higher and managed to flick the flex with my fingers but it hurt.

They were in hysterics laughing at me saying it hurt because I didn't do it properly and try again. So like an idiot I jumped up again. This time I felt a shock run right through my fingers and screamed out loud. My Mum came running in and scolded him for being naughty, and we were both in trouble for messing. This now reminds of Harry Enfield and the Lulu did it scenario. It's no wonder I'm not normal with a childhood like mine.

~ Chapter Sixteen ~ **Wishful Thinking & Gibraltar**

For a while now we've tried desperately to book our holiday. You know the one, three lovely weeks now reduced to a week. And each time, being cancelled at short notice by the delightful Stan. Because schools now stop you from taking your children out of school during term time and employers won't allow more than one person to be off at the same time. We usually ended fighting for the same days off during school holidays. And you can guarantee ninety nine times out of a hundred Stan will have increased his work load by fifty percent. But you will always find one smart arse that doesn't have children but still insists on wanting the school holidays. Even though the weeks prior to the holidays are cheaper than school holidays. They're usually the not so diplomatic ones that whine about not having the right to take time off during school holidays, some even spout why should they be penalised for not having children. Oh the delights of office politics and having to endure such pleasant colleagues.

I think this is Olive's way of getting back at us. She needs to fuel more arguments to make herself feel satisfied. Antonio, in his superb Italian accent says these are selfish people. Why do they have to be nasty. Being Italian and brought up in firm family orientated culture he is horrified at the outbursts. He doesn't understand that they are just sad lonely people who base their whole life around themselves. Sometimes it's pure spite and other times they don't mean anything by it. They have nothing better to do with their lives. Nobody else to consider, no partner or children or parents to worry about, just themselves.

Although at times I do wonder what goes on in minds to feel the need to kick up such a fuss. I can only put it down to being the only way to get attention, that way they feel important to the office, that and the delight of being spiteful. So to the delight of some when it comes to booking holidays you can guarantee a screaming match. I don't really have a leg to stand on by the swapping and changing I've been doing lately. This would only add fuel to the argument. At first when the department was smaller we only had a few to consider. We'd try to work it out between ourselves accommodating each other when ever we could. But as the department grew so did the arguments. You wouldn't want to be in the middle of these arguments they often got intense. Sometimes the 'I've been here longer than you' was pulled. At others it was first come first serve.

You'd get the odd one saying 'I always take those weeks, when asked why 'just because.' If it was to take time off with others in their family you would understand. It would drive you crazy when you know it's just to throw a spanner in the works. Sometimes it's a case of he who shouts loudest gets their way. But who wins in the end, yes they might get their own way but they are shown to be the selfish people that they are. So who did win really. On occasions they would end up backing down through sheer humiliation, which was not to my delight of course.

It got so bad at times we'd end up drawing short straws. You see for a manger to take sides in this would mark their future. They would be seen taking sides with who they've known the longest. Or taking sides with the newest recruits trying to keep them sweet. It was always false economy because in a month or two there would be another favourite, usually it would be those who are the most useful at anyone time.

Yet managers never thought it like that, they thought it more of I'm allowing you to be part of the team. When in fact they had marked not only their own card but the team member too. That's the way it is, there will always be an issue, one that changes daily and one will always end up in tears. It takes a very strong person and a very good manager to manage people. Of all the places and departments that I have worked in over the years I've have seen very few good managers. Some can be good sometimes but not consistent.

Others it would be consistently bad but others getting them out of the mire. Some like have favourites, others are only interested in getting the job done. Very few are able to get the job done and keep a department happy. You can imagine how well I go down in the office, planning holidays trying to book them, alter my days, changing the weeks, cancelling them within weeks before going. They think I'm a bloody lunatic because Stan messes us around so much then wants to go tomorrow, now, yesterday. They look at me like 'what planet are you on Ang.'

Sane people manage to book a holiday, go on holiday and come back from holiday all to plan. Not me. Oh no, we have to make ourselves look like we've just arrived on planet earth. Asking for two days with yesterday and next Thursday thrown in please. I try explaining it's due to Stan's job, never knowing what job he'll be working on or how long it will take. I know only too well in the building game nothing goes to plan and that's without the weather controlling the job too. Look how it affects us daily, do we take a brolly or sandals out with us, and just in case it snows boots, only for a heat wave to hit by lunchtime. Because living in Manchester we have at least four seasons in a day.

You can guarantee that when we finally get near to our holiday Stan would say he's not happy leaving a job half done. Especially if it's plastering then we are in trouble. I've learnt that having to rely on other builders becomes a joke. I'd ask when are the plasterers working, I'm not unreasonable I would try to put our holiday back a few days if it helps. But he couldn't possibly know a simple thing like that and rants 'I can't go altering days off and not know whether they'll turn up.' The ones that do turn up usually do a crap job. Then Stan has to do the job again.

Once Stan booked a plasterer to do a job for him. Just to let us take a few days off together. Not even to go anywhere, we just wanted to spend time together go shopping and relax. The plasterer did a really bad job. Stan went to check on the job and ended up working through the night. He ripped all the plaster off the walls and put new plaster up himself. When the plasterer turned up the next day, he said 'Nice job' to Stan and actually looked proud of his work. Stan enlightened him in the calmest manner he could summon 'This isn't your work, yours was shyte, I've had to redo the lot myself. My dog could have done better blindfolded.' The poor guy thought it looked better the next day. But these guys turn up bold as brass claiming to be professionals and expect to be paid for it. You can't believe people do half a job or a crap job and still expect to be paid for it.

Try explaining that to colleagues, you end up feeling like you moan all the time. If their partners have a regular job then they can fit around each other without any problems. They don't understand that this is real that it affects our life. If my schedule doesn't fit in with his, before you know it a whole year's past by, whilst we are busy doing nothing. Stan and I discuss going long haul again. We want a proper holiday this time. In fact we'd like six weeks to go travelling. I know damn well work won't allow this. Stan and I of course row about it. When he has spare time he expects me to drop everything and go now.

He doesn't understand I could have ten people to fit around. And they have to fit around their own families. He also disregards having fifty two weeks a year to choose from. It so frustrating at times, and I'm made to look the idiot. The last time I asked for more than two weeks off my manager almost fell through the floor. The rest of the department thought I'd gone mad too. I didn't think this odd at all. In fact I wish I had asked for six weeks now. They might have compromised with three weeks straight away. They look at me like I'm halting a production line or I've taken their wages off them. You feel like your one of the ants rebelling, and they say lets make the ant see sense.

You'd have thought I'd asked them for a kidney by their reactions. It times like this I want to scream. Why are we conditioned to having one week per holiday, if you're a really good girl we'll give you two. But dare ask for more than three weeks and the girls gone mad. Let's have her sectioned. I pray for the day the whole office rebels demanding a month at a time. If everybody demanded it then we'd all get it otherwise there wouldn't be any workforce.

Even Ayeisha is accustomed to long holidays, with others in the family going for a few months at a time. At least she won't grow up blinkered. When I approach the subject of moving to warmer climates with Stan, all I ask is visit the places first before going just to look for a property. Even Ayeisha gets excited when we talk of moving abroad. We are desperate to do something exciting before she gets too old, wanting to do her own thing. The problem is leaving family behind. But family and friends can always come and stay for holidays. Stan will probably hide away on fishing trips until they're gone anyway.

As always the right time is never right. Something's always in the way. Neither of us can agree for long enough anyway. Stan prefers a house in the middle of nowhere. I don't mind being in the countryside but not isolated. I'd like to be near the sea or a stream, Stan prefers woodland. Even when we discuss buying property for a business and pleasure, neither of us can agree what business or where. I want to be in reaching distance of family and friends. He wants a hideaway in Papa New Guinea, and with his family around. I do like his family, but I wouldn't want to live with any, nor he mine come to think of it. I'd want a retreat just for us, and our families could stay.

Stan feels I have an unusual family. A family who love the pub, except me. A family who are loud, except me. A family who like to be centre of attention, except me. So most of our time is spent laughing at our family quirks. He thinks I'm born to the wrong family for sure because I am so unlike them in many ways. He thinks I'm a throw back from generations before. I suppose we are a typical family. A large family sprawled about that gets to meet at birthdays, weddings and occasionally Christmas, and then there are those you never see or hear from.

Whilst in work I dream of my ideal. Being away doing my own thing and able to come back every couple of months to see family. But how practical is that. And at what cost. I dream which business will earn a fantastic income, with lots of time off and be fun. Ploughing through my workload I drifting off as you do... It would have to be somewhere nice and hot but not too hot. Where you wake in the morning with sunshine streaming through your windows. With a little balcony or terrace where you can hear the birds in the morning. Yes it's got to have that fantastic holiday feeling you wake up to. Somewhere I'd sit and read.

Somewhere Bash could have friends over too. I suppose we'll need a pool and maybe a tennis court that overlooks a rambling garden. Bash wants it to have a secret garden because she loves the film. With lots of space and maybe a pond. A beach nearby would be nice too. I'd be able to reinvent myself, spend my days painting or writing. Not that I can paint or write for toffee. Although I did do a picture of a horse and a couple of poems at school, does that count? So far I've calculated the house at around 1.3 million pounds, only around 1.25 million to go. That reminds me must remember to put all my wage on to the next lottery rollover.

I suppose we could get Ayeisha a computer for her schooling that way she won't fall behind. I joke there's always boarding school at a push. We don't want her missing out on activities do we so Stan will have to start swimming, cycling and athletics clubs for all the local kids. And we don't want to take her away from friends so we'll just have to introduce her to the local wildlife to occupy her time. She can make friends with the foxes, hedgehogs and rabbits because it didn't do Beatrix Potter any harm did it.

Its alright laughing but you can't always choose your neighbours you don't know what you'll end up with. With my luck who the hell will I end up with next door. Then there's our families to consider, they'd never forgive us for moving away. Its emotional blackmail if we don't see them for a week or two already. I know how much I'd enjoy spending time with family in a holiday environment, pottering about my new 1.3 million pad. Then everyone could be happy. Here I go again talking the talk not actually doing it. I best get Stan to get his finger out then.

Getting back to our genuine holiday, Stan finally agreed to next week off. Thankfully work is okay about it, and before he has time to change his mind yet again, we book a trip to Gibraltar. Now I know I'm actually going I go into giddy mode. We're actually going on a plane to somewhere nice and sunny. We don't care if its not hot. Warm and sunny will make us happy. Work are already taking bets on if it really happens, the odds are looking reasonable, the cheeky buggers.

We looked on the internet for places to go when Gibraltar came up. Neither of us had thought of Gibraltar before. We check what to expect when we get there. It looks quite interesting. In the centre there's a huge square where people congregate and have lunch. It does look charming with historical places to visit and local wildlife to see. I do mean the apes and not the locals. We are staying at the Rock of Gibraltar Hotel. It's a large white hotel built into the top of the rock face itself. It looks fantastic.

I check what the weather will be like and it's looking good. We should have a great time, I can't wait. I have a week to pack, I best be careful not to pack too much. Or Stan will go ballistic if I take everything but the kitchen sink. Best to do it on the last minute hoping he won't notice. I always love the morning going away, checking bags are packed and everything is ready. That's when I'm really into holiday mode. I do a quick checklist for the essentials… tickets, money, lipstick and the oh so lovely credit card, sandals, make-up bag, toothbrush of which Stan still shudders at. And not forgetting the passports at least anything else forgotten can always be bought there.

Stan takes Bonnie to the kennels whilst I finish off cramming things into bags. Just as I thought everything was ready to go, Bash stands in front of me holding two more bags of her own. And this is going light. How she got this bad I'll never know. Stan is convinced she's my twin that we are two peas-in-a-pod. I manage to squeeze them in just before Stan returns. We get the train from Guide Bridge to London then fly from Gatwick. I get giddy again thinking of sunshine, relaxing, eat out and spending time together as a family. Stan arrives back in time to see Ayeisha going into giddy mode too. We're like a pair of kids together making each other as stupid as the other. We laugh at doing a makeup check. Stan looks at us like we've lost the plot. Like that should come as a surprise.

We jump on the train flinging our bags down underneath the seats. I find myself sat facing Stan and allsorts are going through my head. Did we remember to lock up, is the emersion heater switched off. I get a horrible feeling that something might not be checked. Stan tells me it's all checked. In other words don't go spoiling the trip before it's even started. As the train pulls into Manchester I notice a trainer under the seat. It's brand new and looks just like the new ones I packed for Stan. But the bags are zipped closed, surely it hasn't unzipped already. 'Stan is that your trainer under your seat.' He looks down saying 'It's fallen out already that's your packing' he moans.

As Stan bent down to grab the trainer it suddenly moves. I couldn't help but laugh because the bloke sat behind Stan had his leg bent under the seat. And has the same pair of trainers on as Stan's. The poor guy glares at Stan as if to say what the hell are you doing. He thought Stan was trying to mug him. Bash rolls about in stitches whilst Stan looks really embarrassed. 'Sorry mate' he grovels then points at me 'She thought it was my trainer, said it fell out of my bag' then glares at me. I look like I could die. I try desperately not to start the nervous laugh. Now he makes out I want to rob him. 'Blame me why don't you, you thought it was yours too' I moan as we all leave the train. I felt like grabbing a trainer from the bag to prove to the man that we weren't weirdo's. The guy starts laughing realising we were genuine after he sees me and Stan arguing. Stan gives me the disbelief stare and moans 'you idiot, your causing trouble already and we haven't even got out of Manchester.'

When we check-in at the airport he's already asking can he have the window seat. Can you believe it he's worse than a kid. Ayeisha says she's having the window seat. Of course being awkward I tell her she can have it flying out and I want it coming back. He moans 'No your not.' He thinks he's clever laughing at me until he realises I'm before him in the queue. I rush down the isle to our seats first. He couldn't pass if he tried because he had a big bag to carry on board. Ayeisha is amused because she's beaten him too. He knows he'd looked a right idiot pushing past us both like a big kid. So he had to tow the line. And already he looks like he's ready to sulk. Sarcastically I grin 'Ha, I'm the winner.' I remind him it goes in pecking order of most important at the window to the least important at the isle.

Still not amused he whinges for the window seat. He knows I'm joking and only keep it going whilst it annoys him. I'm really not bothered. I'd only have to climb over him to get to the loo anyway. Just to get one more wind up in for the train dig I laugh 'Go on then I'm allowing you to sit at the window.' And ask

Ayeisha to let mardarse swap or we'll never hear the end of it. Can you believe it he sits there grinning like a Cheshire cat. It's worse than having two kids. He should learn some maturity. It wasn't my fault he embarrassed himself on the train. But now I feel better letting him know I'm in control.

When we arrive in Gibraltar the warm air hits you. Oh yes, that holiday feeling is here, you can already smell the sea from the airport. Our hotel looks fantastic lit up on the rock as dark approaches. Ayeisha points to the top of the rock 'Wow look at all the bats.' You can see them against the backdrop of the floodlights. I'm really giddy and can't wait to see the apes. We have to go first thing tomorrow. Our hotel is wonderful and we have a room over looking the front. The first thing we do is throw the bags down then go for a walk around the town. As its a little dark we don't wander far. Just enough to get a feel of the town and plan what to do tomorrow. We decide on an early breakfast then wander up the rock exploring the mountain. Our hotel is already halfway up the rock so it can't be that bad surely.

When morning came it felt like heaven, when we woke to sunshine drenching through our room. We open the balcony doors to soak up the atmosphere, mmm this is what it's all about. We had already tucked into a huge cooked breakfast when we realised we were about to climb up the rock. I suppose we should take a leisurely pace burning calories off slowly. When we start the walk it's already fairly warm and here we are attempting to hike our way to the top. Of course Stan rushes ahead trying to get in front. It's typical 'I'm the leader follow me.' He tries his best to rush us and of course we ignore him. I've just eaten a thousand calories. I'm hardly going to storm the mountain now am I?

The road up winds around the rock of the mountain tapering in until you get to the top. After twenty minutes of trekking up hill in the sun we came across some caterpillars all along the side of the wall. I'm fascinated and stop to take a better look. Because Stan had rushed ahead he hadn't noticed them all. He was too busy looking out for birds instead. There must be hundreds of caterpillars. I shout them both over to take a look. Stan shouts back he knows what a caterpillar is, the cheeky bleeder. I ask him why are they are all in a line. They both burst out laughing at me like I'm the stupid one. 'What do you mean all in a line' he scoffs. 'What's she on about now' I heard him say. I tell them to look at hundreds of them all following each other in a line. Walking over to check it out he laughs 'She's gone mad.' Until they look at the wall and see for themselves. Now they're as fascinated as I am. We're stunned watching them all crawl along the wall a line following each other down the side of the rock and across the path.

They couldn't believe there eyes either. We've never seen anything like this before except for ants. Then again I've never seen more than two caterpillars at any one time. We watch in amazement, then I worry and tell Stan they're going across the pathway. They'll get crushed if people don't notice them. Of course they'll see them he insists. Besides there's hardly anyone going to spot them up here anyway. 'What like you noticed them' I groan sarcastically, we'll have to help put them back on the wall or at least to the side of the pathway' and ask them to help. Of course he laughs at me asking if I'm going to stand here all day to move caterpillars. I tell Ayeisha not to touch them in case they are poisonous. I route through my bag for piece of paper and try my best to break the line from the path flicking as many as I can back against the wall. I felt I had to do my bit to save them.

But as we wander further up the path there are hundreds more again all in lines. Once again we move them from the path. In the end Stan moans we can't stay here all day, we'll just leave them, there are far too many. Reluctantly I leave them and carry on up the mountain. I suppose not many people come here. It's not like they are on the main road. We haven't even seen anyone else. It isn't until we get to the top that we bump into the first people we've seen on the mountain. They've climbed up on the opposite side. Surprised at how we got there, they ask which way we came up. They want to try the other side but part of a wall is partitioned off. You're probably not supposed to go through there. At a squeeze I suppose they could go our way or climb over the wall. We explain to keep going until arriving at the windy road and follow it down until it leads out to the town by the casino.

Out of nowhere an ape appears. It sits on the wall watching us. Its lovely sat there free in front of us and not in a cage. How great not to be enclosed in a car, and just yards in front is a Barbary Ape. It's sitting quite content resting in the sunshine. We were warned to be careful the apes. They'll pinch your bags, sweets and camera anything they can. They'll run off with anything. Soon more of apes approach. A whole family of them.

One has a baby hanging on its stomach. It's the tiniest thing you ever saw. With the cutest little head that would fit in the palm of your hand. They're gorgeous and of course me and Bash want to hold one. But we don't, we hardly want the parents shredding us to bits. They are huge with massive fangs piercing out of from their mouths. They don't mind looking at us, or us at them. So long as we leave it to them to come any nearer they are quite happy. They sit as if waiting for food, but signs 'Do not to feed them' are everywhere. Although I am tempted. There are two young ones playing behind the parents, though not as small as the baby. These two are so cheeky, one taps the other then runs off. The other chases it taps it back then runs off again. They both do this over and over again. Its hilarious watching them swinging down a piece of wire and chasing the other as if playing tick. It's like watching a scene out of the Jungle Book. I could sit here in the sunshine watching them all day. But there's lots more to see, so we stay for a little while then wander further round. The cheeky ones follow us along for a while then run back to the adults.

We walk to the edge of the mountain taking in the view over the Mediterranean Sea. The view is breath taking. The water is an amazing turquoise blue with little boats floating across the water. The place makes you want to melt right into it it's so gentle and serene. As we know I'm not very good with heights. Worried, I plead with Stan to take care with Ayeisha near the edge. I can't help it I'm a born worrier. The first thing I thought of this morning was if my mobile was charged up, just in case we needed it for an emergency. Although Gibraltar is so small I doubt it suffers with crime. But you never know especially in a strange country its best not to get complacent.

As we peeped over the edge of the cliff a young guy appeared from nowhere. Dressed in shorts and carrying a tee-shirt over his shoulder. He just pops up at the top of the mountain from down cliff face, which looks like a sheer cliff face dropping straight into the water. Where the hell did he come from? Surely he hasn't just run up the side of the mountain. We all stare open mouthed at him. He chuckles at the looks on our faces. Stunned we ask where did he come from. He points over the side, but we look at him like he's crazy, that leads to the sea and it looks a pretty steep drop. It hardly looks like a terrain you can just walk, after all we are not in the army. There is an army base at Gibraltar I could imagine the troops being made to run up that cliff face every day.

The young guy laughs again pointing to the edge and saying Mediterranean Walk. We ask can we walk down there. He replies yes. To the bottom, or do we have to come back up. He says in broken English 'Yes, to the bottom but small steps' with hand movements showing a small step. Then off he runs waving goodbye. We looking at each other thinking we'll have to give it a go at least. If we can't do it we can always come back up this way, after all we did want an adventure. If Ayeisha is up for it then it's alright by me, of which she definitely is. She's far more confident and braver than me anyway. I think as you get older you get scared far easier than when you were a child.

Grinning to each other we take our first few faltering steps over the edge. Of course I'm already panicking because of the height. Thinking what if I get stuck how will we get rescued. I only have sandals on but they do have a slight heel which helps to grip the ground. Ayeisha has pumps on and Stan is in trainers. I suppose we should be alright. Stan goes first if, he slips at least we can get back up, only joking! Besides we only want girl power when it suits. As he's the man of the group he has to check it's safe now doesn't he. The stranger was right you do have to be careful of the small steps. But what a view it's amazing. Far far better than just looking across the water from the top of the mountain.

It's full of trees and shrubs all down the side of the mountain and all along the Mediterranean Walk. It's such a beautiful walk with an amazing backdrop overlooking the water. What a view, far nicer that just walking back down the lane. At least we can say we came down the rock face. But nearly an hour later we are still only half way down. Not only is the little step route going down, but it also tapers around the mountain. It's going to take twice as long. It's a good job we had that big breakfast or I'd be starving now.

What if we are still here in another hour and can't find our way out, because I'm sure we have passed this spot already. We only have one small bottle of water between us. I'm not sure if it's the sun or the exertion of the trek but I felt quite shaky. We came across a little hideaway cave built into rock and took a look, but it's only a small space really. It would have been a fantastic lookout post well hidden away halfway up the rock. Enough for someone to hide out and have a little fire going really. Not that I'd like to be down there in the night. Ayeisha claims it to be her little room. Annoyingly people had carved their names into the walls of the cave. What a shame to ruin something like that.

As we walk away from the cave Stan isn't in front of us anymore. And I'm getting a little confident after being up here for over an hour so off I walk in front. I decide I'm being leader of the pack for a while. Yet Stan moans for me to let him through obviously trying to be leader again. I say it's alright I don't mind going in front whilst it's not as steep for a while, knowing this will frustrate him. He's like a child. Incensed he isn't the leader, he rushes forward trying to get in front. Only he can't push through there isn't enough room. If he does push through we could end up falling down the cliff face. Ayeisha laughs, knowing exactly what he is doing. He's itching to get in front, he can't stand the fact he's behind me. Stan tells me to be careful, but I am being careful. Although it is steep you don't feel the full height, because the steps wind around the mountain rather than go straight down the cliff face.

Stan shouts to Ayeisha 'be careful, it's all about being confident, what you need to do is make sure you get a good grip when you put your foot down.' She giggles shouting 'Dad I know what I'm doing.' We both laugh at him because he's being pathetic and can't stand being behind. It's almost like a competition what ever he does, whoever it's with, he has to feel in charge. And if he is not in control he just steam rolls in to take over the situation. 'Bash' he shouts frustrated 'What you need to do is to put your best foot forward and be sure footed.' Just as he says this he looses his grip and his foot slips. All the gravel under him whooshes forward and he falls straight on his arse. His timing couldn't have been more fitting. Of course we find it so funny we can't control our laughter. There he is giving it out to us to be careful. He wants to take a leaf out of his own book, less of the mouth and more watching what he's doing. All because he wanted to be first in line, he couldn't bear to be behind us girls. Don't you just love it when fate has a go. It's like Karma biting them on the backside.

Whilst he has the chance Stan races in front of us looking embarrassed. Then the cheeky git says follow me. But we can't move for laughing, we're almost doubled up. After we wipe our eyes and our stomachs have stopped hurting from laughing, we tease him relentlessly goading what ever you do be sure footed. He's never going to live this one down ha ha. Even though we nearly argued about which way to go, and thought we were going in circles around the mountain. Were knackered from the trek, got stung by nettles, and almost lost Stan on the way down, ok a slight exaggeration. The view was breath taking and well worth the effort. We are so glad we bumped into the young stranger. We'd never have known we could climb down the rock face and definitely wouldn't have attempted the Mediterranean Walk without seeing him do it. The apes were so lovely to watch, we didn't fell threatened by them at all. Even though they were wild and their teeth could do a lot of damage. This is a day we will remember for a long time.

We're really hungry after a few hours trekking. We decide to freshen up back at our hotel first then go into the town and find somewhere to eat. Gibraltar is a somewhere you can relax, and walking about the harbour is certainly serene and calming. We check out the yachts, or houses on water is more what you could call it. Some of these make your house look tiny, they are monstrous bobbing along the waters edge. Yes it's definitely a money place after seeing the size of these beauties. Then you come across a little boat which before we'd have thought it was a great size. Next to those big things it makes it look like a boat belonging to a dolls house.

We wander around the harbour some more when we see a boy fishing along the edge of the harbour. Ayeisha sees Stan clock the boy and rolls her eyes at me laughing. Stan sidles up to the lad asking him if he's caught anything but the boy shakes his head. Stan's eyes nearly pop out of his head when he spots lots of fish swimming around the yachts.

'Look it's teaming with them' he says with his eyes glowing at the sight. Ayeisha looks at me saying he's off is he. A woman comes over to one of the yachts near us. Stan asks her are you allowed to fish here. Bearing in mind we are directly in front of the restaurants, where all the yacht owners are probably dining. She looks at him puzzled saying 'well some of the children do.' Not quite believing he would want to fish in front of the restaurants. 'Oh' he replies sullenly. His eyes shift back to the fish and then back to her then asks 'So no adults fish here then.' Bemused she shakes her head saying no. I think she was quite shocked because she had a look on her face as if to say 'You want to catch fish bugger off and fish somewhere else, this is a respectable area' but she is far too polite. She points beyond the harbour 'try along the sea where some of the men go fishing.'

He's getting embarrassing now. I think we had better go before we are told to. He doesn't have a rod so what's he going to do, befriend a fisherman and ask if he can play. But then again when it comes to fishing, we know his cheek knows no boundaries. Stan's face drops into a sulk. 'For gods sake Stan let the kid be' I mumble. Ayeisha starts to giggle because she knows exactly what he's thinking. Stan turned to me saying he felt like pushing the kid into the water then grins at me. Bash can't believe he wants to push a child into the water just because he can't fish there himself. And laughs 'Dad, that's well tight.' He tells her he knows but at least he'd feel better. She tells him it's a really mean thing to think, and asks 'you wouldn't really do it would you.' But he looks away amused.

Shocked that he didn't say no she asks 'He wouldn't would he Mum.' I burst out laughing because knowing Stan, he'd probably pretend he was looking at the fish next to the boy then slightly nudge him in. I said he probably would after all this isn't the first time he's had an altercation with a child. Perplexed she asks what did I mean. I told her about the time when Stan was trying to fix a fireplace for a friend who rented a house. But the family they turned out to be a bit rough. They didn't look after the house nor its contents. The mother was rather stupid and kept letting her son play near the fireplace with Stan's tools.

Now one thing Stan can't abide is parents pushing brats onto you. Letting them mess where they shouldn't just because it's their child. You know its irritating because it's not your child and there's nothing you can do about it. It's embarrassing to have to tell another parent about their child. He kept telling the boy to move away from his tools it's dangerous. It's not just dangerous but really annoying him too. But the kid carried on grabbing a screw driver and tapping the fireplace. In the end Stan got so annoyed with the lad he grabbed the screw driver off him. Then turned around and holding the boy's shoulder pulled him over. As he did he said 'oops watch what you're doing.' But it looked like the child had fallen over and Stan had tried to grabbing hold to stop him from falling. The boy started crying for his Mum. Stan said oops a daisy picking the boy up and said I told you to be careful didn't I. The mother came in and shouted at the lad for messing and then dragged him off into the kitchen. Stan turned back to the fireplace grinning quite pleased with himself muttering 'bleedin brat.'

Ayeisha stares at me in disbelief asking if I'm making it up. She shouts at him 'Dad, that's really tight.' 'No it wasn't he was a brat and his mother was a clampet. She didn't watch him properly or care what he was doing. What if he'd have fallen over holding a bloody screwdriver. She'd have been crying it was my fault then. We walk away from the boy fishing, its best not to tempt fate.

After a good nights sleep and after our trekking about yesterday we take a leisurely breakfast and wander around

197

Gibraltar town. Stan spots a motor bike shop. There was a massive silver bike in the window. Stan had had a bike as a teenager but never really bothered with bikes since. I suppose it comes down to practicality. Always working, needing a van for work and then having something you wouldn't use for eight or nine months of the year. But this one really caught his eye and it had to be a Harley Davidson didn't it.

Even I know Harley's are a popular bike. But this thing looked huge all chrome and shinny. It was something you would spot in the dark from five miles away. I must admit it was a nice looking bike. He couldn't stop grinning so I knew he was quite taken by it. The owner caught Stan admiring it So Stan has to go and ask how much it was didn't he. Only Eighteen Grand he says. I look at Stan as if to say yeh right, but he's actually thinking about it. I don't think so, we've only come away for a few days of sunshine. And he thinks he's going home with a toy. If he wants a toy he can bring a model Harley home. From the way he's fussing the bike like he's a child on Christmas Day I know he's really thinking of bringing it home.

I have to but in and get him back to reality quickly. 'Stan, if you want a bike by all means get one, but to pay this kind of money for a toy is just a little extravagant don't you think.' You see if I told him he's not having one he'd go and buy it. Whether he wanted it or not just to be arrogant she's not telling me what I can or cannot do thing. But explaining to him, I thought we were supposed to be saving up, if you think it justifies spending that kind of money on a toy then fair enough. Let him think he's making the decision. The right decision being No!

He realises what I'm trying to say and for once without rowing about it. I mean it's not as if he could use it everyday or for work is it. You don't really see a builder turning up on a motor bike now do you. It was nice, and he does works hard. If he really wanted one I couldn't begrudge him a bike now could I. After all he is working six and seven days a week most of the time. But I would prefer it to be a little easier on the purse obviously. He wanders out of the shop drifting in thought, thinking of the cost, how much time, or little time, he'd get to enjoy it. About the cost of shipping it over to the UK.

Walking around for the next hour he looks like a kid who's just lost his favourite toy. I'm sure I haven't heard the end of this one. On the way back to the hotel we take a walk through the botanical gardens. The garden is so pretty, such wonderful colours everywhere giving the garden such a tranquil atmosphere. Whilst it's such a glorious day we want to enjoy it as much as we can. This is the perfect garden where you can sit and read a book and switch off from the world for an hour or two. I could get used to this life. A wander around the beach or the harbour, chill and read a book and then go back to the hotel to dine outside on the terrace. Or even afternoon tea. Yes, I could definitely get used to this.

Walking through the garden we pass a notice at the side explaining what plants and birds you can find in the garden. And then we come across a notice about caterpillars. Intrigued we read on the notice telling us about caterpillars in Gibraltar. There are hundreds to be found. If you're really lucky only at certain times in the year, you can see them migrate down the rock together. They follow in a procession touching from head to toe one after the other. It's like a trail of ants except on a slower level. They all come down from high up on the rock to find soil on lower ground. The notice tells you this is nature it's meant to happen. It asks you not to be tempted to break the line and put them back on the walls if you do see them. Otherwise they can lose there way.

I find I've instinctively held my hands against my mouth saying 'Oh no what have I done now.' Stan gloats 'Ang what did I tell you didn't I say leave them alone.' Feeling really guilty I reply 'No I think your words were there are too many.' Okay so he did say leave them, but not because he thought they should be left alone. I'm not having him telling me he thought he knew. As if I need to be told I was wrong. Ayeisha shouts to me 'Mum you've killed them, all those caterpillars and you've killed them.' Of course not content that I feel bad enough, he has to carry it on 'It's just like your mother to kill something minding its own business. After all we can't even leave a plant with her, she only has to look at it and it dies.' Well okay, this may be true. I do have a very unsuccessful way with plants and things. They do seem to die, very quickly, on me. I don't seem to have much luck with living things, having to remember when to look after it, when to feed, when not to feed. It's such a chore.

Once Ayeisha's grandma gave her a sunflower. I had imagined it be the easiest thing in the world to grow. I mean how hard can it be. A few weeks later she asked how the flower was getting on. Feeling really pleased with myself I tell her its coming on well, it's about three inches tall now. Then I spot hers on the window ledge, it's about a foot high. Oh she tells me looking puzzled, they'll have to be put outside into bigger pots now. Demoralised, I go home to check ours. I point to the sunflower telling Ayeisha how little and pathetic it looks.

As I touch the flower with tiniest bit of pressure the head falls off into the floor! Enough said. But with the caterpillars I feel terrible and on this occasion it was a mistake. I didn't mean any harm to the caterpillars and thought I was helping them. I ask if we should go back up the mountain and try putting them back. Stan says no. Please I plead. He tells me not to be silly they'll have found there way. 'Besides if they see you coming they'll probably scream run it's the murderer and run in the opposite way anyway.' Ha ha very funny I reply sarcastically. But I still can't help feeling terrible. How was I supposed to know.

The great thing about Gibraltar is it's so small, so you can't really get lost. It just a small island with a huge rock in the centre. All you have to do is look at where the rock is to navigate your way around it. The rock has a different shape at either side so you know where you are all the time. The next morning we decide to spend the day at the beach whilst its still lovely and warm.

So we do what Brits do best broad and go paddling in the sea for a while. We take a walk along the rocks. It's great to spend time chilling out together. We should do this more often except Stan won't paddle. He'll walk along the beach, run, play football on it but won't go in the water. In the years we've been together he has only been in the water once. And then it was with a boogie board. Other than that he refuses to go in saying the water and him do not mix. The beach is really clean with no sign of litter anywhere. Not like Blackpool where you're more worried about contaminated water or your kids turning green with rubbish around. Although I must admit I hadn't been to Blackpool for a few years. When we took Bash in the summer the beach was a lot cleaner than I'd seen it had been previously. It looked like they have made an effort.

Ayeisha looks for shells whilst tucking into an ice-lolly. We follow down the beach behind her. Suddenly, stepping onto some seaweed I feel something funny on my foot. If feels sort of heavy as if something is sticking to it. Like when you have a clump of wet sand stuck to your foot. I look down at my foot but it looks like sand stuck to it. I go and rinse it off in the sea. But something is still stuck to it and won't come off. Trust me.

What ever it is its awful dark goo like stuff stuck on my foot. I almost bursting into tears. I try rubbing it harder trying to rinse it off but still to no avail. I try using an ice-lolly stick to scrape it off but no it's still not shifting. Stan bursts out laughing 'for gods sake its always you, your worse than a child.' I look up so not impressed. Now is not the time to annoy me. Somehow I don't feel like making a joke of it. I couldn't even put my sandals back on or it'll never come off my sandals either.

He sees I'm getting really upset because it could be toxic or anything. But the beach is so clean I can't believe happening. Stan asked how I managed to stand in it. But I don't know it must have been under the seaweed and now it won't shift. At this point he feels really sorry for me and goes over to a shop nearby bringing back some washing up liquid. After some scrubbing this finally does the trick. Aww what would I do without my Stan. Hop to the shop showing myself up and everyone seeing what I'd trodden in. I'd be the laughing stock, even more than I am already.

We decide to head back to the hotel around the other side of the mountain. We only got halfway up when I am bursting for the toilet. I didn't realise how far it was to walk. I suppose I should have gone to the toilets back near the beach. But going around the houses we seem to be getting lost. Some of the back streets lead to dead ends, by which I was really bursting. I have two options ask someone nearby if I could use their toilet or go back to the one near the beach. Which ever option I take he's going to go off on one. I tell him rather sheepishly that I need the loo. He tells me we'll be back in a few minutes and to hold on. I moan 'But it's been twenty minutes and we are no nearer because of the dead ends, I'll have to go back.' Of course Stan takes this in the most delightful usual way and starts his 'For gods sake you've got to be joking' routine. I stress I need to go now. 'We're half way up the mountain and you need the bleedin toilet' he rants 'You'll have to wait till we are back near the hotel, there are some toilets there.' But that could be another half an hour.

Its times like this I wish I was a child. That way I'd get away with going in the grid. It's alright for blokes, when the needs must at least they can hide behind a bush. He rants about why I didn't say before we left the beach. That's because I didn't realise until we started up the mountain. He shouts 'I don't need to go every two minutes do I, there's something wrong with you.' I shout back it's not normal to hold it in all day. He then points at Bash saying even she isn't that bad.

She moans to keep her out of this. I offer to go back on my own then catch them up. He just looks at me pouting feeling really sorry for myself. Then stomps past me heading towards the beach ranting 'You can forget looking at me like that.' Because we have to go back to the beach Stan is spitting feathers. Ranting and raving its like looking after a child, yes lets all go back down to the beach'… rant rant.. 'You're impossible, lets just waste half a day.' I get really upset he knows we're only here for a few more days yet he's prepared to upset everybody.

Yes moan a little but he didn't need to rant like its spoiling the whole day. I go into a sulk, and sulk I can. In fact I am probably the worlds worst. Ayeisha doesn't stand a chance poor thing. She's inherited my sulking and his stroppiness in a small way but as she gets older I hope it eases. She has such a nice manner about her, it would be a shame for it to spoil her. But then again I suppose you do take your moods out more at home than you would elsewhere. So I refuse to speak to him. He didn't need to throw such a fit he could have just spoken about it, got a little annoyed then got over it. On the way back he tries speaking to me. But I am not in the mood.

I'm unsure if I'm more upset than angry. He asks 'How long is it going on for this time, an hour, a day a week. You don't have to be so childish.' This is obviously his attempt at a joke, only I don't quite see the funny side of it. He tells me I'm as stubborn as a mule, and that I don't have to carry it on and ruin the holiday. Bloody cheek of it like I've done something wrong. So I needed the loo, did he really need to go off on one embarrassing me in the street like that. He can see that I'm really upset. Then he puts his arms around me telling me 'I'm sorry but you've got to admit you know how annoying you are.' I suppose this is his feeble way of apologising. But I don't want to ruin the holiday. Or it will be thrown back at me at every opportune moment for the next ten years, so I give in.

We forgive and make up, and choose not to mention it again. But I'm sure he will take great delight in reminding me at some point, how I was the childish one. Back at the hotel I want to shower before going to dinner. All wanting the bathroom we fight over who gets it first. Seeing as I take longer to get ready I get the bathroom first. Those two are usually ready quite quickly so they don't get a choice in the matter. Whilst in the bathroom I have to be really careful. All the surfaces are marble, the floor is tiled in marble and very slippy. Although I have had a few days to get used to it, it's been like a problem waiting to happen.

As much as it has been lovely here it does seems to have been a week of it. Today appears to be no exception. I can hear them shouting through the door telling me to hurry up. I'm trying to hurry applying my makeup, which is a little difficult because all the room is steamy. As I reached for the deodorant my hand knocks my face cream. Normally this wouldn't pose a problem but the cream is in a small glass jar and quite heavy for its size. The slightest knock had sent the jar shunting off the side like an ice cube crashing onto the tiled floor. Oh God I can't believe this.

I look down hoping my jar hasn't broken. I don't have anything else to put the cream in. Luckily the jar hasn't smashed. But one of the floor tiles has cracked across the middle. Damn there's no disguising it. It's sort of crunched in one corner with a great big crack across the centre. You can tell it's a brand new crack it's all clean and shinny where the cracks are. I can hear Stan shouting through the door what have I done now. Panic stations, after today's scene I don't fancy another row.

Nothing I shout back trying to think quick. Out of the corner of my eye I spot my deodorant. I shout back it's just the deodorant dropping on the floor echoing. This keeps him quiet for a while. Bloody Hell what do I do now. I quickly grab for the bin trying to cover it in vain. Phew that was close. I carry on getting ready but put my makeup on a towel to stop any more accidents. But then I thought of the cleaners! Damn, the first thing they will do is move the bin to clean the bathroom. Or even worse Stan may move the bin. I start panicking some more.

Oh God, I can feel a trauma coming on. We could get thrown out for damage, or sent a massive bill to re-tile the whole floor. I stand holding my head in my hands wondering what on earth I'm going to do. Then in a flash I catch sight of my make-up bag when a brilliant idea comes to me. I grab my face powder and some bronzer, dab a little onto a tissue and rub it into the nice clean crack. Slowly but surely it starts to go discoloured. I can't help but smile to myself what a fantastic idea.

It looks a little worn, at least it doesn't look like a brand new break. I leave the bin over the cracks for extra security. That and the fact that I can't see it. And if I can't see it, it didn't happen, Bloody genius! I come out of the bathroom draped in a towel feeling quite content with myself. Stan asks what on earth I broke this time. Smugly I reply nothing. He passes by me going into the bathroom to check. He knows I've done something, and he knows I know, but he won't find anything, not that he can prove anyway. I carry on getting my clothes ready on the bed deciding what to wear.

He comes out of the bathroom looking perplexed 'I was convinced you had broken something, what the hell were you doing in there.' Smiling I lecture 'I told you I dropped the deodorant I can't help it if it makes a racket' grinning to myself. He looks at me knowing something is going on but can't quite put his finger on it. He can't figure it out and decides to leave the matter. Which makes me want to laugh because he's itching to know. But if I told him he'd go on and on about it. I'd never hear the last of it. You see he is forever winding me up saying I shuffle plates instead of washing them. He always goes on about me taking my time.

My answer to that is if my way wasn't good enough, then wash them himself. Plus I really don't want to hear over the next few days to be about what I've done wrong. He'd only take great delight in letting me know I have broken something yet again. Do I need to hear this, I think not. I keep this one to myself for a while. Stan asks where we want to go to tomorrow. I tell him I'd like to go back up the mountain and see the Baybery Arpes. As I'd spoken I realised I've said it wrong but hope they don't realise. In unison they both burst out laughing at me because my towel starts to drop down.

Mum! Ayeisha shouts. Of course Stan decides to embarrass me more by saying 'Never mind the Barbery Apes, do you mind putting your own Baybary Arpes away.' I laugh cringingly at what I'd said. I knew they'd pick up on it. 'It's been a long day' I reply. Let's hope it's an event free day tomorrow. The next morning we book a boat trip to see dolphins. I hope we get to see them, they did say we'll get our money back if we don't see any. It would be such a shame to go back home without seeing them.

Lucky for us the of dolphins were out in force. A few of them even swam in front of the boat for ages. A couple of dolphins even had their babies swimming along with us. The speed they chase the boat with is ridiculously fast. They glide through the ocean as if it was made of silk. They are really quite beautiful to watch. What an amazing end to the holiday. I suppose I should be pleased the rest of the holiday went peacefully. It was a nice break spending time together enjoying the beach and soaking up the sun. Although I can't help but wonder what the next holiday will bring.

~ Chapter Seventeen ~ **The Birthday**

Its coming up to my birthday and my family want a party. This is not really something I'd relish in. I thought we were just going out for a few drinks. But I have a large interesting family and lots of friends who would be in their element. A big party lots of attention and all that. Everyone could get drunk, very drunk. And somewhere they could be loud. To my delight they would remember embarrassing stories from years past. Worse still they'd insist on telling them at the loudest and most inopportune moment they could find.

Stan's family are the opposite. A much smaller family who don't drink much. Why drink when instead they can be entertained by mine at their best, whilst they are stone cold sober. Adding to the fact Stan is not really a sociable person. Especially when it comes to parties. Somewhere that he would have to mix and converse with people. Sometimes he comes across as arrogant. Well yes I know he can be. But he doesn't mean to be. He just can't stand being forced to mingle and socialise. Rather than drag him along reluctantly I tend to go to parties with friends instead. Half the time he is working anyway and moans he needs to get up early in the morning.

What's the point of him drinking and be knackered the next day when he'd rather not be there anyway. And if I want to have a dance he'll only end up being sat with some drunks, talking shite as he puts its. That's one thing he can't be doing with listening to drunks waffling on with themselves. I think I'll have a quiet night out with the girls instead at least I won't feel on show.

I've told the gang at work I'm thinking of having my belly button pierced. They look at me thinking I've lost the plot. 'Ang, please tell me your not' they laugh. And insist on telling me they don't like pierced belly buttons. Gertie enjoys telling me how awful they look. Olive asks why would I put myself through it, she cringes at the thought of putting a hole through your belly. Then goes on to tell me how a friend of hers had had it done but had gone badly wrong. Now her friend is left with an horrific scar. How did I know she would put the downer on it and it would have to be her friend wouldn't it.

I've wanted it pierce for some time but never found the courage before. I'll have to have it pierced now because if I leave it any longer I'll be too old. People will start to think I'm some tart just doing it trying to look young. As the weekend approaches I decide its best to call in the piercing shop. I need to find out more about it. I don't want to go jumping into it and then it goes wrong. I mean I'm bound to get the needle stuck in me or something with my luck.

I'm out with just a few from work at the weekend and a few friends, not the usual gang. We are supposed to meet up on Saturday night. I think they're only turning up to see if I go through with it. They're already taking bets that I won't. Now I've told them I'll have to go through with it, otherwise I'll never hear the end of it. They already think I'm a complete wimp I can't give them more fuel can I. As Saturday looms I'm feeling nervous. I really want the piercing but I'm so scared. I don't like needles, I don't like pain and most certainly don't like blood. God I'm such a wimp. Would I be really sad if I got a clip on one. If this lot found out you can imagine how they'd laugh at me.

When Saturday arrives I force myself to visit the piercing shop. Well I walk by three times peeping through the window before bravely pushing open the door. A couple of people are already in the waiting room. A guy is having his nipple pierced I can hear him wincing in pain. Oh God I think I should leave. But a guy pops his head above the swing doors saying he won't be a minute. He's seen me now, I can hardly go rushing out. The nipple guy gets up a minute or two later. Oddly he's looking quite pleased with himself. He watches his nipple whilst listening to advice about keeping it cleaned. But doesn't look like he is taking any of it in. He's too busy admiring his nipple to acknowledge any advice, but does manage to nod in the right places. The girl before me only wants to buy jewellery then leaves with her friend. 'Right then what can I do for you' he says looking at me.

My heart skips a beat and I'd like more time to build up courage. He's a small guy looks around forty and seems pleasant enough. But is this the guy I'm going to let pierce a hole in me. If it goes wrong I have a scar for life. I mumble about a piercing adding 'Only thinking about it for now.' He can see I have the fear of god written all over my face. I go into quiz mode.. How much does it cost.. Twenty five pounds. Do you have to make an appointment.. Damn he can do it now or come back.

As he's telling me I feel my eyes opening wider but can't help it. He smiles and tells me to think about it if I want. Phew, quick do a runner whilst you still can. But I do want it doing. I suppose today is as good as any other. But how do I know it's safe. I ask how is it done and is it painful. He makes a little laugh. I explain my pain threshold is very low, and now look like complete mardarse. He insists on showing me how it's done and holds up a pair of tweezers, these must belong to a giant. 'Christ I didn't think you'd need anything that big' I groan. My eyes almost popping out of my head, I felt myself gasp. He explains it's used to clamp the skin together. It's purely to hold the skin together to enable piercing in one movement, then nothing can slip. You'll feel a tight pinch from the tweezers but you won't feel pain from the piercing because he freezes the area. I sigh a relief.

He explains the clamping hurts more than anything, well not painful but uncomfortable. He stresses I won't feel any pain and will stop at any time. He shows me a little plastic tube which goes around the needle. The ring slides through the tube without any pain or discomfort then slips the tube out, the tweezers are unclamped. It's that simple. All I do is lie on the bed. The equipment is clean and sterile. I feel so much better now he's taken the time to explain the procedure. He's made it look so simple and pain free. Now I know what he's going to do it doesn't seem so bad after all. And he didn't mind being interrogated so he can't be that bad. He's been really helpful putting my mind at ease. 'Right then' I blurt out feeling quite confident 'Can you do it now before I change my mind.' Smiling he asks am I sure. Yes whilst I've plucked up the courage and before I change my mind. He walks me through to choose my ring. God I can't believe myself, I feel really empowered! I'm actually going through with it.

We look at different belly bars but I'm not keen on them at all. He advises a ring is easier to keep clean than a bar. A ring it is then. I'll have to keep it in for six weeks before I change it. I choose a gold ring with a green stone. Everyone else I've seen has silver or red, I haven't seen many with a green stone. Out of the corner of my eye I spot a pretty little opaque love heart. I can't help but feel drawn to it but worried it might look tacky. He thinks because I'm petite and the heart is only small it will look pretty that a large wouldn't look right. Besides nobody else will have one around here because he only has one. I hold it against my stomach grinning, yes this is the one.

I can't believe I've just had an intimate discussion with a guy I've never met before. Now I'm asking him what colour jewellery I should go for, and if opaque love hearts are required. Yes I think I have gone mad. And I feel great. After a few deep breaths it's all over and done with quickly. I feel really giddy coming out of the shop I've actually done it! Just wait until Stan sees this, ha he won't believe is eyes. He already thinks I've lost the plot.

For the next hour I potter around Ashton shopping. I feel quite tingly all over, it could be the adrenalin going. Realising how late it's getting I rush home to get ready for tonight. I best wear a loose wrap over skirt that fits below the waist with a loose fitting top. I don't want it to hurt. When I get home I don't seem to find the courage to tell Stan. I feel like a naughty schoolgirl who has just got a tattoo, he'll think I'm ridiculous. We are meeting early so I don't really have time to tell him in case he doesn't like it. I'll hardly have time to listen to his ranting will I. And I don't want any hassle before I go out. It's best to tell him tomorrow.

I meet up with the others in a pub in the centre of Ashton. 'Well, did you do it' they asked me. I grin but don't tell them straight away. A few of them said I knew you wouldn't do it. I grin again pulling my blouse up a little to show them. 'Aw Ang, we really didn't think you'd go through with it? Did it hurt? I didn't think it would look so nice, I want mine doing now. Aren't these the ones who condemned me before and now they want theirs doing. Next Olive will be taking Gertie to have hers done.

I'm not really much of a drinker only liking an occasional

drink. I never have been able to hold my drink, nor do I like that sickly feeling. I probably won't go down in history as a party animal. The thought of falling over drunk and everyone laughing at me doesn't quite appeal either. It's almost a case of two drinks and I'm anybodies, so I tend to have a few soft drinks in between.

Everyone at work seems to think I'm some kind of weirdo. You know one of those people who doesn't drink so she must have something wrong with her syndrome. They don't understand I only like that giddy feeling and not the drunk feeling. They did eventually get use to me. Either that or they pitied me thinking I'm a recovering alcoholic. They've become sick of saying 'Go on just have one you'll enjoy it, don't be boring.' When I thought I had enjoyed myself not drinking. Our night out is pretty quiet for their standards. All are on best behaviour and none of them appear to be getting drunk. I think they were a little wary of coming into Ashton, as some had heard it was a bit of a rough area. I put them at ease explaining there isn't trouble like there used to be because the police monitor the area now and won't stand for any trouble.

Towards the end of the night everyone is having a great time in a 70's bar. We look out the window to see a huge brawl going on in the street outside. God how embarrassing. If I'm not embarrassed at home with Stan turning up with his oddball pets, now its embarrassment in my hometown with twenty guys battling in the street. Sadie bursts out laughing because she knew I'd told the others that there wouldn't be any trouble. I'm never going to live it down if this lot notice the free entertainment outside. Cheekily I ask if we should go to the other side of the bar away from the door. But someone observant brat asks 'Why Ang, so we don't see what's going on outside.' Laughingly pretending I have no idea what they're talking about I ask why what's going on outside. Only to peer out the window with half a dozen police swarming the crowd. 'I didn't notice' I said I cringe trying to hide my embarrassment. Sadie is finding this hilarious because we usually spend the evening people watching and laughing at them.

I wonder if Bonnie's friend is out there. Best not let him see me. Just in case he wants to get his own back setting his police dog on me. Thank God we are not going to a nightclub tonight, I couldn't do a late one today. Most of us have to be up early doing one thing or another. Thankfully our gang are on their best behaviour, the rest of the evening is unusually uneventful. No fights, no police raids, no drunken sprawls over the floor. For once I'm pleased to go home early. I've only had a couple of drinks when I totter off home.

When I got to my front door I banged my ankle on a watering can. I hadn't noticed the damn thing there. The weight of me stepping forward had jammed it against the wall and into my ankle. Jeez, who the hell left that there, that hurt! When the spout dug into my ankle the pain shot right up my leg. I open the door looking for Stan but he's already in bed. I hobble upstairs sulking. But as I did my body felt strange almost sickly. I limp into the bedroom trying to wake up Stan but he's fast sleep. I felt my body going funny, I'm hot and cold all over. I shout Stan a couple of times but at first he doesn't hear me. Eventually he wakes up startled asking whats wrong. I try explaining that I don't feel well, that I banged my leg on the watering can. But I can't get my words out properly and start slurring. I felt myself going dazed. First my mouth goes dry then wet. I manage to mumble I feel sick. He leans near to me smelling if I've been drinking. Obviously I have had a couple. I hear him start shouting 'What have you been drinking.' I slur 'I haven't been drinking I've hurt my ankle, it was the watering can.' I can hear him rambling on as I try to get undressed. I don't feel right, all I can say is I feel a sick. Then my head goes dizzy and everything goes black.

I came around hearing Stan repeating my name. He was shouting 'Angie, Angie what the hell have you taken.' My eyes open a little but can't focus properly. I feel really weird almost as if I'm drunk. 'For god's sake Ang what have you been drinking' he shouts slapping my face. I come to a little realising I'm sat on the edge of the bed. Stan is knelt in front of me holding me up. I'm wondering why he's holding me up. He shakes me asking what have I taken. What does he mean what have I taken, what is he on about. I try explaining but my words are still slurred. All I can say is I felt really sick. He thinks I'm drunk, worse still I feel like I'm drunk. But I've only had two drinks.

I start focusing a little more. I can see he's not impressed. In fact he's ranting and raving. He's worried sick and he keeps asking if I'm alright. Then he starts pacing up and down the bedroom holding his head in his hands. What the hell have you been doing? I shake my head not knowing what he's talking about. Stan asks if my face is hurting. Come to think of it it does a little. I feel like I've been hit with a stun gun but I don't know why. 'For Gods sake' he shouts, you've just passed out and banged your face on the wardrobe, what's wrong with you. I can't believe your face isn't a mess from that bang, I tried to catch you but couldn't catch you in time.' I try making sense of it all. I start to come round a little more and realised I've had passed out. I felt dizzy from the fall but slowly my speech goes back to normal. I try explaining I've hurt my leg on the watering can. But Stan looks at me like I've gone completely mad. 'What the hell has a watering can got to do with you coming back drunk and slurring' he rants. Coming to my senses I realise he thinks I'm drunk.

'I am not drunk I tell him' in my defence 'I've hurt my leg and it's made me feel sick.' He looks at me in disbelief, but then sees for himself my speech has started to sound normal within a few minutes. He can't figure out what has gone on. 'But you were drunk, I saw you slurring I can smell drink on you' he tells me worried. 'Yes because I've had a drink, that means 'a' drink not ten drinks' I shout at him as if he's stupid.

He looks quite shocked and asks why I was slurring if you're not drunk. 'I don't know, probably because the spout made the pain shoot through me and making me feel sick and dizzy.' He asks what is he supposed to think when I come home staggering and slurring, stinking of alcohol. I shrug my shoulders 'I don't know I just felt really dizzy, and got loads of understanding from you' I moan. 'Ang what do you expect, you just sat on the bed and passed out, you banged your face into the wardrobe, what am I supposed to think' he shouts. 'I can't believe your face isn't all bruised' and kneels down in front of me again. 'You didn't half go down with a whack.'

He was stood at the side of the bed and couldn't grab hold of me in time, or so he tells me. I tell him he's probably let me fall on purpose. To get his own back for the toothbrush episode. But I see he's genuinely worried. He stands up starts pacing the room again, ranting he thought someone had spiked my drink or something. He asks again if I'm alright. My face is hurting near the top of my nose. But it's my leg that hurts more it feels like a pole has been rammed into my leg. He brought me a drink of water. I sit sipping it on the edge of the bed feeling quite sorry for myself. After ten minutes of lecturing he finally calms down and decides sympathy time is over, and he needs his sleep. Standing up, albeit a little shakey, I peer into the mirror checking for bruising. Please don't let me have two black eyes in the morning. My eyes do look a little puffy already, could it be the lighting. My God nobody is going to believe this one!

Feeling rather depressed I undress ready for bed and hunt around for my nighty. Stan moans for me to turn the light out. When all of a sudden he jumps upright and shouts 'What's that.' I look in the mirror not having a clue what he's pointing to. Then I realise he is pointing at me. What's he on about now, have I got a big bruise or something. But slowly it begins to dawn on me. He's not pointing past me to the mirror but at my stomach. With the rush to be out early I realise I still hadn't spoken to Stan about the piercing.

I explain that I meant to tell him earlier but never got round to it and mumble' I've had my belly button pierced.' 'Didn't get chance to tell me, why is that Ang, did you not see me today' he asks sarcastically. Now I feel I am the naughty school girl who's had her backside tattooed. Now he thinks I've lost the plot and trying to recapture my teenage days. 'What do you think, does it look alright' I ask. He looks at me blankly not quite believing what he's hearing. Grinning I crawl into bed. Over the next few days my face is tender around my nose. I'm lucky it's only a little swollen, and I don't have two black eyes.

Back in work I tell the gang what happened. At first they don't believe me. In fact they look at me like I'm covering up a row between Stan and me. It didn't help I've put extra eye shadow on to disguise the swelling around my eyes. I tried a bright colour that looked ridiculous, then tried a dark colour but this was as bad. I've ended up with purple eye shadow going on. But even the guys at work know I couldn't make up a story like that. I mean where the heck would I get an idea of a watering can from. It's so ridiculous it has to be true. And yet again they think its hilarious saying 'Ang it could only happen to you.' And find it even more amusing because I don't drink much. They knew I'd only had a couple of drinks the whole night. Unlike some of them who crawled home in all states. Yet none of them ever seem to have accidents. Except the odd falling down stairs maybe, but other than that nothing ever happens to them.

So me having this accident when I spend most of the year alcohol free seems to entertain them greatly. I think the event free wager on me is becoming as popular as spotting aliens in Manchester. Then again, best strike that because there is always a few hanging around in Manchester. Oh well, at least I'm being of some use to the office. Even if it is entertainment value, again. Sebastian was sorry he didn't make it Saturday night. His friend Martin was having a crisis, having had a row with his girlfriend. Apparently she wasn't impressed he wants to call himself Martin Monday through to Friday. Come the weekend wants to be known as Mandy. Why is it all the interesting people never make if for our nights out. What a shame we could have had such an in depth and meaningful chat.

After all we'd need to know if Mandy shaves or waxes, prefers heels or flats, hair up or down, is it a wig or real. And that's without revealing how Mandy manages to keep the tash at bay. Gertie's face is a picture, she keeps asking questions about Martin. How long as he been a he/she. Is Martin really gay a transvestite or cross dresser. Has he had surgery or does he not want to go that far. Gertie would have been in her element had Sebastian brought Mandy. She'd have interrogated him all night. She'd probably ask if he has boobs or would he like them.

Antonio reckons she would have been looking for tips on getting rid of her own tash. Ha ha. Ouch, I shouldn't laugh it gives me a headache. Besides my tash is almost as big as hers these days anyway. Throughout the week it felt like I'd hardly slept. It feels like a walking headache and I'm supposed to be going out Friday. I've been invited to the pub with friends but I really don't feel up to it. The guys at work tell me to still go that I'll probably feel better on Friday it will cheer me up and I'll feel much better by then. I still don't feel like going out. My headache seemed worse and I've had awful pins and needles feelings all over my body. I'm not sure whether it's through the fainting and banging my head or the piercing upsetting my body. I am allergic to cheap metal it could be that. It hasn't eased all week.

When Friday arrives I feel I've got to get it sorted. I can't carry on feeling like this all over the weekend. I'm worrying myself sick about the headaches, I can't leave it any longer. The others insist I should leave work early to go to the doctor's just check it out. On the way I phone the doctors for an appointment. Because it happened a few days ago they said its best to go straight to casualty, especially with a head injury. Now I feel stupid because it isn't an emergency its just worrying me. I don't want to phone Stan or he'll worry its serious. He'll probably be plastering or something. He'd have to drop off the job leaving somebody's house in a right mess and having him worrying on top. And when all is okay it will have been for nothing. Times like this you just need some sympathy, so I'll go to see Mum.

Mum's cooking in the kitchen when I get there. It was little early for cooking but I didn't take much notice and walked straight into the living room. She follows me into the living room curious to why I'm home early and closes the kitchen door behind her. I explain I'm a little worried that my nose is hurting and about the headaches. I ask if she'll to come to A & E with me but she looks at me startled. I would have expected my own Mother to show a little more concern. I was thinking on the lines of 'of course I will' or 'yes let's go now.' But all she can say is are you sure you need to go. Flabbergasted at her reaction I whine 'Mum I'm worried and want to get it checked out.' Now is it me or is this her way of saying I'm a mardarse. I tell myself to stop being ridiculous. But with the guys at work telling me I should go out when I don't feel well. Then Mum not really looking interested in coming to the hospital with me. I'm beginning to wonder.

Is it me, are they trying to tell me something. Maybe I'm a

hypochondriac and this is their polite way of telling me. Now I feel like a Munchausen addict. After a few um's and ar's and asking if I think it's really necessary to go to hospital, she eventually agrees to come with me. Albeit a little reluctantly. To top it off when we get to the A & E department it's quite full. After what seemed like an eternity finally they shout for me.

The doctor takes a look at me and gives me the once over. It's quite usual to get headaches after a bang to the head. He suggests I have an x-ray just to check everything is okay. Although he doesn't look too concerned. But the whole time he's checking me Mum keeps glancing at her watch. Whilst going for the x-ray I wonder why she seems in such a hurry. I tell her to get going if she wants. Thinking she'd say don't be silly I'll wait with you. Instead she jumps up telling me she has lots to do this afternoon and would I mind her going. I can't believe this I'm waiting for my x-ray results and she wants to go home. I didn't believe for one minute she'd think of leaving me there. But still she flusters checking her watch all the time.

Getting annoyed I tell her to go home if she needs to. Turning to me she says 'If you think its okay only I have a lot to do today, after all the doctor says your okay, I'll check on you later.' I can't believe it now my Mother abandons me at hospital. All I need now is Stan saying why have you gone to hospital when there's nothing wrong with me, for Gods sake. What is wrong with her normally she'd be concerned. I'm feeling very, very sorry for myself sitting alone waiting for the doctor to shout my name.

When he does finally shout me through it's for him to tell me it's only a slight break in the nose. He asks me how it happened, well that just tops it off doesn't it. How do you explain this one without looking a complete Pratt then. Do I lie and make something up, like the cupboard door banged into may face. Which is quite believable because I have done this on more than one occasion. I obviously didn't learn my lesson the first time round. I can't lie but know I'll end up laughing knowing how ridiculous the real story is.

I embarrassingly explain about the watering can, pain shooting right through me, managing to stagger upstairs, and fainting. He asks 'And this was after a night out.' I answer sheepishly 'After only two drinks and I had my belly button pierced earlier that day could it be to do with that.' Okay so I reserve the dramatics, but do look very, very embarrassed. The ever patient doc looks at me and shakes his head like I'm the attention seeker of the day. In fact he almost rolled his eyes. I'm sure it's a reaction to the piercing. But instead of kind sympathy he looks at me like I'm a freak who shouldn't be let out alone. He had this fantastic way of making me feel like I'd phoned for an ambulance to the hospital for a splinter. Sheepishly I leave the hospital alone and pouting. In fact you could have parked a bus on my lip.

Luckily it was only swollen slightly with a little bruising showing. I could get away with some cleverly applied eye make-up, and maybe wear some outrageous lipstick. At least then nobody will be looking at my nose. Doc had said it is normal to feel headaches with a head injury. If it carries on next week then I need to go back to my doctor who can refer me to a neurologist. God that sounds dramatic. Off home I trot telling Stan of my woes. Not gaining much sympathy here either telling me it's okay and asks if I'm still going out.

I shake my head and whine I don't feel too good. Instead of fussing me and showing some concern he asks why don't I go out with the girls as planned. Is it me and I'm in the twilight zone. Why doesn't anyone believe me when I tell them I've hurt myself. I might as well go out then if only to get sympathy from the girls. I suppose I could go, maybe just for an hour or so and if I still feel like crap I'll come home. I feel rotten letting them down after we made arrangements, even though we are only going to the pub.

When I meet up with the girls I tell them of my woes. They can't believe what's happened. Even more so that my Mum left me at the hospital, being ignored, cringing at the Doctor. Annoyingly they laugh 'It could only happen to you.' Not that I mind them laughing, it's just that the 'It could only happen to you' is becoming rather ridiculous. I'm beginning to wonder if my life is never going to change. As we approach the pub my friends suddenly jump in front of me and rush me through the door. I didn't realise the lights were dipped low. Before it registers people start singing Happy Birthday then I notice family and friends sat there. Stunned I realise everyone is looking at me and grinning away. Oh my God I want the floor to open up and swallow me in. I cringe with embarrassment. It's a party for me. I feel my face go beetroot red, what do I do?

Stan had said some people might be out anyway. I didn't realise he meant everyone. I'd grab a seat and down some drinks except I can't drink with these headaches. Plus I've taken tablets, so its night on coke. The pub is heaving with all our lot, and a load of the regulars in too. Stan is sat with Ayeisha. How she kept quiet about this I'll never know. Because she's like me she tries so hard to keep it quiet that she ends up blurting it out. On this occasion she really kept it quiet the little sod. As the party wears on people are only a bit drunk to my surprise. Everybody seems to be enjoying themselves which is a relief. There is a minor domestic going on outside but that's to be expected. As there's nothing like a good shindig to bring families together, and just when you think it's going well all hell breaks through. Why is it when people are drunk they waffle the biggest load of crap. Yet when sober they're really quiet. It's like they've had a brain transplant or something and start talking through there backsides.

That is until the Karaoke started. Bloody Karaoke! My take on Karaoke is that it's great in a local pub for everybody to sing along to or have a laugh with. Even at a children's party is good. But at an adults party and my party. One who can't sing won't sing, I know I'm going to be embarrassed. Who is it organised for. It can't be for me because I'd sound like a cross between Kate Bush and a strangled cat. Stan had said I resemble Hilda Ogden and I wasn't going to argue with him. So it must be for everyone to have a good laugh at my expense. To be fair the pub have Karaoke quite often so thankfully it's not for my benefit.

In my experience the only people who get up and sing at parties are those who are really good, people who are drunk and don't mind making a complete Pratt of themselves. And those who like an audience. Personally, I'm not good, nor do the drunk make a show of myself, and nor do I want an audience. But now its payback on me for all those people who don't like me. Now it's my turn to cringe with embarrassment.

At first some guests try in vain to drag me up telling me I have to it's my birthday. Don't they realise I would need to be drunk or stoned to do that. The only time I have ever got up to sing was when a crowd of us got up and I stood behind everyone letting them sing. The first one up is one of the crowd who couldn't sing for toffee, bless. Yet insists on getting up to sing and do their bit for me. Even trying to serenade me at one point. Doing a brilliant version of a strangled cat is what it is. To make matters worse the poor sod thinks the applause is because of a great performance. But the laughter along with it makes me cringe. Then there's another who's a friend of a friend. She wasn't really invited just tagged along for the fun of it. She gets up not once but three times in an hour thinking she's competing on the X Factor. Blimey looking for an audience or what. I thought this supposed to be my birthday not torture. It does serve its purpose in a way as it takes the limelight off me.

Everyone is wishing me a happy birthday and all I want to do is crawl into bed with a hot cocoa. People want to buy me a drink but I can't drink and feel such a party pooper. I feel I should be tap dancing on the table to let everyone know I'm having a good time. Thankfully the pub is full of locals who pack the place out and join in the fun. This time a friend breaks the ice for me taking her turn to cringe when her cousins get up to sing. Except this time it's just for fun and to be truthful they're not half bad. A little drunk maybe but they do a good version of Meatloaf's Bat out of Hell. They just enjoy themselves larking about making it fun, how it's meant to be.

Then I hear some people moaning about everyone who's been singing tonight. A little bemused I ask why because most people are just up for a laugh. I'm told 'You know, they think they should have made it and kill everybody with Karaoke. They're the type who screech to any record but think they sound great because the music drowns them out. There isn't anything I could say because the guy up swears he's Tom Jones. Doing the impersonation badly what could I do but cringe some more. If I ever get hold of who invented Karaoke, remind me give them a slap.

One time I did enjoy Karaoke was at a birthday party for Ayeisha friend. All the kids where having a go but she wouldn't get up for ages even though she likes to sing. Kids are great fun to watch. You see their personalities coming out on stage. It's really surprising to watch the quiet ones blow you away with great voices at such an early age. They were all really entertaining. Towards the end of the party and with a little coaxing Ayeisha eventually braves getting up to sing. At first hiding behind friends, then when it was her turn to sing she sang so lovely. Parents commented on what a lovely voice she has. I've always thought she has but you don't go telling other people do you. Or you'd sound like one of those horrendous pushy parents that force their children onto people. One of the parents even asked if Ayeisha would sing at her wedding. Ayeisha blushed at the request but was eventually persuaded to sing at the wedding. She sang so softly it was beautiful. It brought tears to my eyes that is something I'll remember always.

~ Chapter Eighteen ~ **The Bonds & Boredom**

Back in work things seems to quieten down for a while. Trudy was a busy bee. Jerry is behaving herself but spending time with Jenifer. They're probably plotting something together. In spite of everything Olive and Gertie are on reasonable speaking terms for once. Even Larry puts in a full week. Antonio is as calm as ever and Sebastian still vying for attention. Lawrence is Lawrence being ever so camp. All is quiet except the subject of holidays. My three weeks vacation is back under discussion. I'm told that I can only take it over the Christmas holidays.

When you think about it they're not giving me anything extra because we're all off at Christmas anyway. I know its Stan's fault swapping and changing it all the time. But the prices shoot up horrendously over Christmas. How generous they offer me two weeks. I wouldn't mind but they all debate in front of me how 'they the team' will cover my work. I seem to remember how 'they the team' forget when we all covered whilst they were off sick and on holiday. I think emigrating to Papa New Guinea is called for. Away from people, work, the daily drivel and the daily road rage to work. Oh the depression. I feel myself drifting off and at my computer again. I'm sure there's a little beach hut out there beckoning me towards it. I think of the reality of having to be here working away like a honeybee but getting nowhere fast. My highlight of the day is getting giddy over whether to have a Cream Egg or Twix. It's a sad state of affairs really.

I keep saying I should join a gym but something always crops up. A stress release coffee with friend's house, a night out, or taking Ayeisha to one of her many weekly activities. I do want to join a gym, but would it be worth it I get bored so easy. I'll pay a year's subscription then only go half a dozen times before the novelty wears off. Lately Stan has taken to telling me my backside is growing *and* cellulite is setting in. He moans 'Once its there you'll not get rid of it, you'll be sorry' he frowns. Okay so I'm not perfect, but do I really need to hear I have the 'C' word. Even thinking of the word brings me out in a rash. Then he delights in saying how he tells be for my own good. I end up shouting 'Really, please tell me some more why don't you, I'm all ears Babe'

Strangely he doesn't take the hint. He then proceeds to ask why I don't join a gym. Even though I had been thinking about it I'm hardly going to admit it to him am I. I'll never hear the end of it. I'd be going to get toned and feel healthy but he'd be telling me 'I told you I was right.' Even though I know, and I say this with gritted teeth mind, that he is right. Again, I hardly want to tell him he's right. I mean, how would he get his head through the door for starters. He insists on telling me as it is whether good or bad. Trouble is the good I can hear all day… I love you, you're beautiful, you're so perfect… but the bad.. having a bad hair day dear… its out of condition isn't it… your arse is getting bigger… those clothes aren't as loose as they used to be are they... is it PMT again dear. Somehow this is nothing I'm rushing to hear. No I think men really need to work on their communication skills.

Maybe I should buy him a book on how to treat your woman. But it would have to be titled 'How to get the best out your woman' that way he thinks he's getting something out of it. To make matters worse he's nagging me on how much chocolate I eat again. After he found all my wrappers in the car when I broke down I can hardly deny it. It has got to the point I've resorted to eating chocolate when he's not around. I don't mean to hide it but it's far easier to enjoy it in peace when he's not around. If Stan knows I'm hiding it he'll tell me I have a problem and probably sign me up to chocononamous.

Its like when Easter comes around I'll buy Easter Eggs a week or two before. I have yet to master the art of not eating any prior to handing them out. Especially if it's Cadbury's. I even buy an extra egg just in case of an emergency. Trying to convince myself the extra egg is for someone I might have forgotten. When I know it's in case I eat one. Trouble is I have never met this someone I might have forgotten. They must be pretty special because I've never forgotten to buy for them yet.

Then I started to by two extra two eggs. One for the temptation and one for the special forgotten person. I still end up eating them both. Some people would be in heaven if they went out on a drinking binge and couldn't remember what they did the night before. My heaven would be to bathe in melted chocolate and have a glass of Baileys to go with it. And the Bailey's would have a of scoop of vanilla ice-cream in it and maybe a smudging of Tia Maria in it. Then soak in a hot bubbly bath with lots of candles and smellies thrown in chilling to soft music in the background. To my defence I have heard chocolate is good for you, something to do with the coco-bean. So there you go I have it on good authority a chocolate orange a day keeps the Doctor away. Stan never did find this joke funny. To be fair he tells me he loves me all the time, and gives in to an argument before I do. But I could argue that's because he's already had his say and wants to end it, whereas I will still be raging.

He always tells me when I look nice. But tells me I should hear the not so nice comments to appreciate the good ones, and this time the fury is the 'C' word. A few days after the 'C' word Stan starts being extra nice. Which worries me, he must be up to something. He's commenting on how nice I look but laughing while saying it. Yes he's is definitely up to something. He's even offered to cook tea for us asking what do you fancy. Then adds 'you look nice today.' Sorry was it a mirage, he's offering to cook *and* commenting on how nice I look all in the same breath. It must be the bang on the head and I'm hallucinating.

I'm wondering where this is leading when he asks if I'm going out at the weekend. I answer 'This one must be good' whilst looking him straight in the eyes. He laughs and asks what am I talking about can't he be nice to his woman. Now I'm really worried and try figuring out what the hell he's up to. I bet it's a fishing trip. Oh well if he's creeping I might as well make it more enjoyable and toy with him now won't I. Just how much will he squirm before he spits out what his plan is. He's being far too nice it's almost sickly. Normally he's pleasant or unpleasant. But this trying to be nice malarkey is far more disturbing.

Then quite matter of fact and out of the blue he asks how much redundancy and savings I have. I did not expect this, it hit me light a bolt of lightening. Where has this come from I wonder.

More to the point where is it going. I ask why he wants to know what savings I have. 'I was just wondering' he tells me looking curious and trying desperately not to laugh. 'Yes but why are you wondering, is what I want to know.' I try to think ahead about what he wants it for, before I can answer how much I have. If he thinks I'm giving, no rephrase that, lending my money for fishing tackle, then he can kiss my sun kissed backside. After some sparring back and forth between us, he finally he spits it out. He's running short on cash, and needs to finish the renovation on the house he's bought. Then he laughs asking 'you could help if I wanted to.' I reply yes I could couldn't I, but that's if I wanted to and I don't.

He moans it's almost finished, he could motor on with a little more cash. 'With my help no doubt' I ask. All he can muster is a wry 'Of course.' and tries to smile. Don't you just love it when its payback time. Keep hanging on in there long enough and revenge tastes all the sweeter. But how much does he need I ask myself. So with a delightful smile on my face and I try not to burst out laughing in his face when I say 'But Stan, I distinctly remember someone saying you'll need me before I'll need you. Now I wonder who on earth could have said that, now let me think.' Yes straight for the jugular and it hit him hard as I watch him squirm.

If it was the other way round I know he'd definitely make me squirm. He laughs knowing it's funny. Especially as he was sooo adamant I would need him before he needed me. I think I'm going to enjoy this moment rather a lot. Oh how the tide is a turning, ha bloody ha! He asks a few more times before I reply 'I'll think about it, but what's it worth. He looks at me stunned 'what do you mean what's it worth.' What else could I reply but 'you'll have to make it worth my while won't you otherwise it's not worth me drawing my bonds out.

He has to walk away into the kitchen, because if he doesn't he'll laugh. Well laugh or strangle me one or the other. Whilst I milk it for all I can of course shouting 'Just one sugar in my tea thanks.' Strangely through the kitchen door I heard a couple of pans being banged about. 'Oh dear I wonder what all that racket can be about' I ask myself out loud. Of course his strop makes me laugh even more. Not out of meanness I can assure you. But all I can picture is Stan's face whilst stropping about. You see one thing he can't stand is not being in control. Plus, to know that I have the upper hand makes him absolutely furious. God forbid he has to depend on me, knowing I won't make it easy for him.

He knows that unless he wants to go through the bank and all the hassle of form after form, all the time it takes then asking for approval and all the rigmarole proving you can repay the money back, he knows he needs me. And more to the point he has to be nice because of it. Which I suppose is a bit like saying I feel like the cat that's got the cream. It isn't as if he hasn't any money and I'm gloating. Not at all his is all tied up. Which makes him more angry knowing its there but can't get to it. 'Oh dear' I say with a smile on my face. We eat our meal that Stan has so caringly prepared, but in a little silence. I'm not going to mention it, and he hasn't mentioned my savings for half an hour now. Half of me thinks he can't want it that badly or he would be asking for it. The other half thinks he's never going to ask because of stubbornness. Never mind time will tell.

An hour or so later and right on queue he braves the subject again. Sulking 'Are you going to help or not.' This means he's getting bored with our little sparring and demands an answer. 'Yes I'm willing to help but what is it worth for me' and I add a sarcastic smile to help ease the pain. He shouts something about me being spiteful. But I'm genuinely not being spiteful. Yes I'm making him squirm, but if I help it has to be to my benefit too. 'Stan my savings are in bonds, I could win next month, but I'm not going to win if you have hold of my money.' I suppose I was slightly stressing my. I explain 'Now come on its only fair now isn't it', Go on Babe, make me an offer I can't refuse.' Now I couldn't stop laughing. I think it was when he starting frothing at the mouth that set me off. I can't help but add I want any agreement in writing. Or the whole deal is off.

Mortified he starts ranting 'What am I talking about an agreement in writing.' I tell him straight if we have a row, he'll say I'm not getting my money back, just to be a smart arse. I didn't think he would take it this well, but after a while he calms down saying 'Don't be so bloody stupid.' But is he just trying to soften me up, I'm not too sure on this one. With a sweet smile I reply 'Not on your life Mr, you want my dosh then I want it in writing, signed sealed and delivered Baby.' I explain that way there'll be no arguing later on, no saying 'I said it was a gift and didn't want it back. I've watched Judge Judy, she says to wise up.

I ask him what is the interest rate is these days. But he doesn't take my sarcasm well. Stan strops back into the kitchen, no he's definitely not enjoying this one. Having to ask me for help and knowing he can't have his own way all the time he sulks. Ayeisha arrived home early and caught the last half of our discussion. She moans at me 'You're well tight on Dad.' I'm not able to hold it in. Grinning I can't help but say 'God its not like I'm going to make him beg or anything.. For long.' I take it he heard me because he's banging the pans about again.

Bursting with laughter I tell her 'Bash stick with me Babe, I'll teach you everything I know.' Well I found it funny, she tried to hide her grin for as long as she could but even she had to laugh in the end. But for some strange reason Stan didn't speak to me for another hour. When he did finally speak he moaned 'I'd rather go five rounds with Mike Tyson than with you, you're like a bleedin' Jack Russell, once you sink your teeth in you don't let go.' I had to laugh to myself but I couldn't let him hear me.

We spent the evening not really talking, just skirting around the issue. Neither of us wants to approach the bonds issue because neither of us wants a row. When bedtime came it felt like an eternity. I hoped to get a good nights sleep but is he going to let me. Twenty five minutes silence in bed was heaven, I knew it was too good to last. Stan not being content to let it go shouts 'You've got to be the most stubborn person I've ever had the misfortune to meet.' Well that's like showing a red rag to a bull isn't it. Of course I don't mean to. But as I'm getting a little giddy from the sparring, and that I have the upper hand, I laugh 'Well aren't you the lucky one.' I knew this was pushing things over the edge slightly, but it was meant in jest to wind him up, not to be nasty.

But Stan definitely didn't see the funny side of it at all. So unless I want a blazing row over a minor joke I have to be nice. Otherwise he'll look for the nearest thing to launch at the wall. I suppose I could grovel a little and say sorry. Sorry for being mean, sorry for gloating, and I suppose sorry for enjoying trying to wind him up. But can I help it if I have a wicked sense of humour. And let's face it he does ask for it at times.

He says if he tormented me like I do him then I would be crying. Well yes I probably would, but it is funny winding up someone else when you have the upper hand. Nor does it mean he needs to enjoy winding me up as and when he feels like it. But he does. We decide to sleep on it and maybe come to some sort of agreement. He gets my money and I get something out of it too, and that is my final thought on the matter.

When I go back to work trust the office to take my mind off things. It's funny how things turn out. One of the girls who didn't like the idea of pierced belly buttons decides to have hers pierced. Is this is the same one who was screaming 'Eeww' at the thought is now having hers done. I find this hilarious. Now the others are blaming me for leading her astray. Are they not grown women who can decide for themselves. Did I march her to the shop saying you will join my cult and have yours pierced. Can you believe them blaming me for being a bad influence. I chuckle to myself that she's being daring. And that I'm bringing the office into disrepute.

To top it off when she went for the piercing she took her sister along for moral support. The sister thought it looked great and only went and had hers pierced too. The only problem was neither of their husbands like piercing. Next they'll be blaming me if they had tattoos. Not quite believing what they had done, they both went home shocked at their own impulsiveness. But next on the agenda is how to tell the hubbies back at home. What on earth are they going to say, I think I've just had an Ang moment. When they arrived home it suddenly dawned on them that their children were listening from in the back of the car. They try to disguise what they were talking about and say the worst thing you could ever say to kids.... 'Don't tell your Dad, it's only pretend.'

Why on earth tell kids don't tell. It's obviously the first thing the brats shout when they get home is Mummy's got a secret. Before they had time to make up a story one of the little brats shout 'Mummy's got a secret in her belly and its pretend.' Her husband nearly fainted at the idea of another pregnancy. Especially when they were supposed to be saving all the money they could find to move to a bigger house. The last thing he wanted was her to give up work for another year to look after a child.

She saw the colour drain from his face and thought he was about to faint. 'It's not what you think' she tells him and quickly lifts her blouse up showing her off her new jewellery. Thank God for that he sighs 'I thought you were'…'butting in she says sarcastically I know exactly what you were thinking, pregnant.' He was quite relieved it was a piercing after all. Of course he blames me for putting the idea into her head. Ha ha who'd have thought it Ang, the rebel. The quiet one who doesn't get drunk leading the office astray being such a bad influence. When I had my piercing the hubbies had said what's she had that done for at her age. Then they run out and get it done. I find it hilarious. I think I'll have a tattoo now, only a fake one. Someone is bound to say I've always wanted one but never found the courage with all those needles. They'll rush out and get a tattoo and then I'll wash mine off actually makes me smile. Oh I am turning wicked.

I think we all get too strung up over things that aren't relevant. We really need to our hair down a little more often. After all you can take a piercing out and let it heal, it's hardly worth fighting about. Almost everybody I've ever worked with in any company they plan their life out. It's a wonder some get through the day if it's not planned out for them in advance. Some even plan what they're going to eat for the next two weeks. I don't mean having plenty of food in the house, but literally what meals they have on certain days. What would they do if their child wants carrots not peas on a Tuesday, are they still going to function.

Its good to be practical to plan but surely you'd want part of your life a surprise. Everybody but Sebastian seems to be planning for the next two years. I think this has gone beyond having something to look forward too. You'd think they were doctors planning around life threatening schedules.

Trudy is planning her retirement. That's a fantastic idea but don't stop living until you do retire. It could be twenty years or more away. How do they know if they are going to be here in twenty years time. What if Trudy's job doesn't last until their retirement. Will she still be married to the same person when she retires. I dread the thought of getting old, I want to stay young forever. Which the others say is quite possible for me because I'll always be in a 21 year old state of mind. I suppose they have a point.

I can't comprehend only planning for my retirement, it would send me nuts. It's one thing planning to enjoy retirement, but only focusing on retirement. Surely an alarm bell should ring somewhere. I don't think any of them would consider booking a holiday a week before going away. They'd need at least twelve months in advance to know where they are going. When I booked a holiday the week before going away I actually saw colleagues twitching with worry on my behalf. I, on the other hand thought it was great and exciting knowing this time next week I'll be on a beach somewhere but have no idea anywhere. Maybe it's me, maybe I'm programmed wrong and everybody else has got it right. But I think I'd rather be in my world.

We all have to plan for time, schedules and money. But when the office talk is deciding what jobs to do on their houses in two years time, and then another few jobs three or four years later, that's when I consider banging my head on the table. I mean we could be run over by a bus next week. I know Stan and I are probably the other extreme. But planning that far ahead is mind blowing. They insist its something to look forward to. Whereas I on the other hand feel its forever away, and half your life has passed you by in the meantime. I suppose you could say I have the attention span of a child. I need it here and now or not at all syndrome. Although I have grown a little more responsible since becoming a parent. Motherhood does make you grow up, but only to a certain extent. The child is within us the whole time, but some of us manage to cover it up better than others.

Like the fact we want to travel, they ask what about Ayeisha. But that's the whole point so that we can take her with us. I want her to experience different countries and cultures. But they look at me like I've gone mad. I'd go mad if I know what the daily drivel is planned for me twelve months in advance. If its going to be the same in twelve months time then I'd rather not know. I need some spontaneity, at least then you get a surprise, something out of the ordinary. Although even I'm not in the same spontaneity league as Stan. He literally is lastminute.com to the extreme. This of course makes for hard work and lots of headaches.

If one of the guys at work wanted to hire a boat and travel the ocean, then I understand this type of planning ahead. Something special, a goal to look forward to. But day to day drivel, knowing what your going to do today, tomorrow, next month, next year. Or knowing what you'll do in two years time. God no, I can't focus on that time scale. Especially if I'm in the same job. My mind wanders, I switched off. I'm picking my spot on a beach somewhere sunny. Drifting away I'm thinking what could I be doing today instead of being at work nine till five. Why can't I find a job that inspires me. I envy those who love their work. Who are stimulated by it and couldn't imagine doing anything else.

I suppose I'm like everyone else expecting the job to come running to us. It's as if we don't need to look for it because we'll end up falling over it, realising it was there all the time. The only thing I seem to fall over is my cornflakes. As much as most of the guys at work can be great fun, living like them frightens me to death. But I'd rather live like them than be like Olive or Gertie, miserable and bitter, acting like the world owes them something. The only thing I want to look forward to in the next couple of years is to live a little. Get the chance to travel whilst we are still young enough to enjoy it together. Well, circumstances permitting.

You've probably realised by now that life isn't always that simple, especially mine. With usually one trauma or another going on. My perfect scenario would be giving up work, take Ayeisha out of school for a year or so and take off travelling around the world. But I mention this to the guys at work and they start having palpitations for me. I explain to the others she would go back to school when we return. But you'd have thought I'd said I was leaving her home alone with the look of horror they gave me. They'd think I've gone stark raving mad. Just think what a teenager would gain having a year out. The experience couldn't be compared to anything. I feel like rushing into school and announcing to the teachers Ayeisha will be having 'time out.' It's her bonding time with Mum & Dad. You can imagine how this would go down. We even thought of getting a lap-top computer so Bash can email homework to school, stopping her from falling behind whilst we're away. But asking school for a week off let alone a few months is like asking pigs to fly, so I don't see that happening either. The school's view is taking your child out then lose your place in school and they'll report you to the authorities. I don't think the Gestapo was that strict.

It doesn't help the matter when I took Ayeisha on holiday last year. And yes it happened to be during school time. But in my defence it was the first week of term. It's not as if they'd get much work done anyway. I reassure myself they'll be on wind down from the half term break anyway. Stan insisted he couldn't go away with us. You know the old workload won't permit time off again. So I took Ayeisha away with my girlfriends which were great fun. But when I thought of Stan at home alone I did feel pangs of guilt. I thought he would relish the idea of peace and quiet. He's always moaning about how he would like time by himself away from us. Something about the house being full of female hormones. Even Bonnie & Jip are female.

Yet he moaned it was quiet and lonely without us. When we came back off our holiday, me being me saw this as a perfect opportunity to remind him just how lucky he is to have me. Cheeky I know. But he said something about me being hard work. Couldn't think for the life of me what he meant by this. Me, hard work, as if. Okay, so I may be a little demanding at times. And I suppose you could say a little temperamental. Well alright then a little stubborn. But what can you do, he knew what I was like when he met me. He can hardly start moaning now can he.

Whilst on holiday with the girls it could hardly go incident free now could it. Although I must admit it wasn't quite on the scale of Gibraltar. Though at first, it did feel like it was starting off like Gibraltar II. We arrived at the airport early as you do because we wanted seats together and try to miss the rush. Only for our flight to be delayed, by seven hours. Of course the airport was heaving and no seats to wait on. What else would it be like when I go on holiday. What was I expecting, someone to collect my bags as my car pulls up. Wheel my though the people like the red sea parting. Check me in immediately and zoom me straight to departure lounge with drinks on hand.

No, I'm not quite at the first class level. More the substandard pilchard level like most of us. I'm lucky enough to get crushed in the rush at check-in. That is if I still have my ankles in tact. I get to waste seven hours reading papers or spending my money in the bar. Ayeisha will want all the books and magazines in the shops so I'll be lucky to be left with ten pounds at this rate. Then if I'm really lucky I get horded through to departure lounge. And just to make my flight all the more pleasurable, I get the big fella with the breathing difficulties next to me like I usually do. Getting to hear snorting and wheezing all through the flight. And if I'm really lucky he'll take up the whole of my arm rest and half my seat. And squash me by taking all my leg room, because he'll hardly have room for his own will he. Gosh, aren't I the lucky one.

I feel drained before we've even begun. It definitely feels like the start of holiday from hell. With a seven hour delay we might as well make the most of it. No point in getting worked up, we'll only make a show of ourselves, for a change. We tried finding the comfy seats but all of them were taken up obviously.

I don't believe it but what choice do we have in the matter. Either seven hours standing or seven hours squashed on seats like pilchards until our flight comes in. Lovely, just bloody lovely. Everybody else I know seems to arrive at the airport with only minutes to spare, gets to check-in straight away and waltz straight through to boarding within minutes. Oh no not us, we have the pleasure of boarding at eight pm. It will be three in the morning when we arrive. We had pictured ourselves dumping the luggage in our hotel by teatime. Then get a look around the town at least. Now we've missed our first evening on holiday. It could have been worse we could have only been going away for the weekend. I suppose I should be grateful we are away for a week.

With nothing else much to do we wander aimlessly around the airport checking out the shops. But what for, it's not like we have any room in our luggage anyway. Luckily a few flights had left freeing up some of those comfy seats. But after an hour or so of sitting our bums are numb. We go for yet another wander to fill the time. I think the kiosk lady thinks were stalking her. Ayeisha stood there reading three books from the shelves already.

Before long we're bored and back on the comfy seats for yet more numb bums. Just when we're nodding off our flight is called. Jumping up a little too excited my bag catches the table. It's just my luck to knock all the glasses on the table crashing to the floor. Thank God most of the heaving crowd had gone. Because everything had quietened down, it makes the sound of the glasses echo round like a ping pong ball. Seemingly going louder and louder. Everybody stops and stares at what the racket is.

I can't look up at their faces because I'm too busy cringing. So I do the next best thing and shout 'Ayeisha try to be careful please' in a sarcastic tone. Poor thing, she's so shocked she stood staring at me open mouthed, then moans it wasn't me. Of which my friends heard and burst out laughing. Its times like this that kids come in handy. We board the flight quickly in desperation.

When we finally arrive at our destination its pitch black. We're collected from the airport by coach. And of course our hotel is right at the top of the mountain. And yes everyone else gets dropped off first. The only sight we get is a few drunks coming back to the hotel arguing over who paid for the taxi. What a great start. As we've missed dinner we're told food has been put aside for us when we arrive. But the food consisted of dried up ham and cheese slices on rock hard bread rolls with the resident flies on a table left out in the hall. Because it's late the restaurant is locked up. The only drinks available are in the vending machine which none of us have change for. Bloody brilliant, we get to sip our luke warm water we still have from the airport back in Manchester. I find a half eaten chocolate bar in the bottom of my bag, at least we get to nibble on the remains.

We wait around for assistance for at least another half an hour as reception doesn't open until seven am. Eventually the security guard manages to get hold of our keys and shows us to our room. We can't get much information from him because his English is not very good, and our Spanish is even worse. On our arrival in the dark our rooms seem to be right at the back of the hotel. We go in lifts downstairs then outside through a maze of pathways past bungalows, and then eventually reaching our rooms.

Our room is two doors away from our friends. At least we are in shouting distance. We had only been there for less than an hour when Maria runs into our room hysterical quickly followed by Sadie. 'What's wrong now Maria' but her face looks frightened to death, then squealed she's not sleeping in that room. She's convinced a load of crawling things are in there and she's sure she saw a cockroach. That's it I won't sleep tonight or what's left of the night. Ayeisha looks at me like I've dragged her to hell. Her eyes are almost popping out of the head poor thing.

Stan needn't have worried of us having a great time without him at this rate. They go off to find the security guard who promptly hands them a can of fly killer. He then points to the crawly things and points to the can. I think this is an indication they have to spray the crawlies themselves. This looks to be the start of another classic 'Ang' holiday. It's too late to sort the crawlies out. All we want to do is sleep. I tell them both kip in our room I have a double bed, with a single bed and a sofa going spare. Although I'm dreading what tomorrow might bring.

It turned out that their balcony door had been left open. Hence the crawlies joining them in in the night. Things finally settled down but we are not taking any chances. We keep a lamp on during the night. We spend ten minutes giving the beds and sheets a good shake down. And then a further ten minutes tucking all the sheets in the beds. Not that we were paranoid or anything. It felt like we'd had an hours sleep when morning arrived.

Starving we decide to brave breakfast. But after the reception we received the night before we were somewhat dubious. To our surprise it turns out to be rather nice. Breakfast is in mid flow with full continental breakfasts, lots of fresh fruit and refreshing cereal in this heat. Now I understand why they say sleep on it things always look better in the morning.

The foyer is bustling with tourists and the reception is back on duty. Great, a chance to get some local currency! There's a lot of staff buzzing around and the restaurant was full. We can't help but be relieved at the pleasant atmosphere. Thank God for that after worrying about early signs this was becoming the holiday from hell. The weather was fantastic it had that holiday smell you always remember. It must be something to do with the ocean air mixed with sunshine. We want to wander into town and relax near the beach somewhere. We are told there are a few steps leading to the town.

I laugh with Ayeisha at least there won't be the Mediterranean Steps. Can you believe it once again our hotel is at the top of the hill. There must be a hundred or more steep steps leading to the town. At first we thought it a good idea to get some exercise. But after fifty steps we're not sure this is a good idea because we're shattered from lack of sleep and a little dehydration from yesterday. We decide to spend the rest of the day lazing on the beach. We all feel sorry for ourselves at who has the numbest bum and weakest legs. Of course I win the whinging competition.

When we get back to our hotel I jump in the shower to freshen up. But as the water gushes out I feel my chest burning. The water isn't hot but it feels like its burning me. I've only gone and burnt myself sunbathing, and it's really sore in the middle between my bikini top. I'm usually quite careful in the sun always putting cream on. I must have missed this bit. Bloody hell, now its going to burn me in between my boobs the whole holiday. I wouldn't mind but it already looks red raw. Brilliant, now I get to do an impression of a tanned lobster for the rest of the week. I wouldn't mind but I'm the dark one, Sadie is pale and hasn't burnt in the slightest. Although it did go hot after lunch I didn't think it was enough to burn. I thought after a good breakfast and a morning by the beach things were looking up until I burnt.

Fortunately the next few days go smoothly. Maria's room is crawly free and we get our room back. Either the hotel is fairly quiet, or we've been put at the quieter end at least. We potter around the town shopping and lazing by the beach. One night after dinner we decide to wander further on up the hill. There were a few bars at the top. Everyone is well behaved enjoying drink outside and thankfully we don't see any drunken brawls. It was still quite warm and the sun was setting. In our wisdom we decide to see what was at the top of the hill. Bash was in heaven, she'd spotted a row of huge trampolines and a bull machine. One of those things that spins you around before launching you into the air really undignified at ninety miles an hour. The one that all the drunks get on thinking they are John Wayne, yet seem to last all of three seconds. I shouldn't really comment because I wouldn't last more two seconds myself.

Of course the guy tries to goad anyone passing to have a go. Normally we wouldn't be seen dead on something like that. But, as there's no one else around, as all sane people are relaxing enjoying a quiet drink somewhere. We decide to have a go, reluctantly at first of course. Now if there is one thing to make you look very unlady like this would be it. Of course I whinge it will be too fast for me. The bloke takes pity on me and offers to keep it slow. I like a fool get on it. But he started it on the lowest speed which for a normal person would be ok. I however felt like I was already on a roustabout.

Then he went to the next level which launched me across the padded floor in thee most undignified way imaginable. Dazed I get up trying to be calm as if it didn't bother me, except I feel like I have whiplash! Knowing my luck I'll probably put my back out. Bash of course stayed on for ages. I think she tucked herself under the bull's ears and tied her belt around its neck or something because he kept turning the speed up and she still stayed on, the little git. Sadie and Maria have a go. Thankfully they didn't last long either. In all we made complete Pratts of ourselves. All except Bash who got the highest score of the night.

It went really dark quite quickly on the way home. All the flies and crawlies were out in force. And all of them seem to be hovering around us. It's like a little cloud of dust hovering above except this one is full of flies. When we walk down the hill back to our hotel I happen to be nearest to the road. When all of a sudden I saw something from the corner of my eyes. It half flew half bounced out of the side heading directly for me. What ever it was it moved fast and looked like its wings were half open. It was certainly no humming bird that's for sure.

I tried to tell the others something had jumped towards me but I froze and couldn't get my words out. Unaware they carry on talking. As it flew towards me near the kerb. The only options were either let it jump on my feet, I push them out of the way or I jump to the right. Within seconds I'd already jumped to the right. But it came back towards me even faster. The closer it got the larger it got. Alright I may be prone to a little exaggeration. But my eyes got wider, this thing felt like it was growing in size too. I mouthed a scream but no sound came out.

I jumped back bouncing from one foot to another desperate to stop it attacking my feet. I don't know why but I start waving my arms around in the air. Like that's going to make a damn difference. This time I jumped to the right and straight into the road. A car came speeding down the hill blasting its horn at me. I'd completely forgotten the traffic would come from behind me. Thank God there wasn't any traffic in the other lane as the car swerved into it to miss me. I heard them shouted something in their local lingo but I was too busy having a heart attack from the shock of almost being killed. Of course all the girls could do was nearly wet themselves laughing. They said I looked like I was doing a ridiculous impersonation of an Indian war dance. Is it our perfume that attracts the crawlies or what. Or is it is me and I'm on holiday something is bound to happen to make sure I don't have too good a time.

For the past few days our hotel seemed really quiet compared to our first night. But then it had to start didn't it. We could hardly go home without having some altercation with the neighbours. This is me on holiday after all. During the night the most ridiculous racket was going on next door. Bang bang bloody bang it seemed to go on forever. It sounded like they were having a fight in the wardrobes. It must have been around three o'clock in the morning. Are these people for real or what. What on earth possess them to behave like that. I could hear a man and woman talking so loudly you'd think they were in my bathroom. Then not content with the racket so far, they decide to stomp along the floor. A tiled floor I might add. Her heels are clomping across the floor echoing around the room. Then just for good measure they start dragging things across the floor scraping them from one side of the room to another.

The sound of scraping along the floor is unbearable. It sounds like suitcases full of lead weights. Then it goes a little quieter so there is a God after all. Half an hour later the banging starts again. It sounds like their wardrobes are coming off their hinges. We try sleeping covering the pillows over our heads but still we hear it. What on earth can they be doing, surely they can't be packing at this ungodly hour.

After what seems like an eternity I end up banging on the wall, hoping this might quieten them down. They are talking so loud you can tell they're drunk. Although there only seems to be two of them they're make enough noise for a room full. Where's the thunderbolt of lightening when you need one. Oh, how I would love to have special powers, god only knows what I'd do to them. All I know is I would really enjoy it.

The damn racket continues and me becoming a mad woman possessed, because one thing I don't do well is not getting enough sleep, I grab hold of a shoe and start banging the heel on the wall. I shout for them to shut up and start ranting 'are you bloody lonely waking the place up at this time of the night.' Jeez, don't they have any consideration. They are so drunk they don't even hear us. After another half hour it finally goes quiet again. The next thing I know its breakfast time.

Thankfully the rest of our vacation goes well and more to the point uneventful. We get to do lots of sightseeing and trips out on a boat. Making sure we keep out of the sun at midday. After all is there anything more unflattering than a pair of burnt breasts, I think not. We enjoyed having breakfast cooked for us, shopping and relaxing together. We phoned home a few times to speak to Stan and make sure he was behaving himself. I thought he'd have put the flags up the minute we'd gone but he really missed us. Aw my lovely, lovely Stan, I can't wait to get home.

~ Chapter Nineteen ~ **Back Home & Dressing Up**

We returned home at the weekend just in time for a friend's birthday. I know I've been home but a few hours when the girls ring. I have to ask Stan if he minds after all it's my first night home. It was a bit cheeky to bugger off out straight away but luckily he doesn't mind too much. The girls are getting together for a few drinks and decide on Stalybridge. Lately known as Staly-vegas. We had been in one of the bars less than an hour when I bumped into Ayeisha's teacher. Now bearing in mind we have just stepped off a plane and glowing with a tan that doesn't look a week old is probably not the best thing to do in the world.

We had told Ayeisha's school a little white lie, that she had been ill. Now is probably not the right time to discuss how she is getting on in school. I can't even look her teacher in the eye. I feel really embarrassed and hope he doesn't ask what we have been doing over the half term. I'm sure to cringe and give it away. Of course the first thing he enquires of is if Ayeisha is over her sickness yet. My eyes open so wide almost popping out of my head. Knowing that I'm telling porkies and worse still I think he knows I'm telling porkies, my face glows bright red. I try to say she's feeling much better and will be back in school soon. I pray the girls don't say anything to drop me in it. But before I can blink and right on queue one of them pipes up 'Yes she's feeling much better now they've got back off holiday.' I almost spat my drink all over him, how I held it in I'll never know.

Trying to think quickly and get myself out of a hole I add 'Yes she must have picked up a bug during the half term or when we returned.' I'm so embarrassed I can hardly make eye contact. I think being a teacher he could suss out a lie a mile away. I glance down quickly to check my sandals, making sure I haven't any sand showing between my toes. That's all I need a dusting of sand to drop out now to show me up. Damn that was close.

As usual I start with the nervous laugh again, starting today because I'm lying, as the nerves can be relied upon for setting it off. The trouble is it looks like I am not bothered or even being ignorant when it starts. I genuinely can't help it and anything sets it off. I resolve that my New Year resolutions will be: Must try to control the nerves; must behave; must stop telling lies, okay only when vitally necessary.

Back at work we are informed our offices are closing down. Apparently it works so much better in the French office that ours get to close. Oh, and just for good measure lets extend the French offices to make them even larger. Now bearing in mind as a general rule only half the staff turn up for work in the French office in any one week. They have to have lots of staff to cover the office because so many of them often throw sickies. Not that I'm bitter that they get away with it. Then there are the long lunches, the holidays, the flexitime and the national holidays. Oh and lets not forget the strikes. At least one every other month is it. They have this odd laid back attitude to the business on one hand. Yet on the other hand they are sticklers for the job. And when they don't get their goods it's a life or death situation. They'll be on the phone demanding answers. Yet when we want staff to be in work, hey lets have a strike.

They certainly don't think the business is priority over lunch time/break time/home time/flex time/strike time. And guess what, we have the pleasure of training the new staff to take our jobs. Oh yes and we mustn't forget the mission statement. Something about providing the best service to our customers. I suppose they could interpret this as when they put our UK Key accounts on hold whilst on the phone. And maybe whilst they waltz about the office 'finding out what they need' only to tell them 'we'll get back to you' meaning can't be arsed.

Oh well good luck to them. So long as we get a decent redundancy package is all I'm bothered about. I'm getting used to being made redundant now. I know a couple of the French staff are really nice and would fit in the Manchester office, they have been a pleasure to work with. But some of the others bring a whole new meaning to the word arrogant. Those I shall not miss.

Its not that big a problem really we can always find jobs elsewhere. Maybe it is time to move on to the next phase of our lives. After all it has to be an improvement on the past doesn't it.

And those who want to keep in touch can. Although I'll probably miss our nights out. Who's going to entertain me now? We'll have to have a reunion with the gang and find out what everyone is up to like a school reunion. Trouble is once you move on you don't get time to keep in touch. Most of us have taken it well. All except Gertie and Olive. Gertie is probably worried who will take her on with her flexible attitude to office etiquette. And Olive just wants to be in the drama of it. But a new place of work, lets face it would we find the same characters again. Maybe, but I'm sure not all together under the same roof. Unless I am really unlucky in life. Which looking at this past year is more than probable. The gang are still saying to me it could only happen to you.

I think the gang are expecting me to have the same characters following me around where ever I go. But surely not am I really going to have a Gertie and an Olive, the madness of Jenifer, Jerry and Trudy, the dramatics of Lawrence and Sebastian and the weirdness of Larry. Could there really be more of them out there in every office. And God forbid I work with another me, I just couldn't cope. Can I not find a thriving office where everybody is positive with no dramas or attitudes.

The others laugh that I'm on a planet of my own. Saying its like I walk around in a zone with this aura around me. And not necessarily a good aura. You see if something is going to happen, you can bet your life it will happen to me or around me. Or to someone close to me. I sometimes wonder if it is me as I do seem to attract something. Maybe I was born on a crossed land line or something or I was meant to be born on the thirteenth.

We are informed the new staff are due to arrive and we are needed to train them on the computer systems. Not enough of the French staff are used to the new computer system. We think it's because they are never in work long enough to learn it. Never mind at least we are here to show them what we do and how they work. They've sent over a girl who has just joined the office for training. Aren't we the lucky ones, we lose our jobs but we'll train you to do it better than us. Oh the irony, only the English could suffer this. Any other establishment would probably be putting the road blocks up as we speak.

We are not ecstatic, but if we do a good hand over of the office we get to earn an extra bonus on top of our redundancy. So the German girl arrives, the office checks her out and decides she looks quite boyish in her dungarees. And her hair looks boyish. We thought she would have been quite stylish wearing a suit or skirt and blouse at least. Already Sebastian starts doing impressions of her behind the door as we try desperately to keep our faces straight. As Sebastian speaks German he speaks with her throughout the morning. She isn't quite what we expected, but then again we don't know what she thought of us either. We settle down start the training, if you can call it settling down. She told us that if she didn't get the job then it would have proved that the company's management team was incompetent. We thought she was arrogant.

You'd think if you were being trained by people about to lose their jobs then a little sensitivity might apply. Oh no not this one. Whilst showing this one, she seems to think we show her once then she'll decide her own way of doing things is better. I agree you'll have your own thoughts about how you work. But you'd at least get the training over with first then go back and do it your way. And not tell those training you 'By the way you've been working crap for the last few years, so let me show you how to do it better! But hell who are we to argue. This goes on for a couple of days.. That is until she goes on visits to our biggest customers. She advises our customers that she will make it work much better for them when she gets back to her new offices. Well you can imagine we were ready to lynch her by this point.

The poor manager and the sales rep didn't know where to put their faces at her rudeness. And we had thought Gertie was bad. Jenifer offered to go with the group on the first visit but quickly declined the second one. Jenifer was incensed at the girl now known as the German. To top it off the German announces that Manchester isn't really that nice a place. That it looked rather grubby dismal and dirty. Now we can say what we like about Manchester, we live here it's our home. But a visitor telling you they think their town is shyte is the last straw.

Who could be that cheeky or arrogant about their hometown

besides Olive. And even she didn't go that far to upset us. We are all livid. Even Sebastian was infuriated because he thinks of Manchester as his second home. We've bit our tongues over her arrogance for a while now we've had enough. If she's not careful we'll show her what we really think of her and we won't be pleasant. The reception she received from the office was rather frosty after that. She put it down to all of us losing our jobs, and nothing to do with her. Trudy and Jerry want to lynch her.

Her attitude makes me think I would like to visit France and see the wonderful countryside there and embrace the wonderful world of long lunches and strikes. We are told to not start whilst she is here. That we should complain to her manager when gets back to her office that she was somewhat 'offensive.' And we are told not to take it personally. What! Don't take it personally, how else are we to take it. We have been asked to make allowances for her. Because her culture is to be much more direct than British culture. And that she should be taken with a pinch of salt. We'd rather boil her in salt.

British people are more likely not to tell the truth but try not to offend people than to go out of our way to cause upset. It's just not the English way. We tend to be a little reserved in that matter. Our manager reminds us of how ruthless and harsh we can be with each other. But this tends to be more when we are joking with each other winding each other up. That is until we are pushed, and this seems to be one of those occasions.

We've bitten our tongue for long enough and won't put up with crap like that. On the second visit Jerry went out with our manager and the German. Jerry made sure she sat in the front of the car making our new friend sit in the back. Just to be polite as you do. Returning Jerry rushed to the car ensuring the German got to sit in the back. Jerry asked her 'You don't mind sitting in the back do you' half expecting her to say yes. She didn't though, she just climbed into the back seat looking rather dejected. Jerry told us it was such a shame she didn't have an ejection seat. Trudy is still stewing over the outburst, she is absolutely steaming with temper. How Trudy kept her hands off her throat I don't know. Trudy is hoping the German accepts a brew off her.

At first I thought she this was rather odd and quite friendly under the circumstances.

Maybe Trudy was still in shock. That is until Trudy told us she wanted to put a few laxatives in her drink before she leaves for the airport. She said what can they do sack me. Unfortunately she doesn't want a brew, just a little water to drink. If this is the start of things to come, then what the hell will the rest be like. If the others think they can come here and rule the roost, then they can think again. Or the laxatives will be making an appearance.

And why are they sending German people to the French office anyway. Can't they get enough French staff to work or something. Apparently they will need a small hub in Germany too. Management decide to brief the next lot coming through for training. They ask them to be a little more sensitive to us whilst in the UK. And try to remember we are after all, losing our jobs of which they do abide by. The rest of them are actually rather pleasant. It's a shame they would be good fun to work with. Why is it just as its getting a little better its time for change.

We have special sayings in the office such as 'yes were happy to help you' meaning tell someone who gives a damn. Or 'I can't help you but I will find someone who can' meaning - *I* don't get paid enough to arse around for your drivel. And 'If you leave it with me I'll refer it to my manager ' – Don't myther me – I have a life outside of work and don't get paid enough to stay behind for you. And 'Of course I realise how important your custom is to us' – Yeh right, sod off and tell someone who gives a s**t.

When we say these phrases they we generally mean it sarcastically. For 'the German' we decide to say 'anything we can do to help you when you go back don't hesitate to ask' meaning now F**k Off we really mean it. Her name goes straight to the top of our office board for our interesting people! Let's hope she rings us, we'll keep her on hold for at least an hour.

To lighten the mood Sebastian tells us of the weekend away he is planning. He's going to Blackpool with some friends. Me being naive asks if he is going to do the lights or go to Funny Girls. 'No' he replies rather glib. But in the next breath announces he hasn't known these friends long. We find this a little strange as you go away with people you don't know. Its not as if he's just met these friends recently and he's really got on well with them, and they as ask him to join them. He admits he doesn't know them well at all.

Again, me being naive tell him there are lots of great Bed & Breakfast places so he won't be short of somewhere to stay. Of which he bursts out laughing at me. Sorry but have we missed the joke here. 'Why, what are you up to Sebastian' we ask intrigued. Is he going to meet someone and he hasn't let on to us. We question him a little more until he gives in. He says 'Well it's a special place I sometimes go to.' Intrigued we stare at him wondering what on earth could be coming next.

'You know what place it is' he tells us with a grin. Sorry Sebastian but we don't know. I ask is it somewhere that one of us might have been to. At this he bursts out laughing 'I don't think it's a place you've been to my friend.' We can't help but laugh, what on earth are we supposed to think of this outburst. All the office is staring waiting with abated breath of what is coming next. Its one of those moments where it all goes quiet and all eyes are upon you.

With the cheekiest smile and quite matter of fact he announces 'It is one of those Hotels, you know where you keep your door open.' Gob smacked I say 'God Sebastian, anyone can walk in in the middle of the night.' Of which he roars laughing. The rest of us laugh at him laughing at us. He replies 'That is the whole point Ang.' Gob smacked I just sit stunned staring at him.

Did I hear right then, I look round to see Jenifer nearly falling off her chair. Yes I did hear it right then. He laughs out loud again saying 'You never know who your going to meet' with a glint in his eye. I look shocked, I must have lived a very sheltered life. Because if I've ever stayed in a hotel the first thing I do is make sure the door is locked. To stop any old drunk or pervert from wandering in when you're asleep.

I keep grinning to myself for the rest of the day, scarcely believing he's so brazen about it. A little later Sebastian asks 'Come on Ang you must have tried it at some point.' Gob smacked I reply 'what, leave my hotel door open, intentionally hoping somebody will walk in, I don't think so.' I ask him isn't it more fun to meet somebody out in a bar, at least then you know what your getting. Having somebody wander in your room, you don't know what you're getting. 'No I don't think so Sebastian' I answer him mortified.

Besides it certainly wouldn't be George Clooney walking through the door. Knowing my luck it would be some scanky one eyed drunk with flees walking through the door. 'Oh come on Ang' he laughs 'I don't think even you would be that prudish.' 'No I don't think so Sebastian I am a little particular who I let grope me thank you very much.' Sebastian thinks this is hysterical. I look around at the others seeing their reaction, of which all are doubled up laughing. Is it me or what? The can't believe Sebastian's latest revelation. I notice they are all keeping quiet. Trudy is grinning and Jerry looks like she's ready to try it. I tell Sebastian Stan and I have been together for years. And, I must say, we don't often stay in a hotel and leave the door open for anything to crawl in. Sebastian tells me I should go wild and live a little.

I'm gob smacked and the office finds this the best fun they've had for a long time. Even Gertie finds this hilarious and joins in the laughter. Either that or she's enjoying laughing at me. Then not content that this is enough Sebastian asks me if Stan is exciting. Jenifer nearly falls off her chair, again. Trudy can't breathe for laughing. Poor Larry doesn't know where to put his face, he feels really embarrassed by this. I have to reply but to say what.

If I say yes he'll think I'm egging him on. If I say no just to shut him up he'll think Stan is boring. I'm in a no win situation. But I have to shut him up, I can hardly leave him to have the last word can I. With a cheeky grin I tell Sebastian 'Yes Stan is exciting enough for me thank you, and *you'll* never know.' Jenifer is trying to type away but still trying to earwig at the same time. Her shoulder is stretched as far across the table towards me as you can get without falling off her chair, again. I feel like telling her to move her table next to me if she wants.

Just when I thought this put an end to Sebastian's Spanish

inquisition he pipes up 'But would he dress up for you' he asks. 'Well of course he does' I answer sarcastically 'If we're going out he'll always gets dressed up. Sebastian stands there laughing, toying with me he replies 'No I mean would he dress up for you.' I'm thinking where the hell is he going here. But I must have been way off line because with his next breath he looks at me intensely asking 'What if you came home one day and caught him wearing your panties.' I was so shocked he asked this I burst out laughing in his face.

Gertie dropped the files she was holding and Olive looks like this is quite normal. But then again she is part Swedish so she's probably quite liberal in that department. 'Sebastian I'd be really worried if he fit in my underwear for a start' I tease. 'No Ang, I mean would you be offended, would it bother you.' Astounded I stare at him open mouthed.

Does he really want my answer, is he ready for my answer. I rant 'Well if I caught him in women's clothes then it would be over between us, sorry but seeing my fella in women's clothes just doesn't do it for me, I like men to be men Sebastian.' He is really shocked at my directness. 'But you don't mind gay people or transvestites he says, your quite open minded, you don't have a problem with other peoples sexuality' he moans at me. 'Yes, but I wouldn't want to sleep with them, just as they wouldn't want to sleep with me.'

Surely I think he will leave it here but no 'Oh Ang' he whines 'Don't be so narrow minded, you are so rigid in your ways you should lighten up a little bit.' 'Yes Sebastian I suppose your right' I mutter sarcastically. 'I think I'll go home now and tell Stan to get my thong on. Oh, and whilst I'm at it I'll leave my front door open to see what dregs will wander in.' I look over and Jen who is holding her stomach from laughing so much. Jerry wanders in doing a poor impression of trying to find files with Trudy next to my desk. Gertie is looking at work on Olive's desk, hovering over her shoulder pretending to look the other way. Yet any other time they can't stand each other.

Sebastian grins away telling me the next time he's going to one of his parties he shall invite me, if only to let my hair down. But the last time Sebastian went to a 'party' it was at a fella's house with other guys he didn't know very well. With the barrister, curator, policeman, solicitor, dentist and company director and an archaeologist. To say he didn't know them very well he certainly didn't waste much time getting acquainted. He had told us how he ended up in the swimming pool with a guy on either arm. Oh well each to there own. I try telling him that I'm sure his party is not for me. Yet he insists on never saying never. For Gods sake where is Lawrence when you need him. I'm sure he'd appreciate my way of thinking. After all he is as camp as they come but he is so not on the same wave length as Sebastian on this one.

Is it me or does everybody get questioned like this. I'm sure others don't have colleagues asking them if there partners dress up for them. After all it is a regular sort of thing you'd mention over a coffee isn't it. Jenifer laughs saying she'll wear her nurse's outfit tomorrow. Jerry said she'd bring her high heels and mini skirt in. Trudy offers to wear her black PVC cat suit and asks 'But Ang, what will you wear only Stan will have your kit on.' I tell them sarcastically 'Ha ha very funny.'

We do laugh about it but joking apart I wouldn't like to see him to get hurt by one of these strangers. He's such a trusting and generous person. Sebastian is one of those annoying people who doesn't like to see the bad in hardly anyone. We would all like to be like that but rarely are. He could so easily be taken advantage of, especially by a stranger. Not like the rest of us. The guys at work say the girls in our office are all 'gobby gits' and they'd be frightened to cross us. All those big guys and they're scared of us. We can't help but smile.

Being northerners we are straight forward talkers. We say it as it is rather than what you want to hear. You'd think people would prefer straight talking but some people do take us to heart. Like when Lawrence worked on the measuring projects for our office a while ago. He had to measure the number of orders we all put on, who invoiced what and when and show management what we are doing. We explained to Lawrence about who did what work, and that some jobs take longer than others.

But his monitoring of our orders was driving us insane. He was forever coming into the office asking questions. He'd get involved in things going on in the office, help drama the situation up then moan he wasn't get his job done. You couldn't help but like Lawrence because he was such a big girl at things it was funny to watch. If it helped to wind Gertie and Olive up we were always happy. But this time the reports made it look like nobody did any work except Gertie and Olive. He knew we did the work but said the figures don't lie he laughs.

Olive thought this was marvellous. Gertie was buzzing around the office like a queen bee saying she knew she worked harder than the rest of us. We of course were ready to lynch her. We warned Lawrence he had better not submit the report under current findings. He sulked that he had to the managers were waiting to see it. We tried explaining to Lawrence it was grossly incorrect but Trudy could see he wasn't listening. Even Sebastian and Antonio said there is no way it could be right.

Lawrence as good as told us the figures shown that we were not doing our jobs properly. It made the figures look like Olive and Gertie were top for number of orders being entered onto the system. What was true was Gertie and Olive put the orders on and had them logged on the system. Then we were left with the donkey work everyday when they were off sick. Lawrence couldn't grasp it when they tried explaining again. After going over it a several times the office was going into an uproar. This was ready to start off world war three. Lawrence tried telling us to stop moaning. But this didn't help the matter because we were ready to tie him to the hot seat and leave him there.

There was no way we could have Olive and Gertie looking like they were the best workers in the office. Can you imagine it, they would say we weren't eligible for the raffle to win the car and they'd walk off with a car each. Why is life unfair and those who take the mickey get away with it. And those who do put the work in never get thanked for it. Yet the company said it was important to reward good behaviour. We couldn't even threaten to go on strike because we were losing our jobs anyway. They'd only get rid of us earlier rather than later. We all wanted to leave with a clean slate and a good bonus.

Trudy walked past and flicked his ear then asked if he was listening to us. This was now a standing joke after Sebastian had been on the receiving end of it before. Sebastian laughed but said he would not be joking if Lawrence carried on this way. Which of course made us laugh seeing Sebastian getting annoyed. His speech became faster and looked like he was ready to rant in Spanish. Lawrence however was furious. Trudy told Lawrence to stop whining and fix the report.

Lawrence thought we were bullies. Of course Olive agreed with him. Well she would wouldn't she knowing it showed her in a good light for once. It's like them losing the race then being given a cake to celebrate winning, and then rub the cake in our faces. Jenifer said she hoped they choked on it. And for one I agree with her. Jenifer told Lawrence to sort it and soon or else. He said there was nothing he could do about it. He stropped around a little then said he was going to speak with our boss. Good we wanted our boss to know because he knew who was doing the work. Lawrence complained we couldn't grasp the report. Trudy told him she'd grasp his neck if he didn't show the true report. We felt awful because we all liked Lawrence but felt the power had gone to his head. He flounced around the room almost in tears. Trying to talk his way out of it and spent an hour of the afternoon trying to explain himself. I told him he could re-run the report only taking account the days we were all in the office.

Lawrence refused to do this at first. Until our boss stepped in saying this was a more accurate way of getting the information. He knew how hard we worked and didn't want a bad reflection of the office but a fair and accurate one. Olive furiously started whispering to Gertie. How strange that they are two peas in a pod today yet most of the time they can't stand each other. I suppose they find comfort in each other knowing they are right and we are sore losers. They were convinced we were picking on them and said they'd complain to tweedle dum and tweedle dee. Trudy shouted drag them into it if you dare. Sebastian didn't know where to look because things were slightly getting out of control.

Poor Lawrence looked like the lamb before the slaughter and

almost got hysterical. Trying to break the atmosphere we told him we can look at the figures again when things are calmed down. Nobody wanted to fall out with him, but he needs to realise a new evaluation is necessary. We didn't want Lawrence thinking we were being aggressive but we did need to show him we meant business. He was still smarting over Jenny flicking him. This was the only thing keeping us entertained for the moment. It was inconceivable to think Gertie and Olive where top dog.

What could we do besides laugh at the absurdity of it. We had to stick together on this one, but hopefully in a calmer manner. We couldn't get over Lawrence stropping about and he couldn't get over us being rebellious. Of course we were but for a purpose and not just being awkward. Gertie did what she does best and stomped about. She knew the new figures would show her in the true light and wasn't impressed. We couldn't help but laugh at her stomping. Normally Gertie would throw a big strop and pick arguments with anyone who disagreed with her. But she knew we were all sticking together and we had the bosses backing. She had to sit it out and wait the outcome.

Lawrence had to trawl though all the dates that everyone was out of the office for holidays and sickness. Then he had to run the reports again. Olive was convinced she would still come out top. Should tweedle dum and tweedle dee come by we'll have to tell them why we think the report is inaccurate. It's about time they knew the truth. But when the new report came back we all had smiles on our faces. Not only did we come out top but it showed we worked far harder as the level of work required to process orders from start to finish showed that Olive and Gertie was bottom of the pile. This pleased us greatly, to say we revelled in it would be an understatement. Of course Gertie and Olive thought we had fixed the report. They told anyone who would listen we made them change the report. We of course laughed at them even more. Well come on who wouldn't.

Olive said it was bullying and trying to show them in a bad light. I shrug my shoulders do I care. All we've asked is to show a true report on a fair basis. There is no way she is winning this one. We will put up both reports if necessary. We've had our victory and don't want to carry it on but if they want us to rub their noses in it we will. We've said our piece and decide to gloat in silence. Olive and Gertie ran to the ladies toilets having a good whinge to each other.

Trudy and Jenifer tap dance across the office. I hold my hands up to Jerry pretending to do the Charleston trying to count sets of hands. She thought it was funny considering the last Charleston dance. Sebastian couldn't help but laugh and joined in. Lawrence in his defeat allows us to be friends and realised what made us angry. He pouts a little but agrees with the report. We quietened down once they returned to the office after all we don't want to make it any worse than it already is.

Just as we thought the office was getting back to normal Edith popped in to see us. We all hid behind our computers pretending we were busy. Edith was from an office down the corridor, but often had to call in our office complaining of one thing or other. She was really sweet and didn't mean to harass but was a stickler for detail. But harass she did and often, shouting as us for not filling forms in correctly. Each time we filled the forms in you could guarantee she'd give a big sigh because as she found something else to be amended. And on it went each time finding another fault. She informed us at great length how this affected her VAT reports. We were usually on the phone to a customer when she came in the office. So she'd hover over our shoulders.

Olive was sure Edith hovers over to hurry you up on the phone. But then again Olive was always spoiling for trouble and ready to create an atmosphere. We ignored her comments because what ever you said she would turn it into a row. Soon Edith's visits became a weekly saga. When she came into the office she'd stand next to one of us desperately trying to rush us off our phone calls. She'd waft papers around in her hand. Then you would hear a little tap on your desk. If that failed then you'd feel papers being floated around the side of your face. It was anything to catch your attention. It was hilarious, can you imagine trying to be on the phone with all this fluttering around your face.

If we were lucky we would hear her footsteps coming along the corridor. This allowed us a few seconds make a grab for the phone. We would phone anyone so that she would ask one of the others, hopefully Olive or Gertie. But they had this knack of always looking busy when Edith arrived. It didn't mind how important your phone call was, or how stressful, they would leave her standing there. She usually stood by my side, thankfully today it was Trudy's turn. Just when Trudy was about to get tempered, Edith would give you the sweetest smile. Then you end up feeling guilty for it.

Why do people have the ability to make you feel bad even when it's not your fault. I must try to master this one and use at appropriate times in the future. This time Trudy was deep in conversation with 'somebody' on the phone when suddenly the light on her phone went off. Then the phone started to make a high pitched noise. You know that noise associated with a phone being left off the hook. Everyone realised what it was stopped what they were doing and looked up at Trudy.

The sight of her face being caught out lying was priceless. Poor Edith she knew it too. At first we weren't sure if she was upset or angry. But it was so funny we just couldn't help bursting out laughing. Edith on the other hand did not find this funny at all. And started ranting about her Vat reports having to be right. That she could do with out coming into our office to correct our mistakes. Edith shouted 'Vat this' and 'Vat that' which caused us even more hysterics. How do you keep your face straight when someone loses their temper. It sets me off in a fit of giggles even more.

She knew what we were like for winding people up. And shouted about not being impressed by our jokes and her being on the receiving end. Then gave us an informative lecture of office procedures. We should have realised this was time to stop. But us being us, we carried on laughing. To be fair it wasn't entirely our fault. We just weren't used to seeing Edith losing her temper. We didn't mean anything by it. But she then tore down the office shouting for us to take it more seriously saying 'It's for the Vats sake.' And with that she stormed out of our office and down the corridor threatening to report us all to her manager.

Usually we would stop there, but because this set off our silly mood this just made us worse. Before she had chance to make it back to her office the urge overtook me, I shouted at the others 'For vats sake.' Jen thought it was hilarious because it sounded like 'for f**ks sake.' We all roared laughing. Trudy shouted 'Vats not right.' And on it went all day seeing how many times we could get 'Vat' into a conversation. We tried it out on a few unsuspecting colleagues at first. Who just thought we were being strange until we couldn't hold our faces straight any longer.

They realised it was a joke being played on them but couldn't fathom out why. When our boss came back we tried it out on him for a while saying 'Vats right its Vat one, I'll have to do Vat again.' He wondered what was going on. Until Edith came in saying the Vat report needed updating that he twigged. He gave us such a stare. One of those looks which was enough to make us stop. Being a sweetie Edith forgave us after a while. She was a stickler and enjoyed a good laugh, but not necessarily at her expense.

~ Chapter Twenty ~ **It's almost Christmas**

Its only nine thirty in the morning and I'm already on my second coffee of the day. I thought it could have been a quiet day just for once. The phone rang it was the bank calling about my Letter of Credit documents. We had dealt with the bank for a while now and we were used to dealing with the same people at the bank. Luckily for us it worked well as we got to know them over time. You could guarantee our Letters of Credits would have hundred and one requirements. Asking for six copies of this document, seven copies of that document. And there could be anything up to ten different documents required. They usually requested every document ever invented short of your dental bill and your birth certificate. I don't suppose it would be long before they asked for those too.

You can imagine the amount of paperwork needed. After collating every page we stapled them together ensuring no documents get lost. If there is a discrepancy the bank rings to advise one of us. Usually they'd ask for the missing page or advise what needs amending. We felt this was quite reasonable, and as the bank know each of us it makes life much easier. But now the bank in their wisdom decided to have a whole room full of contacts instead of the few we dealt with before. Now each time we ring the bank a different person answers every time. And we won't know any of them. Now being human, we prefer to speak to someone we know rather than a new person every time. It just helps when dealing with people that you know.

This morning when the call came through it was from a woman we'd never heard of before. Instead of acquainting herself with us she went straight into complaint mode. Moaning about one error on all the documents. I advised our new friend I would courier the amended copies over to the bank straight away. I knew if I didn't send them immediately, any delays on processing the documents could result in our orders being held in containers at the arrival Port. And they could be stuck there over the Christmas period.

My new friend said she would get to them when she could. Well this got my back up to start with. Any of the others would have looked out for the courier and processed them straight away. I let this go, I didn't want her to hold up my documents, they were already on a tight deadline as it was. Nothing unusual there then. She then proceeded to whinge about them being stapled together. I went into diplomatic mode explaining its easier all round if the documents are stapled together. That way no copies could get lost, as had happened before.

Now me being human thought this made sense, she however thought differently insisting on them not being stapled. I explained for the last few years dealing with the bank this is the way we have done things. She whined 'It takes time to undo the stapes, next time send them without.' Well the tone alone she spoke in got my back up even more. I could feel the hairs on my neck start to prick up. I just had to have a go didn't I. 'Well this is the way we prefer to do things' I explained, being a customer I thought she would have taken the hint. But she didn't take the hint. And again stressed she wanted them without, again using a tone.

Again, I wasn't able to stop myself 'Aren't we supposed to be the customer, don't we pay you for the services we ask you to do on our behalf, isn't our account a rather large account for you.' But it was like water off a ducks back, still insisting without staples. Before the conversation ended I asked for her name. I then slammed the phone down, ranting 'Mrs Woods likes documents without staples then does she.' I turned around to see a crowd of faces looking at me. The office saw I was furious.

I moaned 'God Damn clowns at the bank, now they're moaning we shouldn't staple documents together. Staples, I'll give them bloody staples.' Not being petty minded I print a copy of every document required for the order and not just the one's she complained of. That way our new friend would have to take time checking every page instead of accepting the one document she needed. And just for good measure I stapled each page to the next one. All forty six pages of them. Only to make sure they don't get lost I can assure you.

Lawrence gets giddy in the excitement and runs over adding a few staples too. This must have cheered him up because he was definitely in the mood for some fun. By the time we had finished there must have been over fifty staples all across the top of the page. Immature I know. But there was no way I was going to let her have the upper hand. Still not quite satisfied we decided to complain to her manager. We've worked with the bank for so long we wanted things to run smoothly again.

And, since it worked well before we felt it should do again. Speaking to her manager I subtly remind them that we are a big customer of theirs. It's a sad thing to do I know, pulling the do you know who we are stunt but she deserved it. Her manager understood perfectly and advised she would have a word with Mrs Woods. For once it had been our turn to give payback and make someone else grovel. It felt very therapeutic. Especially pressing down on each staple, that was so good. I addressed the envelope to our friend. Oh dear, do you think she'll get the message now. The thought of her opening the documents with over fifty staples attached brought a smile to our faces. When I got home that night I told Stan about our day. He said we were a load of bitches but even he had to laugh. For a while afterwards he called me nasty knickers.

As this was our last Christmas in work together we decided to dress up our old Christmas tree. Well if you could call it a tree. It was more like a twig with a few leaves held together with tape that looked like it had been through two World Wars. Seeing that we won't be buying any more decorations again we decide to spruce the tree up really special this time. We found every bauble and piece of tinsel we could lay our hands on. Some were so old I'm sure they dated back to the last century. We put that much tinsel on it the poor thing it glowed from three miles away. And that's without the lights switched on. It had to be seen to be believed. People from other departments came to have a look. They couldn't believe what they had seen either. You'd have thought a dozen children had been let loose on the poor thing. Whilst dressing the tree we decide the more outrageous the better. It might as well see the New Year in with a big bright light. To say it was hideously tacky was an understatement.

It was like a creation from Hancock's Aphrodite at the Waterhole where only the creator could see any greatness. But even we had to admit it was beyond outrageous, more on a par with glow worm at the waterhole. You know when children from kindergarten are let loose with the paint and it's just horrific and you desperately try to see what the picture is. Well that's what people were doing, checking that there was in fact a tree underneath. One colleague even asks if it was ready for the trash. Can you believe it, our masterpiece ready for the trash, it was so unfair.

In walks Tony who takes one look at the tree and comments very nice sarcastically. Lawrence tells him not to make fun of our creation. Joking Tony tells him 'I'd be careful if I were you or I'll be sitting you on the top of our Christmas tree in the warehouse. Lawrence took offence and walked into the other room sulking 'what are you insinuating.' Bemused, Tony shouts back 'Insinuating, I'm not insinuating anything I'm just saying I'll stick you on top of the tree in a minute.' Lawrence flounces back in and with a big strop shouts are you trying to say I'm a fairy?

Now we can see where this was going, we had wondered why he had taken it so personally. Now everyone stands there embarrassed not knowing where to look. Tony isn't sure if he should laugh or rage. He can't believe how this is turning out and moans 'Christ, I only came in to get the worksheets for the warehouse, what's going on around here, is it hormones or what.' We are dying to laugh but desperately holding it in because we don't want to upset Lawrence any more that he was.

His face already looks like he is ready for a drama, after all he can get a little temperamental. Tony tries reassuring Lawrence that he didn't mean it like that and doesn't he understand our humour yet. Lawrence says he only came into our office to be cheered up not fall out. But Lawrence sees the look on Tony's face and realised Tony was quite offended. Thankfully Lawrence realised he was a touch too sensitive and decides to let it go. Tony goes into another office moaning 'what is it with everyone around here, have they got the Christmas jitters or what.'

Even given the temperamentals of late we worked hard the

weeks leading up to Christmas. Desperately trying to get all the orders processed and shipped out in time. It was long hours and we were all feeling the strain. Come Christmas week we were on top form as usual. To say we were giddy was an understatement. We brought a radio in for the last week of Christmas. We finish on Christmas Eve so there won't be much work done then.

Because we were all too busy with our own families to meet up after work we decided to bring cd's into work. At least this way we could all have a laugh and dance in our room. Everyone is in a great mood, they all seem up for it even Gertie. We put the music on quite loud. Surely leading up to Christmas Eve there won't be any phone calls now, or rather they better not. Poor Trudy had come into work with one shoe on. She spent the best part of an hour trying to glue her heel back together. She looked ridiculous and tried normal household glue. They fell apart as soon as she stood up. Lawrence laughed and gave her some of his chewing gum to use. But every time she walked her heel stretched from the floor then stretched back again. We couldn't help but laugh at her.

After a few songs from the cd's Lawrence decides he's the Christmas choreographer and decides to teach the office some dance moves. He's brought along his Abba songs of which some had been big dance hits again. Desperate to show off he swanks around the room giving us the new dance steps. Here we are trying to learn the moves but each of us looking ridiculous. I've seen six year olds doing far better versions. We think we look good but are all in fact left footed and certainly no rhythm at all. The only thing we do well is manage to turn the wrong way throughout the whole routine. Because of the racket we were making yet again, people are popping in to see what is going on. But we can't help it it's almost Christmas.

Even Gertie seems to have gotten over the reports incident for today. She seems to be in a great mood and joins in the fun. She must be happy we'll soon be off work for a few days over Christmas. Olive is still smarting and phones in sick. Oh what a shame. I wonder if she'll manage a few hours and manage to come into work in the New Year. After all it isn't too difficult to put in a full week occasionally. We will be leaving soon, you'd think she would at least make an effort before we leave.

Lawrence was like a dancing queen holding court in the centre of the room. He tries in vain for the steps to sink in for us. But decides we are all a bunch of lost causes. He pushes us out of the way and takes to the floor showing us how it's done. All he is missing is a sequined all-in-one and a tangoed face like he's on Come Dancing. He's keeping us entertained anyway. We're all in hysterics watching him show off. But the next minute the office door swings open in pops a colleague from down the end office. At first we thought he'd come to join in, until we saw his face. He was not amused in the slightest. I thought if you barged into a room full of giddy people that it usually rubs off onto you. But not this time. He bellows down the office to turn that racket downs shouting 'Some of us are trying to work around here.'

Point taken that he's still working. But bearing in mind its Christmas week and we finish for the day in the next hour. I thought he could have been in the festive spirit a little. It isn't like we asked him to be the life and soul of the party, and dance on the tables or anything. We stand there stunned with our mouths wide open not quite believing yet another outburst. He walks out the office slamming the door closed behind him. We stare at each other in disbelief thinking hang on a minute is it February, that we've all got it all wrong. That was until Jerry bellows furiously 'Excuse me but it is Christmas or haven't we noticed.'

We all burst out laughing and turn the music on full volume. If he hears the music going louder he might just get in the spirit of things. Jerry still not satisfied shouts 'Bloody scrooge and I bet his wife loves Christmas with him.' This brought on even more giggles. Just for the hell of it we try to make even more noise than before, if that's possible. A little obnoxious I know but he did ask for it. We've had a year of it so far, and we didn't intend for the New Year to end the way it has been all year. We've all brought in nibbles and a few low alcohol drinks for the last few days. We decide to finish off the nibbles and enjoy the rest of the day whilst we can. We're all so looking forward to finishing for a few days.

I'd recently bought a car off a mate of Tony's. He said it would be a nice little run around for me. And after seeing it I thought it was just right. My car was getting a little worse for wear, plus it was costing a fortune in petrol. When I got my new car I had to take the old one off the road. Otherwise both of them had to be taxed and insured. During the Christmas holidays only a few people would be in work. They didn't mind if I left it in the security bay until the New Year. At least then I'd have the time to put it up for sale. I did have one slight problem with the old car though. The lock on the boot was broken.

You only had to push the clip on the boot and the boot opened. But who would notice this at work. And it's not as if anyone would be using the car. Apparently somebody had noticed. Tony had remembered I mentioned the broken clip. He decided to make good use of it. Although he didn't drive the car, he used the boot as a fridge whilst it snowed before and during Christmas. He'd come back to work with his Christmas shopping and thrown the bags in the boot until his Mrs came to collect him. And to make matters worse, a dodgy mate Tony knew gave him packs of steak for his family. Since they had nowhere to store them again they left everything in my boot.

Tony told me it was a good job it snowed leading up to Christmas because my car would have had a right mess in it. I didn't have a clue what he was talking about until he told me he'd used it as a freezer. Tony is the type of guy that if he couldn't help you then he knew a man who could. I could have strangled him using my car as a middleman with his dodgy dealings. It would be just my luck for the meat to get caught in my car. Would I still be responsible even though I didn't have anything to do with it. God it doesn't bear thinking about. I don't even have to be there and I'd still be at the centre of trouble yet again, and I'd probably be told I'm the ring leader. Of course Tony thought it was hilarious.

Thankfully its home time and what a day. The car park is a few minutes walk away in an isolated area. During winter when its dark and I'm finishing late, if nobody else was walking to their car I'd ring Tony. He never minded walking me to my car. There is no way I'd walk alone in the dark to my car. Especially with all the weirdo's around these days. Tony would always spare a few minutes because that's what mates do. And if he needed a favour one of us in the office would happily help. So long as it was legal and didn't involve cars. Tony and Sebastian had become good friends too. Tony often took Sebastian home for dinner with his family. I think Sebastian amused Tony with his stories and wicked sense of humour.

Tonight we left as early as we could. A minute longer in work during Christmas week was more than we could bear. We already dreaded having to come into work the few days in between Christmas and New Year. So when a guy at work said in a smart arsed way 'Are you sure you can manage walking to your car on your own' I wasn't impressed. With a sarcastic grin I replied 'Seeing that it's still light I think I can manage.' It struck me as an odd comment to make. But it was more the way he said it, like it was a joke with a hidden meaning. What was he getting at and why would somebody doing a favour for me bother him.

Normally I wouldn't have bothered and just laughed it off. But the way he said it got my back up. Not satisfied at leaving it be I told him I'm thankful to have Tony as a mate. He'd rather spare two minutes for a colleague than come into work one day and find myself or a colleague harmed by a pervert hiding in an isolated area near the car park. He looked startled by my stern reaction. But obviously not startled enough. He says it only seems to be me that Tony walks to the car. Now I'm stunned at his comment. Has it not crossed his pea brain that the others often leave an hour earlier than I do, and when others walk to their cars its together. By the time I leave there are very few people leaving. On these occasions I'll ring Tony.

And I also had to get another comment in. I could hardly let this Pratt get the better of me. I asked him if he thinks it's a nice thing to do for a colleague and a mate. The little git, he looked a bit sheepish as if he'd been caught out trying to imply something untoward. One more smart arsed comment from him and I'll end up smacking him in the bloody groin. Hopefully he won't get up in a hurry to comment then. I think to myself if that's what he's thinking then good let him. If he has to invent stories about other people because his own life is so sad and pathetic then what a sad arse he is. It was then it crossed my mind and why not enjoy winding this idiot up. I could go out of my way to ring Tony up and ask him to walk me to my car.

Hopefully we'd bump into 'idiot' then I could shout be careful we might be spreading rumours. But God knows what he thought when Tony wasn't in and I asked one of the other guys to walk me to my car when it was dark. Of course idiot probably thought I'm working my way through them eh. I never liked idiot anyway. I had thought he was alright until he asked if I had my belly button pierced. When he asked if it was still painful I just thought he was being nosey. Until he added have you got anywhere else pierced.

What a freak, you just wouldn't ask a colleague this would you. Is it me? Do I attract all the freaks? I could feel the hairs on my neck stand on end. So just to be awkward I said 'Yes I have actually.' I thought try toying with me and you'll get it right back. His eyes open wider. You could see all sorts were going through his pathetic mind. Until I added that my ears are pierced as well. He mumbled Oh but looked really embarrassed knowing he was trying to imply something else. I felt quite smug knowing I'd shown him up. I mean, what on earth did he think I was going to say. Even if I did have piercings elsewhere did he really think I was going to tell him or all people. I wonder if he would have been so inquisitive if his wife had been present, somehow I think not.

I dread to think if Stan had heard him talking to me like that he'd have probably have given him a smack in the mouth. Then he'd have pierced some part of idiot's anatomy and tell him now you don't need to ask women where if they are pierced now you've got your own. The worrying thing is before this episode idiot was quite pleasant. If Tony wasn't around I would have asked him to walk me to my car. But the freak he was he would have misunderstood this as me wanting his attention rather than asking a colleague for a favour. It makes you wonder what goes on in other people's minds. Eww, the thought makes me cringe.

I'm quite an open person, I either like you or I don't. You'd have to be really horrid for me not to be polite to a colleague. After all you do have to work together. What's the point in bitching and feeling crap all day. But I'll only be pushed so far. Then I refuse to play their games and take pleasure in ignoring them. I act like they don't bother me then they can't get to me. Otherwise they'd only get under my skin.

Gertie and Olive however, manage to drive me to distraction. It was bad enough tolerating idiot, without taking their patheticness too. I couldn't be bothered with either of them. If I needed to speak to them I kept if brief and work related. Because again Gertie was changing like the wind. Before I'd have taken their attitude with a pinch of salt to keep the peace. But after months of their saga enough was enough. Surprisingly I became quite firm with them, enough to make them take notice anyway. They'd often been rude or arrogant to me then expect me to be nice in return. This time round I didn't do nice and ignored them completely. Which actually bothered them more because it was the reaction they were looking for. Before they'd sulk but by the end of the day they thought it was alright to become life and soul of the office. To say it was ridiculous was an understatement.

Gertie would be moody then Olive vyed for the attention of the office. Whenever Gertie noticed Olive getting attention she would start saying how unhappy she was at home. Low and behold somebody would give her sympathy and fuss round her and she'd wangle going home early on these days. Then we noticed a pattern formed around Monday's and Friday's. Pretty convenient don't you think. When she did get her own way she'd be nice to everyone and giddy around the office. But low betide if she didn't get her own way then you knew about it. She became horrendous.

She'd slam files around, be gruff with everyone bang doors and slam phones down. We can all slam a phone down we'd just think you're having a bad day. I thought that with the Christmas festivities she would at least be pleasant for more than a day. But with Gertie a bad day became almost every day. Often causing terrible atmospheres and other departments had started to notice too. Leading up to Christmas she was on a high or low. But since then even customers began to complain about her manner. In the end our boss had to have a word with her hoping to stop the behaviour.

She turned the taps on of course, pleading how unhappy she was at home and it was difficult for her to do full time hours. We had all been supportive and sympathised with her in the past. But now we had no more sympathy to give. She had got her own way and her hours got reduced, hoping this would help to stop the moods. We wondered if she carried her mood swings on at home or was she a different person there.

It also crossed our minds whether she went home blaming work for her moods. Because what ever situation she was in there was always somebody else to blame for her mood. For a few weeks the less hours seemed to work and her manner changed for a little while. Then slowly but surely the moods crept back in. Every time we thought we could have a moan free day it became an obstacle course around temper and sulks. Which invariably brought other colleagues into the equation and we felt it was all for attention. This time the problem grew between Gertie and Olive.

It became a competition between them of who had the most ailments or worst condition. And if they didn't have them then they sure would know someone who did. I think Gertie bit off more that she could chew because Olive was in a class of her own. There is nothing Olive didn't suffer from, and if not her then a family member certainly did. Once Olive announced she had suffered from cancer. I actually felt sorry for her this time. That was until she said it was skin cancer then proceeded to order a sun bed to be delivered to her house. I couldn't believe my ears, what on earth was she doing this for. Hello, if you've had skin cancer and fortunate to be given the all clear then you'd be careful in the sun. You'd get spray tanned or something for sure.

I thought she would show at least a little concern. But her face actually glowed when people fussed around her. Antonio and Lawrence told her not to go on sun beds after her skin cancer treatment otherwise it could come back again. Instead of registering the danger and seeing their shocked faces, she said she'll only use the sun bed to get a quick tan over the winter period. Apparently she wants to glow when she goes out. Telling us you've got to go at some time meaning death, it might as well be now. How ridiculous, she's actually revelling in the attention of possible death. Even more when told it's not worth the risk. Why do people act like this. Is it for sympathy or what.

I feel like shouting some people don't have a second chance. What would be the point in that she'd only revel in more attention. The girls aren't impressed with her and ignore her at all costs. I refused to comment on the 'ailments' and be led into giving her attention. I can't stand people in your face pushing for attention at any cost then the whole office have to fuss round them. Should it be true then I doubt you would risk it. Surely the last thing you would do is parade around gloating about it. I can hardly believe it. She knows people die of cancer every day, to make mockery of it is despicable.

I cringe with embarrassment for her. The battle between Olive and Gertie is so ridiculous at the moment you'd think they were both suffering from Munchausen's Syndrome. Sometimes we'd torment them both by making up symptoms just to see if they would fall for it. They never let us down. I told Olive once that I dyed my hair and it turned green. Can you believe it she said 'So did mine.' Except her doctor said hers was caused by all the medication she was on. I knew she'd say it happened to her. I just didn't realise she would have to top it.

Another time Jerry said her brother's children were really tall for their age. Olive said so was her niece but her niece was so tall she had to go for specialist treatment which might end up her needing taking special medication to reduce her hormones. We thought it was hilarious listening to her spin this yarn. You could see her head raised in triumph that she had an audience. I had to hide behind my computer whilst they teased her with this one. It was so ridiculous I couldn't keep a straight face. I daren't look up at the others or they'll make me laugh for sure. I have to pretend I'm on the phone again. Sebastian asks Olive if her niece has to go to Ormond Street Hospital for this specialist treatment, oddly she said her own doctor treated her. We knew she would take the bait. One person who didn't enjoy the banter was Gertie. She noticed somebody else was getting attention in the office she reverted into colleague from hell.

Gertie went into such a fowl mood and refused to chat to any of us. And only spoke when absolutely necessary. And even then it was miserable as could possibly be. She returned to grunting instead of saying speaking. Eventually she asked to move her desk to the end of the office away from the rest of us. Claiming the rest of us distracted her too much. And, to top it off poor Larry had been in a depression for the last few days. Apparently the girlfriend needed some space over Christmas whilst he contemplated spending it alone without her. Surely things had to improve in the office soon. How much stupidity are we to endure.

~ Chapter Twenty One ~ **That New Year!**

I intended Christmas to be a quiet affair spending time with family. It will be the usual I'll end up watching half my family get drunk. And yes, I might have just a couple of drinks myself to the usual annoyance of everyone around me. It's always the same at that time of year. People insisting 'Go on have a drink it's Christmas don't you know how to enjoy yourself.' At least if I'm not going to parties I won't get the lectures of why I should drink. It's always the same at this time of year when you have to explain yourself to why only want a drink or two and not twenty two. I've often wondered why you need to force drink down your throat just to please others rather than just enjoy themselves.

It's almost like you're not normal if you're not staggering about. They don't understand I can enjoy a drink if I'm out with the girls having a dance. Even Ayeisha laughs at me saying 'Go on Mum be a devil have a Baileys' the cheeky little sod. Years ago when out with friends we wouldn't stay a pub long enough to drink a drink. I'd spend the night giving all my drinks away. They'd be downing them as fast as they could. I can't believe the money wasted on drinks, especially on those I gave away. I'm sure it would have paid for a car. When I arrived home Stan announced 'Our kid has asked if we are going out New Year's Eve.'

I didn't mind as we hadn't made plans and it would be a nice change spending time with his family for a change. We could go round to their house for drinks then see the New Year in in the town later. This sounded alright a nice pleasant evening and forget your stresses and hope that this New Year will be a better one than the last. I'm not asking much, just a peaceful year, work only three or four days a week and maybe a lottery win. Sometimes at New Year I call into the local pub and see my family before the drinks flow too much. If the evening goes well we could always go into the centre of Manchester to see in the New Year.

When New Year's Eve came the evening was enjoyable. We

had something to eat before going out for drinks in their local pubs. Pretty low key really, no drunken parties or anybody throwing up all over the place. A few people were drunk but giddy drunk and not stupid in your face you need a smack in the mouth drunk. Everybody seemed to really enjoy themselves. Although at one point Stan did get on my nerves a little. Of all people he had to say 'go on why don't you have a drink.' Because he'd had a few drinks he was convinced I wouldn't enjoy myself if I didn't have a drink. Normally Stan never mentions me drinking. Of all nights to start it has to be when we're out with his family.

Once Stan has a drink he harps on about it without realising and it gets on your nerves. Luckily it didn't cause a row I just ended up laughing at him. The pubs were busy, people of all ages mingled with each other. Thankfully it wasn't bombarded with the usual gangs of teenagers getting legless and making complete parts of themselves. For most of the night it was the usual cheesy Christmas music played. That was until they played the Band Aid record. It totally depressed me listening to the words.

Yet everybody else was happily full of festive cheer happily singing along. It was horrendous listening to words of people in poverty and starving. How could you sing along to it as if it's a great Christmas jingle. Don't they listen the words and understand the meaning of starvation. They act like they don't feel anything. I felt really guilty having a home, a car and know my fridge is full of food whilst others have nothing. Yet here is everybody smiling and singing away to 'Feed the world' then giving each other kisses. This really put a dampener on the New Year. After a pleasant evening we suddenly felt we shouldn't be there and decided to call it a night. We go back to their house and have a drink but the atmosphere was less than jolly.

The Band Aid record made us feel really uncomfortable. We certainly didn't feel in the mood to be celebrating. Neither of us was sober enough to drive so we rang for a taxi. Trouble was the taxi couldn't be here for almost an hour. Great! Any other time it wouldn't matter we'd just stop another hour and wait. But tonight after the mood dampener, nobody was in the mood for chatting anymore. It had become one of those moments where the atmosphere changed within a split second and you know you can't get that jolly fun feeling back.

It became like a false smile that you wear and everyone feels awkward. Each passing minute felt like ten minutes, the taxi couldn't arrive quick enough. I felt awful but there was no way we could have stayed longer. It went from a fun jolly evening to each of us making senseless polite conversation. I almost felt as if Stan would say it's because that I had spoilt the evening through not drinking. But even he knew it was impossible to enjoy it after 'Feed the world.'

Eventually our taxi arrived and we said our goodbyes. Climbing into the taxi I noticed Stan picking something up from the floor of the taxi. I presumed it was his money and just thankful he didn't drop it before we got into the taxi. Can you imagine having no money to pay. That would be so embarrassing. When the driver asked where we were going he had the strangest look on his face. And his tone seemed really odd. I thought to myself is it me exaggerating the moment because of the dampened atmosphere. But I glanced at Stan, he had registered it too. In fact he looked at me with 'What was that look all about.' So it wasn't my imagination running riot I'm not mad after all.

Usually drivers make small talk and ask if you've had a good night and so on, especially at New Year. But not this one, he acted like he just had somebody in his cab who argued about the fare and did a runner without paying. Maybe he just hated his job or he was in a mood at having to work New Year and took it out on his customers. There was definitely something going on you could cut the atmosphere with a knife. I felt like saying don't work New Year if you're going to be miserable. Then again he could have drawn the short straw working New Year so I'll let him off. After all I wouldn't like to put up with a drunken crowd at New Year. People drunk and being sick in your cab and having no money to pay the fare. I suppose I'm being a little harsh on him.

We drive down the lane towards the main road when the driver starts to slow right down. If the atmosphere tonight wasn't odd enough then this certainly was. Stan looked at me again as if to say what's going on is he slowing down to make more money out of us or what. Just then the driver said 'Look, I'm not messing around right' with a really stern tone to his voice. I was really taken aback and didn't know how to react. I just looked at Stan with a blank expression. Then he said 'I'm being serious now.' My reaction was he wants the taxi fare upfront. But even I was not prepared for what was about to come.

It has to be me who everything seems to happen around doesn't it. If there was a cloud raining on one person then sods law it would be over me. If there was a rock slide you can bet your bottom dollar it would be heading towards my direction. I don't know why this sort of weirdness happens. It seems to follow me around and tonight was no exception. The driver carried on again 'I'm not messing around right.' I could see he got Stan's back up and asked 'What's your problem mate.'

My throat felt really dry because I wasn't in the mood for being thrown out of a cab in the middle of nowhere in the early hours of New Years Day. When the driver said 'Its not a joke right, but if I pull over just phone an ambulance.' Stan looked at me with a I think I'm sobered up now look. I got nervous and laughed half expecting Jeremy Beadle to jump out from a car behind saying 'Ha we got you.' But the driver slowed down almost stopping the car, he turned around to us looking really weird and said 'I'm not messing around I don't feel well if I have to pull over phone an ambulance right away.'

His face looked far too worried for it to be a joke. But still I couldn't help but think it has to be a joke. I mean come on, we've only come out for a few drinks and bring in the New Year. And hopefully a little better than the last one. The driver then carried on driving slow and said he felt pains in his chest he was worried he was about to have a heart attack. I stared at the driver in disbelief again. Surely Jeremy Beadle is definitely going to jump out with his microphone now. This isn't funny at all. Its one of those surreal moments that you can't comprehend and wait for someone else to take the lead. Stan asked if he was alright does he want Stan to drive. Of which I'm worried because Stan has been drinking. Now who do I want in control of the car, Stan drunk or driver feigning heart attack. But the driver said 'I'm alright now it seems to have stopped for a while but if it starts again then please phone an ambulance.'

By this time we could tell he wasn't joking around and the seriousness had sunk in. I'm really worried and ask him to pull over. He shouldn't be driving in this condition and want to call for an ambulance anyway. We can get out and wait for another cab. But no he insisted 'You're not getting out.' God now I'm worried. What is it with me? Why am I on my way home on New Years Eve, and trapped in the cab with a driver who is going to keel over at any point. And refuses to stop to let us out insisting on dropping us off.

I appreciate he's not well, but for his sake and for ours we should phone an ambulance. Then what do I say, send me an ambulance were in a taxi driving at the speed limit heading towards the hospital and the driver is insisting on taking us home. If it was a five minute journey we could pray we all make it and laugh it off later. But we have a thirty minute journey down country lanes and main roads. It was one of those times when your in shock and don't think sensibly. Especially with a little drink and tiredness setting in you just sort of go with the flow. Now looking back if it happened again I would insist he pull over and phone the bloody ambulance.

But it was one of those scenarios that's so surreal you don't quite know what to do. Is this really happening to me or am I going to wake up shortly and realise it was all a silly dream. By the time we get to the main road the driver announces he'll have to go straight to the hospital, he doesn't feel too good and the chest pains are starting again.

Frightened to death we are going to crash Stan and I both shouted 'Stop the car, and let us phone an ambulance.' 'No' he shouts 'I have to go straight to the hospital, I'll get another driver to come for you, I won't charge you for the journey' as he puts his foot down on the accelerator. Stan and I look at each other not quite knowing what the hell to do now. I feel my stomach churning.

He grabs his radio and shouts in a panicking voice 'This is an emergency, please can another taxi come collect his ride and to meet at the hospital I'm having a heart attack.' They radio back that another taxi is on its way. But now I'm in shock. I shout at him to stop, Stan or I will drive him there. Even though we've both had a drink, I think this would warrant an emergency. But he still insists it's alright. He carries on for a moment then asks for an ambulance to be called.

Luckily we are near the hospital. As the radio announces an ambulance has been called for he starts to hold his chest. Stan jumps out of one side of the cab and I jump out the other side. As we fling his door open he looks like he's starting to gasp for breath. Take deep breaths I shout trying to take control of the situation. Stan does his impression of a headless chicken. I hope he can do mouth to mouth because I don't know how to. Although we could bang on his chest if it stops. I'm sure I've seen that in ER somewhere. He looks really pale, panting and ready to keel over yet still insists on waiting for the other taxi to arrive. We reassure him the taxi is on its way. But more importantly the ambulance arrives first.

Thank God it arrived within seconds. It did help that by now we were minutes away from the hospital. He tries telling the paramedics to wait for our taxi. Thankfully they ignore him and start loosening his clothing. They give him oxygen which calms him a little. Then he asks if we can radio for somebody to collect his cab. Stan grabs hold of the radio and tries asking for help like he's in the police force. You'd have thought he was sending an army out to fight the way he took charge.

Thankfully our taxi pulls up. Our new driver locks the cab up giving his keys to the paramedics. We eventually climb into the new cab and watch the ambulance leave for hospital. Leaving another stunned taxi driver to drop us off. The new driver a little confused and asks what's happened. We tell him of our saga, of which he nearly crashes his cab because he's too busy looking into his mirror at us in shock. Finally arriving home we bring in the New Year with about as much enthusiasm as a dead sparrow. We open the door and decide to go to bed hoping a better New Year starts again in the morning, or so I thought.

I'm just about to throw my shoes off when Stan says 'At least we didn't get charged for the first taxi, or it would have been a fortune at this time of the night.' Flabbergasted I stare at him for a moment unable to speak. He then says 'Look what I've found.' It looks like a he's holding a little black purse. Now I know he certainly didn't go out with a girl's purse. Nor did he talk to any women so where could it come from. He said he found it tonight. Then it dawned on me that's what he picked up in the taxi. I asked 'Why he didn't hand it in to the driver.' He said 'You never know whether they hand it in or keep the money, besides with tonight's events I didn't have a chance even if I wanted to.'

I can't believe him, he knows the driver knew where the girl is from because he's probably only just dropped her off. Unless he dropped her off at a party. I told Stan I'd be surprised if the purse had any ID in it because girls usually only carry money and make-up and keys. We could always ring up the taxi firm somebody might have phoned in asking for it. Stan recons he might as well look inside the purse just in case, it won't do any harm to check. Inside the purse is a little loose change, a key, a college identity card and a driving licence. The college ID had a photo of a pretty young girl who looks in her early twenties.

The driving licence shows her name and address which is in Denton, only about ten minutes away from our house. In fact I recognise the address. I'm sure a friend of mine lived on the same street I can take it round tomorrow. No doubt she'll be relieved to get it back. But then Stan has a brain wave and decides to take it round to her now. Bearing in mind its gone two o'clock in the morning. I tried explaining it's a little late. But because he has had a drink and like most men who've been drinking talk crap. He thinks its a good idea. I try to stop him but this only gets his back up thinking I'm the nagging wife when he's trying to be the hero and all. Now I'm ready to loose my rag with him.

He's really irritating me. I end up shouting 'It's gone two in the morning for Gods sake, I don't think her parents will appreciate you knocking on their door at this time of the morning.' He claims they won't mind and heads towards the door. I end up shouting louder 'Stan she might have not gone home, what if she's gone onto a party and you come along and wake up their bloody house.' If she is a student she'll more than likely live at home but stayed over at friends house partying. What is wrong with him, and why does he want to play the knight in shinning amour to some girl he's never met before in the early hours of New Years Day morning. If he goes waking her parents up they'll probably worry to death about where she is and how she'll to get home with no purse. I'm sure if she needs to get home she'll ring them.

But try convincing that to someone who's had a drink. It's virtually impossible, it's like speaking to a brick wall. So we row some more. What was supposed to be a quiet night with family has turned out a bit of a nightmare. I shout at him that if he goes round there don't be surprised if they are worried sick, and it's on your conscience. Hoping that this will satisfy him. But oh no he decides its best to phone them instead just to let them know we have their daughters purse and not to worry. 'But you don't have their number' I shout and almost ready to throw the phone at him. He looks at me like I'm the freak then tells me he'll get it from directory inquiries. I don't believe it, is it me. Do I have the problem and everyone else is sane. Can I not just have a quite New Years Eve.

I rant 'If you want to play bloody hero then take it round tomorrow morning' and with that I stomp off to bed. It will take him at least half an hour to walk round there and half an hour back so he might turn back half way there when he realises its cold. I'm pretty sure they won't be impressed and I'll be furious if he drives because he's been drinking. Thankfully he decides against both and shortly after comes to bed although neither of us are speaking. He knew I was right so why didn't he accept that in the first place. Further more why can't he apologise and tell me I was right. Yeh, like that's going to happen.

He can't stand being wrong, worse still me being right. It must be a guy thing. Although I fall short of telling him so because it will lead to another row. And then I won't be able to stop myself gloating so it's best to leave it, for now anyway. I can always remind him how right I was when he sobers up. And I will savour this one.

The next morning after what seems like only a couple of hours, its time to wake up and collect Ayeisha from her friend's house. In the cold light of day Stan realises all by himself that maybe it wasn't such a good idea to have a strange bloke turn up at your front door at three in the morning after all. He then has the cheek to ask why don't I drop it off on the way to pick Ayeisha up. My God his cheek holds no boundaries does it. He probably feels a bit of an idiot ranting like he did over something so pathetic is more likely to why he prefers me to drop the purse off. I find the street it was near my friends after all. Whilst looking for the house number I see a police car parked a few doors away, and an officer waits in the van. When I walk towards the house I notice he glances over towards me. I put it down to some wild party last night and must be taking statements. I think to myself it must have been some fun for them last night, at least they had a good time.

I'm feeling quite pleased with myself being a Good Samaritan. And knocked on the door ready to bear good news. A woman answers the door looking slightly tired and bewildered. Oh dear I don't suppose she got much sleep last night after the neighbours party. Or could she have been at the party the old devil. I asked if the young girl lives here. Looking quite surprised she answered yes. I hand her the purse and ask to give it to the young girl explaining she must have dropped it last night. That we had found it in the taxi explaining we'd more than likely got into the taxi after her. Looking even more shocked she takes the purse from my hand politely saying 'I think you'd better come in for a minute.' I presumed she wants the young girl to thank me for returning it.

But she looks at me rather worried. I walk into the vestibule but feel like an intruder. Trying to justify myself I stress there wasn't any money in the purse, but there were some personal items I thought she'd want back. I'm feeling worried now, I can't help but think what if there is money missing. I hope she doesn't think I've taken it. I wait in the hallway as the lady quietly says she's is so thankful I've called, that the police are here maybe I could help them. Now I'm a little taken aback. I stand there looking very worried wondering what on earth is going on. Surely the police don't make personal calls for a lost or stolen purse even if it is New Years Day.

With a worried frown she says 'It's my daughter, she came home last night and doesn't know how she got home. She's in a bit of a state and isn't sure whether she's been attacked.' I gasp out loud and mouth Oh my God. I couldn't have misheard what she just said could I. But her face told me I did hear right. I feel my eyelids widen and can't stop myself blinking.

What on earth do I do now. Ask if everything is alright. Do go home and ask the police to call at my house. What does one do in this situation. I feel a lump grow in the back of my throat. It's the nerves kicking in again. I don't have a clue what to say even if I could speak. The lady is obviously her mother. She's so polite to me under the circumstances. In her situation just thinking what might have gone on I'd be hysterical. She thanks me for bringing the purse and she stresses 'Hopefully you can fit some of the pieces together.' I follow her through to the living room. The young girl in question is sat on a chair in tears talking to a police officer. Her mother explains I've called to return the lost purse.

I don't know where to look. The police officer is in the middle of taking her statement. She looks up at me as surprised as I look at her. Timing or what. I could have gone there at any time of the day. For the police to be there at the moment I innocently arrive with lost property. I feel like such an impostor and shouldn't be there. A complete stranger in their home at a most private moment. I feel terrible. The last thing you'd want is a total stranger sat listening to the personal things being said. Cringing I don't know where to look. The poor girl looks so embarrassed and I feel embarrassed for her. I don't know how the police do their work. I suppose we take our boring jobs for granted.

The officer asked me a few questions like where was the purse found; who found it; what time was it, did I know which taxi firm it was or did we flag a taxi down. Luckily I had an idea which firm it was as we had phoned for a taxi. I explain I couldn't remember the name off hand but would recognise it from the phone book. The poor mother rushes towards me passing a telephone directory. I look down the list of taxi firms when the name jumps out at me. The officer takes down the details of the one in question. The young girl is in tears but still thanks me for taking the purse round. Saying at least she can find out what happened as she didn't even know how she got into the taxi.

I feel terrible, should that be my daughter I'd want to get a shotgun and hunt the attacker down. If something untoward had happened that is. But I suppose it could have been anybody that she was out with last night. Then came the question I was dreading about the driver. The officer asked if I'd recognise the driver again. Taking a deep sigh I blurt out 'Well I can do better than that.' As they all look at me bemused I carry on 'You can find out from the hospital who the driver is.' It feels like everyone in the room stopped breathing. All eyes are on me wondering what on earth is coming next. I feel really uncomfortable, almost like I'm about to make a ridiculous story up. I have to hold my own breath for a moment to stop the nervous laugh kicking in. I can already feel it start to tickle the back of my throat.

I can hear myself praying please don't laugh, not now. I explain the saga of driving home the taxi driver acting a little weird, then took ill and had a heart attack. That an ambulance came and another cab had to collect us. 'I'm sure the hospital would have records of Accident & Emergency arrivals.' Now they all look at me stunned as if they have just met an alien. Alien or idiot that is. You can tell they are thinking whether to believe me or not. Now it's like I'm doing a Jeremy Beadle and they are waiting for Jeremy to jump out from behind the door. They still sit looking open mouthed. I'm thinking I must be mad, that it's all a bad dream and I'm about to wake up to reality. Do they believe me or am I some ridiculous person who suffers from lack of attention syndrome or more to the point Munchausen Syndrome.

The events surrounding me lately are like something out of a film. I can't quite believe them myself half the time. But really, this is getting ridiculous now. Even if I was a Munchausen sufferer I don't think even I couldn't make this kind of thing up. I should be getting paid for script writing or something, I think I'd make a bloody fortune. I'm sure the officer has heard allsorts before. But even she looks at me unsure if I'm telling the truth or not. Which obviously makes me feel like I'm making the whole thing up even more. I look at their bewildered eyes looking back at me. Even the young girl looked at me and stopped crying. I feel like jumping up and shouting 'Surprise I fooled you.'

You could tell from the look on our faces that our minds were working overtime. The girl comes home in a state, can't remember getting home, thinks she's been attacked and then the taxi driver is suddenly taken ill with a heart attack. It does make you wonder. I think we're all ready to brand him or something. I tell myself to get a grip we don't know what has gone on. It could be something perfectly innocent. The girl is at a party drinks too much and cops off with a lad. If she's drunk she isn't sure what's happened, the next morning could think something untoward has happened. The poor taxi driver could just be working too many hours, strain has taken hold, he gets chest pains and takes ill.

I think its best to leave it to the professionals. Although we do look at each other rather confused trying to make sense of it all. The officer takes down all the details and says she will check it out with the hospital. I want to apologise but what do you say. I just say I hope to God everything turns out alright for the young girl. I get up to leave and tell the Mother I hope everything gets sorted out and that things turns out alright. As I walk out of the front door I suddenly remembered Stan almost called around at three o'clock this morning.

Can you imagine what they would have thought if Stan had taken the purse back. It doesn't bear thinking about. He'd be hauled off for questioning, fingerprinted and swabbed before you could blink. My God how suspicious would it have looked. She thinks she might have been attacked then a strange bloke comes around claiming he had found her purse. It really would look like he was the last person to see her home. Try explaining your way out of that one. I took great pleasure in telling Stan how right I was. He was so shocked he was positively nice to me all day. Even though we had rowed he was so grateful I had stopped him.

Back in work they all said what a boring time they'd had over Christmas. Watching Granny get drunk on Sherry, Aunty Mabel trying to get everyone up dancing, and out came the game twister. And all of them regret eating and drinking so much. Then they ask me how my New Year went. Well you can imagine how long this one kept them entertained for. They were in hysterics, not because of the seriousness of what happened but that it could only happen to me. They couldn't believe it. How many people go out at New Year, and the most that they experience is a drunken night with the local letch and maybe a karaoke or two.

To hear these events happening around me yet again they are convinced it's like the pleasure and pain thing. All this happens around me like a grey cloud and some git is experiencing a lot of pleasure on the back of it. If I could meet the git I'd surely give him a slap. A couple of weeks later Antonio heard a news report on the radio. Apparently a taxi driver had been arrested on the other side of Manchester on suspicion of attacking girls who where drunk. He picked them up late at night after they came out of night clubs then driven them to an isolated area. Because they were drunk they didn't have a clue where they were going. At first I thought it was the office's idea of a distasteful joke as I can clearly remember the 'cat' incident.

But Gertie and Olive insist that they've heard it too. Their faces do look genuine. Surely not even these would joke about such a thing. I begin to feel quite ill and almost have heart attack myself. Then I realised it couldn't have been the same taxi driver. Firstly the Police would have taken an official statement from me. And they would have known where he worked when any attacks had taken place. Secondly, once I'd got a grip myself I realised that the taxi firm didn't work that area of Manchester. But for a brief moment a wave of sickness swept over me thinking it could have been the same guy. I presumed that all turned out well with the young girl as I didn't hear from the Police again.

The last note

Our office is leaving soon due to being surplus to requirements. We decide to clear out our desks as you do. We have a few weeks to get sorted and do the transfer of work. It feels weird now its actually happening. We will say goodbye to friends, and finally getting rid of those who drove us mad. Its now time to get rid of the accumulation of crap gained over the years. There are files on our desks that must been there for at least ten years and only opened once. Even then it was a mistake. Dusting them off we wonder why on earth we ever hoarded all this. It was one of those never used items but sure they might come in handy one day. Although we are ready for change it does seem rather sad letting go. I suppose that's just fear of the unknown kicking in.

The guys had spent the last few years either trying to organise me or trying to get me married off to Stan. Well they've more or less succeeded on the first account. But the latter will have to wait for a while longer. I tell them we're still checking to see if we are compatible ha ha. I never thought I'd be sad to say goodbye. I think of all those times I prayed of leaving work. The times I could have said stuff the job and bugger off somewhere. Now it's happening I felt almost tearful. Most of us feel the same but need to get on with the job in hand.

A lot of the old files have already been boxed ready to be sent to the new offices. I wonder if they can understand my illegible scribbled notes on some files. I imagine the thought of the new staff crowding round my files asking 'Does anybody have a clue what this could mean' actually leaves me with a smile on my face. Most of the time I couldn't read my own notes let alone make any intelligent sense of it. And for them to try doing it without any knowledge of our customers, phrases or local slang, and in a second language, perish the thought. Antonio ever the perfectionist insists on telling me I should make clear notes and put one in each of the files. That would take at least fifty hours. I don't think so we are all in wind down mode.

We spend the next week packing the last few items that are going. Some staff are needed to stay for a few more months and pop in to say goodbye. At least we thought it was to say goodbye, to see how we were getting on and maybe wish us good luck. Instead they have called in to see what furniture we have, and thought our tables and chairs can be theirs. Can you believe the cheek of it. Sebastian's infuriated and goes into a drama queen strop and stomps up and down the office ranting something in Spanish. Trudy flips and shouts 'If you don't mind we haven't even gone yet.

I'm stunned at the insensitivity of it all yet can't help but laugh. Then again what else did we expect. I'm only surprised they haven't tried wheeling our chairs out of the office whilst we are still sat on them just to check if they look alright in their own rooms. Tony gets wind of the palaver and promptly arrives in our offices armed with a tape measure. He pretends to measure all our tables asking if he can have any furniture for his office. Apparently his lads need somewhere to stick their coffees. This struck a raw nerve with the others and they are not amused. I however, find it hilarious. Although eventually they do see the funny side after they have cooled down. A day or two later.

Olive and Gertie on the other hand are waiting for any excuse to cause problems. As more staff call in our office both of them choose to use this to their own advantage. Both sighing loudly 'What are we going to do now we're losing our jobs.' They're using this to make all of us feel as badly as possible. I think they forget we are all losing our jobs and we have all had the chance to leave with full redundancy. And those who stay on for the few extra weeks are getting a bonus for assisting the transition. We all took the latter. I'm just pleased I'll have extra money whilst looking for another job. But they are intent on grinding down anyone who will listen. If it wasn't bad enough before it sure as hell is now. We all cringe with embarrassment when they start moaning. The only good thing out of it is they get rid of unwelcome guest quickly. A few minutes in our room and they run like hell. Couldn't they be nice just for a few weeks, then we can all leave in good spirits.

After the disgruntles we desperately want to cheer ourselves up. Lunch times have become fun to say the least. We've had lots of 'Mmm what have you got there, pasta oh look Angie's got Pasta.' Or we get 'Look what so and so's got in the fridge today, she's having salad today she must be on a diet.' If it wasn't enough to delve through the fridge for who had what they decide go through the freezers. Strangely, as each department have their own fridge/freezer some people thought it was alright to rummage through other departments freezers. I thought if the food doesn't belong to you then don't delve through it.

Lawrence and Antonio kept saying they wanted to leave something in the freezer like a dead worm to see who screams. At least that way we'd know who was opening our packages. Now we are leaving we wondered whether we should leave a little present for them. Fortunately for them none of us really wanted to go that far. But Antonio wasn't saying no to playing a little game or two. After everyone had left the canteen area, everyone but Gertie and Olive, we went into the canteen. Lawrence said 'Oh look and what do we have here then, is this the finance departments freezer, so it is. And what are we going to have for lunch today then.'

Lawrence then struts around the room making us laugh. Behaving like a naughty school boy when the teacher left the room and thinks he'll get away with it. Trudy takes the food from the finance department's freezer putting it in the purchasing freezer, then puts the purchasing department's food into the finance freezer. Sebastian empties whats left of customer services food and leaves it in personnel's. Because we leave at the end of the week our food is leftover bits. At first glance they will think we've eaten their food. This tickles me as food etiquette at work is so predictable and some things are just so faux pas.

To use another department's fridge is like asking to be whipped. It is the nearest thing to taking the kitty from Sunday service collection that you could get. Yet even so they still insist on rifling through ours. We think the food swap may set a few tongues wagging to say the least. Then we have a brainwave, let's leave our name tags on the tables in the canteen. We set the tables for dinner as if we are officially dining their. Even putting wine glasses out for added effect. With the kitchen area swapped around and the tables set we put the finishing touches to and leave our left over Christmas Crackers.

We laugh at the thought of colleagues walking in on Monday morning to see the table set. We chuckle at the thought. It looks so nice we hope they appreciate our finishing touches. It almost brought a smile to Gerties face. Oh well maybe next year she'll smile again. You'd think she would want to smile knowing she is finally getting rid of us.

Now we are leaving our boss wants to take our offices for a night out on the town. He's already received his new posting and was a little worried that he wouldn't get chance to say goodbye. But it's already started. Gertie doesn't want to go out drinking. Olive doesn't want to go out for a meal because she's on another diet. Great stuff, what shall we do then go and watch a football match. Antonio said she can always eat salad. Sebastian quips salad is what she should have been eating. I laugh and tell him 'Meow, put that cream away. And I suppose your going to tell her yourself then Sebastian.' He shivers and said he would never be that brave or that foolish. What a wimp. Although a great cat fight between them both would have been compulsive viewing. I wonder who would come out on top. I know Sebastian would give a little run for his money. Until she caught him that is.

Trudy is ready for a night out and Jenifer and Jerry are keen to come. Although they have been warned to be on best behaviour and no drunken antics so we shall see. Poor Larry wants to come but is unsure because he doesn't know if the on/off girlfriend is going to be available. Or should I say ready for a night out with him. Sebastian spoiling for a reaction asks Larry to bring her after all we haven't met her yet. Nor are we likely to.

Apparently Kimberly doesn't like crowds. I'm sure he means anyone who isn't in her crowd. Sebastian is not letting it drop and whispers he could always bring someone to impersonate her, like someone he met on the internet. Poor Larry, he's convinced he can woo her back. He's been sending her roses every few days since before Christmas but to no avail. You'd think he might have got the message by now. Antonio asks Larry whether it might be time he moved on from this relationship and found himself a nice girl without ties. He might meet her on our 'Hope it will happen' night out. At this rate Larry will be joining the exodus with Gertie and Olive.

I was hoping to have a really good night out and wind down with the gang so we can say goodbye. And I suppose even the others thought it through gritted teeth. We've had more takers from the other departments who want to come. But our boss doesn't want to mix our night with other departments. This is a thank you to us for all our hard work. Sebastian isn't bothered if Gertie and Olive don't come. He said they never did any hard work, except for being ill. Oh dear I think Sebastian is on a roll now. Maybe it's a good thing if they don't come. Otherwise we can't be responsible for Sebastian's mouth when he's had a drink. It will probably end up in a huge tongue lashing and few home truths spilt along the way. What a pity I could have sold ring side seats.

They then realise we are not that bothered if they don't come. They can sulk till the cows come home we're not fussing them that they actually come round to the idea of a night out. Larry eventually listened to Antonio's diplomatic advice and realises maybe he shouldn't put himself out for her. Why miss out on a last night out with his colleagues. God! Is it me or what, its like dealing with a bunch of children. In fact you'd probably get more sense from children.

We throw a few ideas together of where to go. Our boss mentions Belle Vue racing saying it would be good night for us all. He's really keen and he hasn't been to there for years. We all think a flutter at the races sounds like a great idea. Those who want to eat can and those who don't want to can watch the races. Those who want to drink can and those who don't want to don't have to. We can all have some fun together there. Plus it has the added advantage of sitting next to who we want. And we get to avoid those we don't without it being awkward. But more so we can keep separate anyone who might feel the need to be a little outspoken shall we say. What a perfect choice. I'm only gutted I didn't think of that one. I'm quite looking forward to it now.

We had decided upon a raffle for the goodies sent as a thank you from our customers and traders. Colleagues from all the offices we deal with around the world had also sent us presents. They had been sending goodies in for the last two weeks. This was really nice of them after all we have only just seen Christmas through, and they had sent lots of presents then. Everybody is really excited about the races. Everyone except Gertie that is. She feels a headache coming on and might not make it. She asked can we do the raffle now. Sebastian is ready to scream because he knows what she is up to.

Gertie had already eyed a particular parcel full of wine. Funnily enough they were also the most expensive bottles. She thought she was going to get the full set until our boss cottoned on and split up the bottles for separate raffles. This clearly narked her because she stormed off to the ladies toilets apparently feeling unwell. Sebastian said 'Fancy making yourself ill over a bottle of wine, surely it can't mean that much to her.' I found this hysterical because this is the same stunt she has pulled since joining the company. Trying to get her own way one way or another but knows its not going to work this time.

Our boss insists the fairest way is each pick a number out of the raffle tin. The lowest number has first choice of the goodies and then the next lowest number following suit. Each has a turn to pick then start again. Whilst we wait for Gertie to return Lawrence said he really wanted to pick one of the expensive wines. But feels he can't pick any now because she'll throw a tantrum. I tell him if his number comes up first then and he wants the wine then he should pick it. Even the others tell him to take it. But I'm not too sure if they say it just to wind Gertie up. Antonio is such a sweetie he says if I don't pick it then he will because he wants to give it to me. I laugh telling him I don't like wine if he gives it to me I'll only use it in my cooking.

They all fall about laughing, all except Olive. She didn't like it at all and noticed how we refused to fall for the tantrum. She looks a little stunned. Just to top it off Larry said he'd pick it because it's a nice bottle to give his girlfriend. For Gods sake after all we've talked about he just doesn't learn does he. When Gertie returned we all picked numbers, and we purposely let her

287

go third then she couldn't accuse us of fixing it. God has a funny way of working because her number was the highest. She had the misfortune to watch all the nicest things being picked first. Lawrence wimped out and picked the cheaper wines.

Antonio on the other hand did not wimp out and picked the most expensive bottle. Gertie was still sobbing, falsely I might add, from the sudden illness that had mysteriously surfaced. Antonio gave a broad smile and passed me the bottle saying this is for you my little friend. I couldn't help but give the biggest smile back. I added Stan will love you because I can use it in my cooking. Gertie immediately stopped sobbing and glared at me. I could hear the others gasp at Gertie's reaction because she was so stunned she didn't know what to do. She then looked out of the window then towards the door and whined 'That's right leave the crap for me.'

Our boss was fuming and told her that no present was crap, some are just a little more expensive than others. When it came to Gertie's turn she made such a pathetic performance of what should she choose from the delights saying it could take her all night picking. Its cringe worthy because now she's going to the other extreme being overly nice. It's almost sickly. Antonio recons it's because she has learnt her lesson. Trudy said fat chance of that, more like she's smarting and won't give you the satisfaction of a performance. Her way will be to snub us at the races, she'll probably turn up late so we will be too late to eat. Or not turn up at all to try and spoil the evening. Lawrence said 'Her not turning up like that's going to spoil it for us.'

We all finish work early eager to get ready for the races at Belle Vue. We chose it for the greyhound racing. It's local to the motorways and quite easy to get to. Our boss told us to book taxis through work and put it on the company account. That way we can have a drink and not worry about driving. Deciding what time is best to meet up we all think seven o'clock is fine. Gertie however seemed a little hard to pin down on what time to meet. She wanted to order her own taxi. This all indicated on a no show from her but she insisted she was still coming.

Almost everybody arrived in good spirits. We were all excited about our last night together. Gertie didn't come on time after all and chose not to answer her phone. We try ordering food without her but they can't get ours ready until she arrives. Forty five minutes and a few drinks later we're told if we don't order food now it will be too late and end up ordering. Gertie will have to make do with Chips from the café part.

As the first race is due to start we excitedly choose the names of which dogs we hope will win. Each table picks a dog for first and second place. Our table came last and next to last. It dawned on me that after we had placed our bet I'd said I liked the look of number three. And number three won the race. Lawrence mocks I could have told them that before. Again we choose the names we like for the next race. After placing the bet I saw the dogs and said we should have picked number two. Sebastian laughs that if number two wins I'm picking the dogs for the rest of the night.

With anticipation we watch the race only for my number two to come in at second place. I can't believe it we could have won money for second place. Lawrence laughs giddily that I've got the psychic eye that I should pick from now on. Antonio jumps up standing behind me he laughs and rubs my shoulders. Everybody laughs at Antonio saying 'Now concentrate on the winning dog.' Nervously I wait for the dogs to be walked by in front of us. I don't look at their names but just watch the dogs, waiting to spot the one. I pick again this time choosing number four. It looks rather cheeky why not. From looking at the names I'd probably have gone for number two. But we decide to go with my instincts and settle on number four.

Now three out of three could this really happen. As the race starts we are shouting and cheering so loud the whole place stops what they are doing to watch us watching the race. Our dog is only second to the finish again! I'm absolutely stunned, they are stunned and our boss is flabbergasted. He asks if I come here often and if there any other gamblers in the family. I can't quite believe it myself answering 'Well actually there is one or two in the family.' This is turning out to be a really good night. The atmosphere is electric. We are so giddy we can't contain ourselves. We thought it would be fun but not as exciting as this.

Just as we're getting giddy about the next race we notice a familiar figure walking towards us. Sebastian sniggers look what the cat's dragged in. Gertie swanks over without a care in the world, totally disinterested that she's held our meal up by an hour. I joke maybe when she heard seven o'clock she meant eight o'clock. Antonio says no it just took her longer to get ready. I wouldn't mind but we had tried to phone her numerous times but she had switched her phone off. She moans to Olive that she doubts she's missed much anyway.

Lawrence tells her she'll have to order her food separately. She sneers that she doesn't want to eat anyway and just wants to get drunk. Our boss isn't impressed with her at all. She knows he didn't have to do this for us. Sebastian says he's not bothered because we were having a great time without her anyway. I can't help but laugh, she is choosing to go out the same way she has performed all the way through. Olive befriends her yet again even though they couldn't stand each other before. It's amazing how things turn out. Olive takes delight in her new found friend. I wonder if she will think the same when we have all left as she used to snub Gertie in the past. And to think the occasions we had to separate them both. I wish them luck they are going to need it.

We were having such a good time we didn't want to waste our energy moaning about them two. The waiters were trying to serve our starters as we chose the next race. We all get excited as Lawrence shrieks we have to go through the same routing thing we did for the last two races. He tells me to take a sip from my drink then put my glasses on to look at the dogs walking in front of us. He insists we did that previously. I suppose it can't do any harm and we end up in hysterics that it could happen again. Olive doesn't like that I'm choosing the dog for next race. I'm not bothered in the slightest either way. But I do think it's fair that we all have a go. Our boss says he is happy to go with my choice going off my record so far. Olive sulks to Gertie. To make it fair he tells Olive's table to pick a dog too. Whilst the dogs are getting ready to line up we get so giddy we can hardly contain ourselves. I've chosen number three for our table.

Olive's table chose number one shouting because they are number one. The dogs take off with number two and three in the lead. As they approach the first bend number one approaches the lead. Damn, we so don't want them to win. We are up on our chairs screaming for number three. As they take the last bend Olive's dog is almost parallel with mine. But when it takes the last straight my dog leapt ahead almost like it was being pulled in front. We can't help but shriek with delight. This is fantastic I can't remember when I last had so much fun. We were all cheering and shouting, and it felt so good celebrating in front of Olive and Gertie.

Of course they sulked that we were just lucky. Antonio tells them not to be such sore losers. Gertie was not amused and slowly gets drunk thinking we are just showing off. Well of course we are and if she'd have been a little kinder and cheerful she would have been celebrating too. The fact she's sulking makes the win even sweeter. Still smarting Gertie claims that we won't win again. Our boss laughingly asks me if I'm going to take up gambling. I smile towards Gertie telling him I think I've found my niche in life, I'm going to come to the races every week.

Can we be any more successful. Should we call it a day now we are ahead. Grinning to each other we have to have another go and this time I pick number six. Olive picks number three hoping it will bring her table luck. At the start off we are all pretty even until the last bend then number six out paces all the other dogs. It takes the lead by metres. I think Olive is ready to pull her hair out as we are still on top.

Our table is making such a racket you'd have thought we were winning thousands. But the thrill of winning was just as much a high. We can't believe our luck yet again. Lawrence is on his chair and Sebastian tells me to take a sip from my drink and put my glasses on. Whilst Antonio massages my shoulders telling me 'Come on you can do it, concentrate on the lucky dog.' Trudy is so giddy she can hardly contain herself. Jenifer squeals with delight. Gertie is very much drunk and very annoyed but we don't give her attention or it will feed her fury. Poor Olive looks so disheartened. We are supposed to be eating our meal but nobody seems hungry whilst all this excitements going on. We offer to join forces and we can choose the next two dogs together going for first and second places. Olive however refuses to join us even after saying we'd share the winnings at the end of the night. She'd rather cut her nose to spite her face.

Gertie on the other hand is drunk and thinks it's a good idea and insists our table join theirs. This time I pick number five there table picks number two. At least we get something for first or second. As they take off from the starting line my dog flusters at first then joins the leader. Olive's dog scrambles for last place. If it goes any slower I think our dog will lap theirs. We are all on our chairs screaming them on. Even though we have pooled together we secretly want ours to win. Mean I know but we can hardly have them basking in our glory now can we. We can't help but scream for our dog to win. Now we are all stood on our chairs when our dog is heading towards the lead in the last few yards. It just happened that our number five came in second and their dog came in last.

They don't want to celebrate but do seem keen to share the winnings. We are so giddy that we don't care about the money it was just great choosing the winners. What a fantastic night considering I usually have more chance of picking a three legged donkey than any winners. Tonight we were on a roll. We are all on a high when we notice that Gertie has shared the money out.

Although I remember choosing the winners I know I didn't get a penny from the winnings. And to think our boss was generous offering to share the winnings out. He'd be mortified if he knew that just a select few took the money. It doesn't matter of the amount it was the principle. Oh well, some people will never change. They will go through life taking all they can to feed their own egos.

At least I don't come away with false hopes of people redeeming themselves. Some will always be selfish no matter what you do for them. As we say our goodbyes we are quite tearful which I didn't think we would be. I think it's because it was another era of our life over and a new phase beginning.

I suppose if we're honest, as much as we look forward to the future we know we are scared about the unknown. Worried if we will settle in our new roles. Worried if we will meet nice people and will we encounter the same enemies. Unfortunately I'm sure I will inherit the latter. After all this hazy cloud does have a tendency to follow me around. Maybe next year will be different. Of course everyone had lost their money on the wager on me. As every week there seemed to be another event.

Most of us insist on keeping in touch. Although over time I'm sure it will fizzle out it always does. I'll be very surprised if our gang are still friends in the future because people's lives change. When you're not surrounded by the same people unfortunately you do move on. As we had taken our photos and personal items off the wall at work it was kind of sad. Yes we all wanted to leave and receive a nice redundancy package, and we all want a new start somewhere. But now it's actually happening it's slightly daunting. What is out there for us? Will we forge friendships like we have here? Yes we argue all the time but we do actually enjoy each others company, especially out of work. Well most of us do.

It's great to work with interesting characters even though they may drive you mad. They make your working life so much more interesting otherwise how monotonous would it be. It's like one of those love hate relationships. You drive each other mad during work but come the evening and all work issues are forgotten about. I think most of us are out to have a really good time. And it does help if I'm not the only source of entertainment. We had promised to keep in touch and meet up occasionally. But people always say that don't they.

Other departments had called in to say goodbye and wish us luck. They ask what will we be doing but none of us have the foggiest idea what we want to do. We all got a little tearful and rushed our goodbyes. Sebastian asked me what I thought I'll be doing for the rest of the year. But I don't really know. I want to have a break and enjoy a few weeks off whilst looking for a new job. Maybe plan our trip to Australia we may get there one day. I joke I might write a book. Well you never know there may be someone out there bored enough to actually read it. He smiles and says 'Ang, it could only happen to you; you must write it and make sure you write about all our interesting times.'

~~~

Oh well another year bites the dust and a new phase begins. I wonder if the next one will be as entertaining as the last. Surely not? I feel my stomach start to tingle because I hear through the grapevine Bruce Springsteen's planning another world tour. I wonder if I can get closer to the front this time. I'm already getting giddy at the thought and its months away yet. I can but dream. Let's hope it tops the last one, and I'll let you know how it went.

~~~

Printed in the United Kingdom
by Lightning Source UK Ltd.
120524UK00001B/166-243